THE MAN
from
ESSENCE

THE MAN
from
ESSENCE

CREATING A MAGAZINE
FOR BLACK WOMEN

EDWARD LEWIS

WITH AUDREY EDWARDS

Foreword by Camille O. Cosby

ATRIA BOOKS

New York   London   Toronto   Sydney   New Delhi

ATRIA BOOKS
A Division of Simon & Schuster, Inc.
1230 Avenue of the Americas
New York, NY 10020

Copyright © 2014 by Edward Lewis

All rights reserved, including the right to reproduce this book or portions thereof in any form whatsoever. For information, address Atria Books Subsidiary Rights Department, 1230 Avenue of the Americas, New York, NY 10020.

First Atria Books hardcover edition June 2014

ATRIA BOOKS and colophon are trademarks of Simon & Schuster, Inc.

For information about special discounts for bulk purchases, please contact Simon & Schuster Special Sales at 1-866-506-1949 or business@simonandschuster.com.

The Simon & Schuster Speakers Bureau can bring authors to your live event. For more information or to book an event, contact the Simon & Schuster Speakers Bureau at 1-866-248-3049 or visit our website at www.simonspeakers.com.

Interior design by Kyoko Watanabe

Manufactured in the United States of America

10 9 8 7 6 5 4 3 2

The Library of Congress Cataloging-in-Publication Data has been applied for.

ISBN 978-1-4767-0348-0
ISBN 978-1-4767-0350-3 (ebook)

To the women in my life who have been the wind beneath my wings: my wife, Carolyn Wright-Lewis; daughters, Nicole and Haydn Wright; my mother, Jewell Spencer Lewis Clarke; and my maternal grandmother, Mary Spencer Croner.

ACKNOWLEDGMENTS

To my partners: Although none of the three men I went into business with consented to contribute to this book by agreeing to be interviewed, I must nevertheless first thank Clarence Smith, Jonathan Blount, and Cecil Hollingsworth for the founding partnership that gave *Essence* life. We were the four bold black men bodacious enough to believe we could start a magazine for black women and make it soar. We did.

To the Essence and Time Warner team: Memory is by nature the most unreliable of human attributes. I would therefore like to thank all of the CEOs, editors, managers, salespeople, attorneys, board members, investors, and consultants associated with Essence and Time Warner whose voices are heard and identities revealed throughout this business memoir. Their recollections either jogged my own memory, confirmed events as I remembered them, or helped to correct misperceptions. The writing of a memoir always involves the reconstruction of events that may be imperfect in the telling, but represent the author's best approximation of what occurred many years ago. Through the collective memories recounted here, along with my own, I arrived at my best truth.

To the early riders: Thank you, Carolyn, my beautiful wife, who rode shotgun on this from the very beginning, encouraging me to tell my story and then reading every word with a keen and observant eye throughout the publishing process. Thank you, too, to Mary Ellen Gardner, who knew from the start that the Essence story needed to be told, and did many of the initial interviews for the book. The critical comments of editors Pamela A. Johnson, Frances E. Ruffin, and Sandra Satterwhite who read early portions of the book are also much appreciated.

To the experts: Thank you, Dr. Icilma Fergus-Rowe (FACC), cardiologist at Mount Sinai Medical Center; and Captain Ron Emenheiser, former Air Force pilot and corporate pilot for Fortune 500 companies, for making the complicated accessible, whether discussing the inner workings of a plane's engine or the delicate workings of a human heart.

To my friends and business associates: Thank you, James Dowdy and Nat Lehrman, former Essence board members; George Hirsch and John Whitehead; and Don Cornwell and Tom Burrell, my business buddies and best friends, for being there exactly when I needed you to be. I am grateful to Suzanne Warshavsky, my legal counsel, and would also like to thank Constance Robotham-Reid, my assistant for many years, for her loyal support and good counsel. To the staff at Solera Capital, thank you for providing the space, the support, and the serenity that allowed me to effectively work with focus and purpose. Much thanks to Young & Rubicam for its early advertising support.

To the publishing posse at Simon & Schuster: Thank you to Judith Curr, the leader of the pack at Atria Books, who so enthusiastically signed on to publish my story. And to the incomparable editor, Malaika Adero, who brought her always sharp editing eye to the project, I give much gratitude. I also thank her assistant editor, Todd Hunter, for masterfully staying on top of all the logistics involved in getting this book into production.

To the cover girls: What can I say about Mikki Taylor, president and creative director of Satin Doll Productions, Inc., and Sandra Martin, who have been with me practically from the beginning, first as editors in the *Essence* fashion and beauty department handling the magazine's cover shoots. I am so thankful to have had their expertise in executing the cover of this book. They are the absolute best!

To fabulous Faith: Faith Hampton Childs, literary agent extraordinaire, who always goes the distance, and then some, in giving invaluable feedback and nurturing support, I give highest praise and deepest respect.

To my collaborator Audrey Edwards: Audrey listened to me, heard me, captured my quiet voice, then pumped up the volume with stellar writing that gave me a voice ringing true and clear. Thank you!

To the Essence *readers:* I give much gratitude to the millions of African-American women who have supported *Essence* for more than forty years. Without you, there would be no story to tell.

CONTENTS

PART III

Getting Through
(1970–1980)

PART IV

Getting Over
(1980–2005)

FOREWORD

Camille O. Cosby

I know why Ed is Ed. Edward Lewis was born in the Bronx, New York, but he spent ten summers of his childhood working on his grandparents' land in Farmville, Virginia. I know that area very well. My mother was born and raised in Shores, Virginia, a mere fifty miles from Farmville, a small town located between Richmond and Lynchburg. With a current population of fewer than 9,000 people, Farmville is the birth town of Ed's mother, Jewell Spencer Lewis Clarke. She was raised there, along with her eight biological siblings and five stepsiblings.

Mrs. Clarke did not want Ed, her only child, to be in the Bronx during the summer, so within days after a school year ended, she, along with numerous other northern black parents, sent their children south—on buses, trains, in cars. The purpose was "to keep them out of trouble," their parents would say. Ed was sent to Farmville every summer from the age of 5 to the age of 15.

What a town Farmville was in Ed's youth—rural, communal, considerably Baptist—and a place where children, without most exceptions, showed respect for family and neighbors. The community was self-sufficient, growing its own food and making its own clothing. There was a strong emphasis on teaching values and manners.

Farmville was also a town, like all southern places in the 1940s and '50s, that was legally segregated under a powerful, enduring apartheid system in the United States of America. Incredibly, it was the U.S. Supreme Court that institutionalized American segregation in public places, the workplace, and schools with its decision in the 1896 *Plessy v. Ferguson* case. That decision stated that public accommodations could be segregated by race as long as they were "separate but equal." The infamous ruling stood until 1954 when an unequivocal, unbiased U.S. Supreme Court overruled *Plessy v. Ferguson* with the historic *Brown v. Board of Education* decision. That ruling essentially outlawed segregation by pronouncing "separate can never be equal."

It was Ed's cousin, Barbara Rose Johns, who at age 16 galvanized students to walk out of Farmville's black, segregated R. R. Moton High School. The school was purposely underfunded, and had no desks, blackboards, cafeteria, or teachers' restrooms. Young Barbara's 1951 walkout became the basis for the lawsuit *Davis v. Prince Edward County*, brought by the famed and courageous civil rights attorney Oliver Hill. The case was one of five that comprised the plaintiffs in *Brown v. Board of Education*, the lawsuit tried and won by the NAACP's mighty chief counsel, Thurgood Marshall.

As Ed's cousin was demonstrating the leadership skills that would later characterize his own life, one can only imagine how America's intractable, shameful racism affected his emotions during his youth. But like so many of his northern relatives and peers who spent summers with their southern kin, Ed was told by his grandparents that they expected and needed him to work. And work he did. As did all of his ever so many relatives who were busy on the farm during the summer picking cherries and tobacco; plowing fields, canning vegetables, tending the chickens, horses, pigs, and mules; harvesting squash, lima beans, corn, and tomatoes; growing peaches, apples, onions, green vegetables, cabbage, and blueberries. And, even cutting logs with a manual saw!

It was common for people in Farmville during the 1940s and '50s to live without the conveniences of electricity or plumbing. Ed's grandparents, like mine in Shores, had an outhouse, and fetched their water from a spring that flowed on the property and from a well. They used kerosene lamps for light after dusk; bought ice to keep the milk cold; kept warm and cooked with stoves filled with wood; collected rainwater to launder clothes on washboards; and slept on beds made from straw.

From a child's perspective (at least from mine), the lack of modern conveniences did not cause inconveniences. It was a way of life that was full and important. Everyone was expected to do something in collaboration with others. Farmville, I think, was an environment that aided Ed in developing a solid sense of himself, despite the ubiquitous racism. He learned to value humans, to communicate well, and to work with diligence, responsibility, and passion.

In 1985 Ed Lewis invited me to lunch. I had never met him, but I certainly knew who he was, having been featured with my husband, Bill Cosby, on the cover of *Essence* magazine in the late 1970s. There would be another cover featuring just me, and later, other articles in the magazine about Bill or myself. Ed had invited me to lunch to ask that I join the board of directors of Essence Communications Inc.

As a public person married to a very public man, I have met innumerable people, but I can explicitly say that I have not met many men like Ed Lewis. There he was at lunch, a positive paradigm of black manhood, the result of his single mother's loving upbringing—and of all those matrilineal relatives in Farmville! He had great eye contact, forthright questions and answers, and an open transparency and great respect for black women. He was also an astute businessman who, of course, possessed great intelligence.

The outcome of that lunch meeting was my joining the Essence board of directors, one of only three women outside of *Essence* female senior staff to serve as a director. The first one was Harriet Michel, then executive director of the New York Foundation; the second was Congresswoman Maxine Waters, and I was the third. I held the position from 1986 to 2005, the year Essence was sold to Time Warner.

A couple of years after joining the board, I purchased Pioneer Capital's shares of Essence stock. Pioneer was the investment company that had bought its shares from Playboy Enterprises, an early investor in Essence. The purchase made me the second-largest shareholder of Essence stock behind John H. Johnson, the founder and publisher of *Ebony* and *Jet* magazines.

I knew Ed was a sound businessman and a good leader, so I never saw buying Essence stock as a risky investment. Moreover, *Essence,* a magazine founded by four young black men in 1970, grew into a media powerhouse essentially because Ed Lewis remained the steady cofounder, CEO, and publisher who navigated that entity during its thirty-five years of black, independent ownership.

The story of *Essence* magazine and Edward Lewis is as exciting, dramatic, and instructive as any of the extraordinary stories in the annals of American businesses.

When the board approved the sale of Essence Communications Inc. (ECI), to Time Warner in 2005, I served on a special finance committee along with fellow board members J. Bruce Llewellyn and Frank Savage. Our objectives were to negotiate some of the financial matters as it related to the *Essence* senior staff, and to be certain Ed's wishes were honored by requesting that the mission and integrity of Ed's beloved Essence Communications Inc. be sustained as an independent voice under the ownership of Time Warner. The fact that Time Warner paid the largest amount of money it had ever paid for a single-titled magazine company when it bought ECI, speaks to the remarkable influences of black female voices and intelligence.

Essence Communications Inc. would not have developed into the sought-after, financially sound, and creative workplace it became without Ed's calm and focused leadership. He has often been underestimated, but has always prevailed, thanks to his substance of character, perseverance, and a background rooted in a large, loving, and magnificent family. What a family it was and is: one that has been filled with resolute and caring black women and black men.

That family nurtured the man who would in turn help launch a magazine that has affirmed, celebrated, and communicated to black women for more than forty years. So when Ed wooed and won his exceptional wife, Carolyn, nearly thirty years ago, he was a man already steeped in a deep respect and an enduring serious-mindedness about women. It is no wonder he would emerge as the last man standing at *Essence* magazine.

The Last Man Standing

I know what they say about me—that I am too quiet and low-key, unassuming, even clueless. Not the one you'd expect to be the last man standing after the smoke has cleared and the body count taken. Yet here I am, in the position to tell a remarkable story as the only cofounder remaining on the masthead of a multimillion-dollar magazine I helped launch more than forty years ago with three other black businessmen.

We four partners were all young bloods in the beginning, emboldened by a rather extraordinary, even revolutionary idea: that there could be a profitable business in starting a magazine that affirmed the strength, beauty, style, and achievements of American black women. My being here may seem as improbable as that idea was back in 1968.

What was groundbreaking at the time was not just the idea of a business partnership among black men, but the notion that the American black woman constituted a viable economic market that could be sold to Madison Avenue as a demographic force distinct and different from the general women's magazine market. A force to be recognized, reckoned with, and valued.

Coming as it did on the heels of the civil rights movement and the cresting of the women's movement, a magazine "For Today's Black Woman" proved to be one of those good ideas whose time was right on time. But like any seismic social movement, it was an idea that would take shape in struggle and upheaval, given to both enormous expectations and bitter disappointments. There would be boardroom fights and courtroom fights, firings and mass defections, hostile takeover attempts, petty shakedowns, even warring partners packing heat—and always, a skeptical Madison Avenue that had to be convinced of the worth of the black female consumer market.

The first fight was early and probably inevitable. What do you *name* a magazine created for black women rising in the dawn of a new decade with its new possibilities? The name had to resonate, connote depth of spirit and primal agency.

The story of *Essence* is in many ways the story of American business, black style. With little history to draw upon from black businessmen and women competing in the larger American marketplace, the men and women behind *Essence* had to forge a new business model along with a new magazine in a still largely racially unwelcoming marketplace, accompanied by an old, and sometimes debilitating, black mind-set. There would be casualties along the way, for sure, but also historic victories. I consider myself one of the victors. Not only because I helped build what turned out to be an enormously successful magazine enterprise, then sold it thirty-five years after launching it and walked from the table with a fair amount of the chips, but because of what I learned getting to the table.

What I would first learn is something that Suzanne de Passe, the legendary Hollywood producer who headed Motown Productions, commented on thirty years ago when there was talk of Motown being sold: "In a certain way black people seem to feel that black companies owe them something extra," she said in a magazine interview, "the kind of something extra that cannot be given if you want to stay in business."

So true. What distinguishes black businesses from the business enterprises of other ethnic groups is the sheer intensity of emotional investment that African Americans often bring to a black venture. And I have found that the more successful a black business is perceived to be, the more strident the investment is on the part of the general black public. There is a very real and consuming sense of propriety—that the business somehow belongs to *them*.

The trouble with this, of course, is that it can become exceedingly difficult to make business decisions if it feels like an entire race of people is scrutinizing your every move. This has pretty much been the case with *Essence* from the beginning. A magazine for black women would by its very definition turn out to be a fragile totem on which to lay all the hopes, aspirations, wishes, desires, and even fantasies of a people long denied affirmation. Virtually every fight and skirmish in the big and small battles that would rage at the magazine for thirty-five years has been over what was thought to be *owed*—or perceived to be owed—not just to the people involved with running the magazine, but to the larger black population as well.

In some ways this phenomenon is a part of that curious "black tax" African Americans are inevitably made to pay, whether it be for the cost of being black in America or for the much higher cost of being a black success in America. It is pretty much an axiom in black American culture that enormous individual black success gets experienced collectively as race success. But it is also just as true that enormous individual black success can typically lead to black resentment on the part of all those other blacks who are not as successful.

We call it "player hating," a specific and venomous envy that gets directed at any black person who seems to have figured out how to play what's often thought of as a white man's game—and win. Or sometimes to play any game and win. I have certainly been the target of much player hating in the four decades following the launch of *Essence*. But I am not really surprised. Compared to the men I went into partnership with, I was always the quiet, soft-spoken, cool, and unassuming brother in the room. Not as tall or handsome as some, or as charming, loquacious, or flashy as others. This would appear in some ways to make me the least likely to succeed.

But the thing about being quiet and soft-spoken is that you most likely have a greater capacity to listen. The thing about being cool is that you have the ability, as the British poet Rudyard Kipling put it, to "keep your head when all about you are losing theirs and blaming it on you." And the thing about being understated is that you don't lead with ego or arrogance, and are therefore less likely to fall into that career-ending booby trap set with the two deadly distractions fatal for many men: women and sex. All of these "unassuming" qualities turned out to be the very virtues that contributed to my victory as the last man standing at *Essence* magazine.

From the beginning this partnership with a band of young brothers, diverse and distinct, yet bodacious enough to believe we could make money selling to the market of black women, would try and test us as we set sail on a new business course. Through waters that were uncharted, murky, and perpetually troubled. Prior to 1968, most African-American businesses had been established as solo or family-run enterprises, starting with and usually ending in the ego-driven vision of the founding father or mother. *Essence,* on the other hand, was started as a legal *partnership* by men who were neither related by blood nor even known to each other before a fateful meeting brought them together in 1968 around the idea of "black entrepreneurship."

A black business partnership was not only an anomaly when *Essence* was started, it was no less than downright radical, for the success of the venture would depend on the ability of the partners to do something that has historically eluded African Americans: act in concert and unity by subsuming personal ego and ambition in order to elevate a larger collective vision. In other words, if the business was to survive, succeed, and thrive, four black men would have to learn how to work together. Sounds simple enough. But the fact that I alone am the partner left standing after forty some years speaks to just how difficult executing that simple idea continues to be.

Surprisingly enough, it was in my partnership with four black men that I learned some truths about power. I discovered that real power—the kind that effects change and is lasting—is about understanding the nature of shared dependency. This is what a partnership really is. Each partner brings a set of unique skills and talent to the enterprise and must rely on the specific strengths of the others to make the business run. There is no place for one-upmanship, competition, or egos getting in the way of doing business if the business is to run profitably. In a successful partnership power has to be *shared,* otherwise it won't work. And neither will the business.

The defining feature of *Essence* through all the struggles that would mark its ascent has been its ability to remain successful and profitable over an incredible forty-plus-year run. From its launch in May 1970 with a circulation of 50,000, to the day it changed hands in 2005 with a circulation of 1.1 million and a total pass-along readership of 8 million, the magazine turned a profit every year after 1977, except 1978, 1979, and 1984. Magazine publishing, it turned out, could be a huge cash-generating machine capable of enriching all those who had some ownership in it. But let's be clear: *Essence* specifically was a huge cash-generating machine. The same could not be said of the dozens of other publications that had gone before and would come after.

The key to *Essence*'s success would be the very market it was created to reach: black women. In some ways the magazine has always benefited from simply being the first publication of its kind: The first to ride through on the crashing waves of two tsunami-like American social movements—civil rights and women's rights. The first to tap the colossal sleeping beauty that was the black women's consumer market. The first to recognize black women as both a political and cultural force who brought creative savvy, intellectual prowess, and a singular talent for heavy lifting to a shifting American landscape. And the first to acknowledge, applaud, and continually affirm the beauty and elegance of black women's style, grace, and remarkable achievements.

The partners who started *Essence* may have been men, but we always agreed on one essential thing: We were the brothers "holding it down" on the business side of the magazine, but it would have to be the "sisters," black women, who let it fly on the editorial side. None of the partners were arrogant or crazy enough to presume that we actually *knew* what black women wanted in a magazine directed to them. That insight would come from the visionary women who have edited the magazine for more than four decades. It was their ability to strike the note of empathy and recognition in editing a magazine for women who looked like them, dreamed like them, had the same longings and aspirations, experienced the same pains and disappointments, and ultimately claimed the same victories that always made *Essence* an intensely personal experience for its millions of devoted readers.

I would daresay that no other publication has enjoyed as fiercely loyal an audience as the readers of *Essence*. Its editors-in-chief, the top management women who set the editorial direction and mission of the magazine over the years, have been viewed as crusading leaders as much as thinking editors by the women who look to *Essence* for guidance, and not just information. This is perhaps the linchpin of the magazine's success.

Still, when *Essence* started there was absolutely no history of black women running magazines for themselves, about themselves. For that matter, there was no history of black women running much of anything in corporate America. So like the partners on the business side, the women on the editorial side of *Essence* would experience the same birthing pains that bring forth any new, seismic movement.

With no history of black women magazine editors to emulate, the editors of *Essence* had to forge their own path to higher ground, often operating on intuition and instinct, the two particular strengths women bring to enterprises. As the award-winning novelist Toni Morrison said about the tenacity of black women in an essay she wrote for the fifteenth-anniversary issue of *Essence*, "She had nothing to fall back on; not male-ness, not whiteness, not ladyhood, not anything. And out of the profound desolation of her reality she may well have invented herself."

It would be the male partners of *Essence* who invented the Essence Woman, an advertising demographic marketed to Madison Avenue. The Essence Woman was a striver, a doer, smart, educated, ambitious, with tremendous purchasing power that advertisers would be wise to recognize and court. On the editorial side the Essence Woman was no less real. She was a woman in the vanguard of change, sometimes conflicted, often vulnerable. She cared about her relationships with her man, her children, her family, and her community; she wanted a career and not just a job; she wanted to look good and see herself reflected in all her varying beauty; she was political and artistic, business-minded and race-conscious.

Essence was not only the first women's magazine to embrace the total-ity of its readers, it was the first magazine to think in terms of *empowering* its readers—specifically black women who had historically been denied power. This became the editorial mission of the magazine—to not just inform, educate, and celebrate, but to *elevate* the thinking of black women regarding how they saw themselves, the larger world, and their place in it. This idea of an editorial mission in running a magazine proved to be a bold, new editorial approach to magazine publishing and a harbinger of such magazines as *Ms., O, The Oprah Magazine,* and *More,* all publications coming after *Essence* that would speak to the power inherent in a niche female demographic outside the margins of traditional women's magazine markets, whether it be feminists or women over 40.

For black women and men working in media, *Essence* became the nat-ural forum for their talents as writers and editors, illustrators and photog-raphers, models and fashion designers, hair stylists and makeup artists. No other single publication directed to the black community offered so many employment opportunities to a black freelance artist community. It is no wonder, then, that the top editorial position at *Essence,* its editor-in-chief, the one who has final decision-making authority in assigning and hiring from this vast talent pool, is perceived as the seat of exalted power among black women in media. Twelve women have occupied the editor-in-chief's chair since the magazine was launched, wielding the kind of power that certainly was not possible for them at nonblack magazines.

Status and glamour, high income, celebrity access, and a national constituency of loyal readers are the perks now typically associated with the editor-in-chief's position at *Essence.* It is hard to believe that during its first stormy year of operation, the magazine had four editors-in-chief. Great and not-so-great editors have run the magazine since then, and I had a say in hiring all of them. I would occasionally butt heads with some of them, and even fired two of them.

But for the most part, I had the good sense to just get out of the way.

Like my partnership with the men on the business side of the magazine, I recognized that the women on the editorial side of *Essence* were in a working partnership with the business side. The men and women who worked in sales on the business side were charged with selling page space in the magazine to advertisers, while the women and men who worked in editorial were charged with delivering magazine content to readers.

Each side was dependent on the other to produce the twin revenue streams—advertising and circulation—that make or break a magazine enterprise. Just as I knew I would have to rely on the strengths and talents of my business partners and share power, I knew I had to rely on the strengths and talents of my editor-in-chief and her editors—and also share power. I had to have faith in her ability to make the magazine "fly"—to reach the circulation levels that would make the magazine profitable.

Given this, I rarely tried to dictate editorial by telling the editors what to write about or whom to feature in the magazine's pages or on its covers. As the magazine's publisher, my job was to oversee the business side of the enterprise: the advertising, accounting, circulation, public relations, and human resource departments. If editorial decisions affected any of these areas on my watch, then I stepped in. Otherwise, I pretty much let the editors run the magazine as they saw fit.

The truth is, I have always been comfortable with women running things, clearly another virtue at a magazine directed to women. I have my own roster of personal "sheroes," those women I adore and respect unequivocally, from my grandmother and mother to my wife and two daughters—and numerous women in between—who have helped shape and influence me, contributing mightily to who I am today. They are a large part of the reason I am here still standing, not so much as the last man, but as a better man. They are the reason I am now telling my story, which is inextricably also the story of *Essence* magazine, and the story of every black woman longing to see her better self reflected in American media.

The story starts in struggle with four black men trying to turn a business idea into a profitable magazine amid turmoil from within and racism from without as they continually fought to sell the black female market to resistant advertisers. The story ends for purposes here when that magazine was sold thirty-five years later to the largest publishing company in the world for the highest cost-per-page of any purchase in its history. By then a publication called *Essence* had reached a circulation of 1.1 million readers, with 8 million pass-along readers, and grown into a virtual business empire that included at various points in its expansion a television show, an awards show, a music festival, a book partnership, other magazines, and licensing ventures. I was the surviving partner at the table who did the deal in the sale of the magazine, and the surviving partner who was accused of "selling out."

As I said earlier, the story of *Essence* is the story of American business, black style. And that means it is a story filled with all the pathos and drama, high points and tragic lows, and familial dysfunction that typically accompany black life, with racism always in the mix. I survived to tell the story not because I was necessarily the best man among the partners, but maybe because I was the strong man with tenacious staying power. Like those survivors of the horrific Middle Passage on the transatlantic slave crossing to the New World, I was the one who refused to die.

A few years ago I had the wonderful opportunity to have dinner with Condoleezza Rice, then secretary of state in the George W. Bush administration. The enormity of the historic moment was not lost on me. In fact, I was somewhat overwhelmed by it. Here we were, two African Americans whose shared history of slavery, oppression, and discrimination could never have been a predictor of the transformed world in which we now found ourselves. That predictor, it turned out, would be *Essence* magazine, the publication that for more than forty years has been showing black women they can be anything and everything they want to be. I had no idea whether Condoleezza Rice was an *Essence* reader or not, but what I do know as surely as I know my name is that without *Essence* there would have been no black female secretary of state. And no black first lady in the White House.

Just as I know that without *Essence* there would be no me, standing in victory.

—EDWARD LEWIS, NOVEMBER 30, 2013

PART I

Getting Started

(1968–1970)

CHAPTER 1

The "Godfather" Calls a Sit-Down

1968. It was a very bad year, perhaps the worst of times in a nation rocked by political assassinations, urban riots, underground revolutionaries, and defiant protestors. Visionary leaders were violently killed: Martin Luther King, Jr., gunned down on a Memphis hotel balcony in April; Robert F. Kennedy shot in a Los Angeles hotel kitchen in June; black riots erupting in dozens of American cities following the killings. The Democratic National Convention in Chicago had been convulsed by rioting and confrontations in August as the city's notorious head-bashing cops knocked heads outside the International Amphitheatre, ferociously beating down thousands of angry black and white protestors who were threatening to tear apart America as we knew it. A grim national report on the civil unrest, commissioned by President Lyndon B. Johnson, was released that year and warned that the country was in danger of moving toward two societies—one black, one white—separate and unequal.

Yet if 1968 seemed to be the worst of times, it also held out hope for some for better times, and I, for one, needed that. I had already suffered through my own miserable times, losing a college football scholarship to the University of New Mexico, flunking out of law school in Washington, DC, six years later, and finding myself, now at 28, back home at the St. Mary's housing projects in the South Bronx, living with my mother and stepfather.

Like most blacks, I was furious over the assassinations of King and Kennedy, but I knew violence was not the answer to the many problems besetting us as a people. Money was, pure and simple. Not money for the

3

sake of lavish spending or grand profiling, but money for the real good it can do in improving lives.

I cannot say it was money alone, though, that drove me to apply for a position with First National City Bank three years before. That year, 1965, I just needed something constructive to do—needed to feel I was back in *somebody's* game. I had returned to New York in the fall, after a seven-year absence, having spent six years in Albuquerque at the University of New Mexico and another nine months in Washington, DC, as a student in Georgetown University's School of Law.

I washed out after the first year.

Devastated, I spent the summer working for an antipoverty program in DC before heading back home to New York. Still reeling from what I considered a colossal failure, I was too ashamed to tell anyone, not even my mother, I had flunked out of law school. In fact, I was so dislocated I actually rode the subway two or three times a week from the Bronx to Columbia University's campus in upper Manhattan, where I would hang around the law school, pretending to still be a law student. I told my mother I had transferred from Georgetown to Columbia. This went on for weeks. How pitiful was *that*?

But nobody wants to dance with you at a pity party. Shortly after flunking out I called Howard Mathany, dean of men at the University of New Mexico, to confess the awful truth. The dean had been an early mentor while I was a student at the university, helping me to remain in school after I lost my scholarship. I stayed in touch with him when I left Albuquerque to go to Georgetown. And now I trusted this white man enough to call and pretty much spill my guts.

"Dean Mathany, I flunked out," I blurted into the phone. "I guess I just don't have what it takes to be a lawyer. I never saw myself as an intellectual heavyweight or anything, but—"

"C'mon, Ed!" Dean Mathany cut me off impatiently. "You've always had many interests, and you *do* have a master's degree." True. I had lost my football scholarship my freshman year, but was able to return to the university the next year through some string pulling and end up with both bachelor's and master's degrees six years later.

Dean Mathany casually mentioned that he had a friend who worked in personnel at First National City Bank (now Citibank) in New York.

The bank was looking to hire talented minorities in its executive training program in New York City. "Maybe you should think about applying," the dean gently suggested.

I realized this was Dean Mathany's easy way of telling me that one setback did not mean I was without prospects. I still had skills. Failing law school did not mean *I* was a failure. It just meant I had not done well in a particular situation. That struck me. And I would continue to be struck throughout my life by all the people I would meet—people I admired and respected—who saw a winning prospect in me when I often could not see anything at all.

I was drowning in shame and self-doubt the day I called Dean Mathany to say I had washed out of law school, but he was not about to listen to any "po' is me" riff. Instead, he threw out the life preserver of faith and affirmation by suggesting I think about applying for a position with First National City Bank.

Just a thought. But sometimes that's all you need to turn around a life.

I applied for and got the job at First National City Bank, and three years later, in the fall of 1968, got the call that would transform my life. It was from Russell L. Goings, a vice president at the Shearson, Hammill and Company investment banking firm.

"Ed, I'm inviting a bunch of you young bloods to a meeting down here at headquarters," he boomed over the phone. "I want you to come. It's time we sit down with these guys here at Shearson and get them to put some money behind their liberal rhetoric."

Then in his late thirties, Russ Goings, whom I would later come to think of as the Godfather of *Essence,* was a great hulking bear of a man—handsome, articulate, confident, imposing at six foot four, with a large, brash personality to match. He understood that the real battle for civil rights would be won not in the streets, but on the economic front of black entrepreneurship. He had played professional football for the Buffalo Bills, but as Shearson's first black vice president, Russ knew the winning game in the late 1960s for young, educated American Negroes (as we were then called) was black capitalism, and he was in the forefront of getting Wall Street to aid in that effort.

———

I didn't know any of the guys at the meeting Russ was holding that evening of November 8, 1968, but we were all pretty much alike. Young and black, tall, short, dark-skinned or light, we were smart and educated, professional, well employed, and had one thing in common: We wanted to be real players in the American game of business. We wanted to make a difference in the lives of our people—at least I did.

Russ, sitting at the head of the large conference table in one of Shearson's meeting rooms at its Wall Street headquarters, was telling us that the most effective way to do that was to *own* our own businesses. This is why he had called the meeting, he said. He wanted to discuss business ideas and ways to raise capital to fund them.

"Now, I'm not talkin' about no mom-and-pop operation you could fund with your Christmas Club savings accounts," Russ thundered, leaning his large frame forward. "Let's think big and bold. Come up with some business ideas I think these Wall Street boys will want to invest in, and I'll guarantee you a meeting with them. Shearson will help you put together a business plan, identify funding sources, give you technical support, maybe even some seed money—anything you need to get a business going!"

While black militants were threatening armed revolution during the urban violence that marred the last half of the 1960s, black capitalists like Russ Goings were storming American boardrooms, telling white businessmen to open up access to capital if they wanted to make black peace. Russ was one of the big guns Wall Street had in its arsenal of weapons aimed at quelling black urban rage. For if anything defined America in 1968, it was all the exploding violence, among its black youth in particular, that had shaken the country to its racially charged roots.

What was clear by 1968 was just how enraged much of America's black underclass really was. There was rage over police brutality in poor black neighborhoods, rage over poor schools in poor neighborhoods, race discrimination in job hiring, poor housing, inadequate social services. The hundreds of urban riots that followed the first one in the Los Angeles neighborhood of Watts in 1965 had white America running scared by the start of 1968, the year political and social violence seemed to spiral out of control.

Even President Johnson looked a little scared on July 28, 1967, the day he announced he had commissioned a panel to investigate the causes of and possible remedies for the urban violence that was tearing up the cities. Headed by Otto Kerner, the governor of Illinois, the commission released its findings in February of 1968. The Kerner Report was a scathing, damning indictment that charged white racism with being the primary cause of urban violence. Among the remedies proposed were the creation of jobs, the building of new housing, and the hiring of more blacks in mainstream media to more accurately reflect and report on the country's underserved black population.

The Kerner Report became the lightning rod for an assortment of social and economic programs following the rebellions by disaffected blacks in America's cities. And black capitalists like Russell Goings expected Wall Street to play as major a role in leveling the playing field as any government-sponsored social programs.

"Black men don't need a *handout* from business," Russ liked to tell the white guys on Wall Street. "They need a *hand up* in the way of access to capital so they can start their own businesses." Like the James Brown song said, "I don't want nobody to give me nothing. Open up the door, I'll get it myself." Equal business opportunity. That's what Russ was about when he called that fateful November meeting.

I first met Russ shortly after going to work for First National City Bank. He tried to hire me away. Russell Goings didn't exactly run Shearson, Hammill, but he was arguably their corporate conscience, and knew how to work white corporate guilt the way a three-card-monte hustler could work Times Square tourists. And there was plenty of white business guilt being fired up in 1968 as America's institutions scrambled to be a part of the solution to black civil unrest. Russ had even convinced Shearson to let him open a branch office of Shearson in Harlem, known as First Harlem Securities.

If young, educated black men such as myself had the opportunity to become business owners, we would be in a position to create jobs for our own people, to build our own better housing, and to turn around our own beleaguered communities. That was Russ's idea, anyway.

"You need to think big and bold like those two fine young men down there in Mexico City," Russ was saying, looking around the room at all of us. He was referring, of course, to the two black athletes who just three weeks before had raised a clench-fisted Black Power salute during the awards ceremony at the 1968 Olympics in Mexico City.

Tommie Smith, 24, representing the United States in the 200-meter track and field event, had won the gold medal, setting a new world record, and John Carlos, 23, also representing the United States, had won the bronze. Standing on their respective podiums, they lowered their heads and gave the Black Power raised fist salute as "The Star-Spangled Banner" played and the American flag waved in the winners' circle. Smith wore a black scarf to symbolize black pride, and Carlos wore a chain of beads to honor, he said, "those individuals that were lynched or killed that no one said a prayer for, [for] those who were thrown off the boats in the Middle Passage." Both men were shoeless, wearing only black socks to highlight black poverty.

The gesture was defiant. The raised fist was daring. And it had the effect of an exploding Molotov cocktail being heard around the world.

"Man, I don't care what anybody says, that shit took some guts," one of the guys sitting at the table was saying.

"But check it," said another. "Do you believe Carlos, with his dumb-ass self, left his gloves back at the Olympic Village?" A few of the guys snickered at that one. Smith and Carlos had planned to do the Black Power salute wearing black leather gloves if they won any of their events. But John Carlos had forgotten to bring his gloves. So Tommie Smith gave him his left glove to wear, which is why in all the photos of that defining, defiant moment, each man is wearing only one glove—Smith is raising a gloved right hand and Carlos is raising a gloved left hand. It *was* pretty funny. But the act itself was pretty damn heroic.

To me and the other men at the table, Tommie Smith and John Carlos were hardly dumb-ass. Bad-ass was more like it. They had set it off, not by torching a city, but by igniting black male pride. Standing on their winners' box that day in Mexico City on October 16, 1968, they became, during a very bad year, the international symbol of the American black man at his personal best: athletically superior, politically conscious, and brave enough to raise the fist of Black Power in challenge to a racist system.

The American government may have been embarrassed, but we black men were just really proud. And one of my proudest moments was having the opportunity to tell Tommie Smith and John Carlos exactly that forty years later when I had the privilege of meeting them at the Beijing Summer Olympics in 2008. After years of being ostracized because of their daring act in 1968, they had been invited by the Olympic Committee to attend the 2008 Beijing games as honored guests.

Russ was shrewd enough to understand the business implications of Smith and Carlos. Investing in bold black men with bold business ideas had become an attractive idea to the Wall Street players—the investment bankers and the venture capitalists who were looking to back new ideas with profit potential as well as the potential to do some social good. To be sure, bold black men who were also educated professionals were certainly less threatening than the ghetto boys who were burning down their own neighborhoods—or the athletes who were throwing a fist at the American flag. The smart white money would be on investing in black men who were not quite so angry, or at least not so up in your face with it. Goings knew this. He wanted us to think like the bold brothers Smith and Carlos were, but act like the polished professionals we also were.

I have often thought about the irony of that day. Here we were, twenty-five or so sharply dressed young black men in our midtwenties to early thirties—looking good in our wide-lapel suit jackets, bell-bottomed trousers, and platform shoes—having a sit-down on Wall Street called by a black man. We knew that there but for the grace of God went any one of us, because any one of us could just as easily have been one of those ghetto guys burning down their neighborhoods.

Russ was winding up his presentation: "Remember, fellas, the route to black capitalism runs through Wall Street, which leads directly to America's financial temples—the investment banks, the commercial banks, the stock exchanges. This is where we've got to now be throwing down our buckets. Forget that forty acres and a mule bullshit. Ain't none of you ever gonna be farmers! Wall Street represents the one American god in which we can all trust: money."

Russell Goings wasn't the only one preaching the gospel of black capitalism in 1968. The first true believer was Richard M. Nixon, elected president of the United States on November 5, 1968. It was Nixon who had coined the term *Black Capitalism* in April of 1968 while campaigning for the Republication nomination right after King's assassination. Black Capitalism was the centerpiece of what Nixon was calling his Bridges to Human Dignity program, emphasizing black self-help through business development rather than continued dependency on government social programs.

I am one of the few people I know who would have voted for Nixon if I'd been old enough to vote when he ran for president the first time against John F. Kennedy in 1960. I was 20 that year, a year shy of the legal voting age of 21. For some reason I didn't really trust Kennedy on civil rights. He seemed too old-line Boston, too rich, too Brahmin, which to me made him too disconnected from the issues affecting the lives of the country's minority caste. Unless he was forced to, I didn't think he would to do right by black people.

Richard Nixon, on the other hand, was no guilt-ridden liberal. He understood business. And, like Russ, by 1968 he recognized that the best way to help a disenfranchised minority class was to help turn it into an entrepreneur class. Almost as soon as he came into office, Nixon signed Executive Order 11458, establishing the Office of Minority Business Enterprise (OMBE) within the Department of Commerce.

Commerce Secretary Maurice Stans would give the order teeth and bite with the creation of MESBIC (the Minority Enterprise Small Business Investment Corporation), which became the venture capital arm of the government for minority businesses. For the first time in our history, small black businesses had access to capital through a government program mandated specifically for them. And we had Richard Nixon to thank for that.

Nixon also named Robert C. Weaver to head the Department of Housing and Urban Development, the first Negro ever appointed to a cabinet position. And Arthur Fletcher, a Negro in the Labor Department, was the deputy secretary who almost single-handedly administered the Philadelphia Plan, a government program aimed at giving more federal contracts to minority construction firms. People used to think I was crazy when I would say Richard Nixon was the real father of affirmative action.

It was the Godfather, however, who was now pledging that Shearson was on board to assist with any solid business ideas we came up with during the meeting. To prove it, Russ introduced Michael Victory, Shearson, Hammill and Co.'s number two guy—an executive vice president, partner, and heir apparent to the number one spot. For purposes of at this meeting, Michael Victory was apparently also Russell Goings's wingman.

Victory was as soft-spoken as Russ was loud. He promised that Shearson would give us all the help we needed to get a business going—advice, support, seed money, access to capital. "Just come up with a good business idea," he said with the slightest trace of a Cockney accent. I honestly do not remember any of the ideas that were getting tossed around, but I do remember Victory throwing out a "for instance" that grabbed my attention. "I would think there could be a need for a Negro women's magazine, for instance," he said offhandedly.

A hand shot up: "*I* have an idea for a magazine for Negro women," said a light-skinned brother with green eyes who was sitting across the table from me. He told the story of seeing his mother in the living room when he was a kid, thumbing through a women's magazine, looking at all the photos of white women, and then overhearing her mutter, "I wonder why someone can't do a magazine for Negro women."

"That's not a bad idea," Russ said. A few more ideas were floated, then at the end of the meeting Russ broke us up into smaller discussion groups. "If a particular idea interests you, then get with the gentleman who presented it," he told us.

"Jonathan, you might want to talk to Ed Lewis over there," Russ suddenly said, gesturing to me as he talked to the brother with the magazine idea. "Ed knows something about finance."

Besides me, there were two other men that evening whose imagination had been captured by a mother wondering, *Why can't someone start a magazine for Negro women?* We pulled our chairs up to talk with Jonathan, her son.

"Why *can't* we start a magazine for Negro women?"

"You heard Russ. Not a bad idea."

"In fact, it might be a great idea."

"This could be a serious moneymaker."

We introduced ourselves, talked some more, exchanged business cards. Russ called a second meeting, and at this one another guy joined with the four of us who had met at that initial meeting. We talked some more. Over the next few months four of us from the original group of five would become business partners. It was the first step in launching a magazine for Negro women that would become bigger than anything we could have ever imagined as 1968, a very bad year, drew to a close.

CHAPTER 2

Four Black Men and a Magazine, Baby

Clarence Smith. Jonathan Blount. Cecil Hollingsworth. Phillip Janniere. *Who the hell are these guys?* That is not the question I asked, but maybe the one I should have. Because by March 1969—four months after the November 1968 Wall Street meeting to talk about black entrepreneurship—I had quit my job at First National City Bank, dropped out of graduate school, and gone into business with four men I didn't even know.

Well, one of them, Clarence Smith, I sort of knew. I had seen and talked with him during those occasional times when I made the after-work bar scene. He liked to hang out at a bar called Cheers, a popular spot in midtown Manhattan. Clarence came to the second meeting Russ Goings had called on black entrepreneurship, and ended up joining the four of us from the first meeting who had gotten together afterward to talk about starting a magazine for Negro women.

Clarence, at 35, was married and the oldest one in the group. A regular cruiser among the after-work bar set, he was big on drinking, eyeing the ladies, and smooth talking. He was actually brilliant at smooth talking. His voice was deep and melodious; his words persuasive and articulate. This, combined with being good-looking, made him a natural in sales, his chosen profession. He sold life insurance for the Prudential Life Insurance Company, and was a top producer, consistently in the "Million Dollar Circle."

I used to joke that Clarence could sell the rattles off a snake back *to* the snake. He and my colleague Earl Graves, founder and publisher of *Black Enterprise* magazine, were the two salesmen I knew who could sell their asses *off.* They were the best I had ever seen. Clarence never sold *me,* however. I always considered it something of an achievement that I had never been seduced by a glib-talking smoothie into buying life insurance, something I knew I didn't really need back then as a young single man with no children.

As for the three others in the partnership, Jonathan Blount, 24, single, was the youngest and by far the most colorful and controversial of the group. He's the one who had the idea for a magazine directed at Negro women. Or at least his mother did. Like Clarence, Jonathan was smooth, handsome, charming, and also successful in sales. He was a salesman for the New Jersey Bell Telephone Company's Yellow Pages in its South Orange office. A tallish, gold-colored man with piercing green eyes that women would tell me "seemed to be looking right through you," Jonathan's pretty-boy looks, as it turned out, concealed emotional instability. He could be mercurial, unpredictable, yet brilliant; crazy, tempestuous, but profoundly astute. You never knew what to expect with this guy, which would cause problems from the very beginning.

Cecil Hollingsworth, 27, was the only partner who already owned his own business. A former second lieutenant in the U.S. Army Reserves, he was a graphics consultant who designed catalogs, brochures, and sales promotional materials for such clients as Warner-Lambert, the Lorillard Corporation, and Merrill Lynch. Like Clarence, he was married. He also had an office and stationery, which gave him a business *presence.* So did his sculpted heart-shaped Afro, handlebar mustache, and natty dress style.

Phillip (Tony) Janniere, 27, single, was simply the best-looking one of the group. Standing six foot two, muscular, suave, with what some of us still call "good hair," he, too, was in sales. And he worked in the very business we were talking about starting—publishing. As a salesman for the *New York Times,* Tony at least had some idea of what publishing actually was, and that was more than the rest of us could say.

And finally there was me, Edward Lewis, 28, single. The only one in the partnership who had finished college, had an advanced degree, and was not in sales. I came out of banking and knew something about financing, managing cash flow, and credit analysis. Quiet, reserved, of medium height and dark skin, I wore a full Afro, a full beard, and preferred the somewhat flashier look of pale-colored pinstripe shirts and double-breasted suits. Though women have told me I am handsome and have a great smile, I have never thought of myself as particularly smooth or charismatic. Certainly not compared to these guys who had just become my business partners. We were, however, all united in the desire to have a business of our own.

I don't think any of us ever dreamed we would end up in the magazine business. Not even Jonathan, who claimed to have always had a magazine idea. I just dreamed of owning a business, period. It was my mother's brother, my uncle Tracy Spencer, who used to tell me repeatedly, "Sonny [my family nickname], if you want to have control over your life—over your destiny—the only way to do that is to have something of your own." He was a logger who ran his own logging company in Farmville, Virginia.

As a kid, I would spend summers down in Virginia doing all sorts of chores and also working for my uncle. He is 95 now and, from what I can see, still in charge of his destiny. It was because of Uncle Tracy that I wanted to have something of my own. And I wanted to be judged by what I would be able to do by having something of my own.

The other thing motivating all five of us was the growing frustration we felt working in white corporate America. We were considered to be among that rare breed of new middle-class black men known as a BMW—a black man working. But not just any black man working in any job. We BMWs were the high-end brothers, the professional black men who were young, single or married, college educated, and well employed in lucrative new occupations that were starting to open up for the most "qualified" among us following the urban riots of the late 1960s. Fields like corporate sales, law, investment banking, Wall Street trading, financial planning—all professions at the very center of American capitalism.

The black guys working in these professions were the ones thought to have an actual shot at a top slot in corporate America. Competing in careers that carried status, power, and the potential for wealth, we were popular with the ladies, envied by the working-class brothers, and sometimes a little full of ourselves, fueled by a powerful sense of our new possibilities.

We were the ones cruising the upper-tier, after-work bar scene, hitting the popular drinking spots that catered to a newly minted black professional crowd. Places like Mikell's, Rust Brown's, the Cellar, Under the Stairs, Cheers, where men in the crowd bought drinks for their buddies at the bar or for the women who caught their interest, or just talked into the night about all the things all men talk about: women, sports, money, politics, the job.

I met two men who became my best friends during this time— Hughlyn Fierce, a young banker at Chase Manhattan, and Frank Savage, who was at First National City Bank like me. Hugh would go on to have a distinguished career in international finance with Chase, and serve as chairman of Freedom National Bank, while Frank would also have a great career in international banking, corporate finance, and pioneer financial investing in Africa.

In those days, though, when we were all just starting out, Hugh and Frank and I would regularly meet at Cheers on Fridays to talk shop and give each other moral support in our new, pioneering careers. These ad hoc get-togethers usually drew other young, professional brothers, too, and were really the forerunner to the black professional networking organizations that were started in the seventies.

My male generation of pre-baby boomers were the first blacks hired in corporate professions who paved the way for the handful of black men who came behind us to reach the highest rung in corporate America: head of a Fortune 500 company. Men like Kenneth Chenault, chairman and CEO of American Express; Richard D. Parsons, former chairman and CEO of Time Warner and former chairman of Citigroup; Kenneth Frazier, president and CEO of Merck pharmaceuticals; Ronald Williams, former chairman and CEO of the Aetna health insurance company; Don Thompson, CEO of the McDonald's fast-food corporation. These were the men who became the blazing stars in a corporate galaxy of new opportunity for talented blacks.

But let's be real. Top corporate slots are still few and far between for even the most brilliant among us, black *or* white. In the nearly fifty years following the urban riots of the mid-sixties that opened up new opportunities for blacks in all areas of American life, only twelve black men and one black woman (Ursula Burns, CEO of the Xerox Corporation) have run Fortune 500 companies.

Many more, to be sure, have occupied senior management positions as corporate vice presidents, division presidents, directors, or partners. But in 1969, when we five guys formed our partnership, none of us was naive about the game being played in the corporate workplace or how far we could expect to rise. There was still racism to contend with; insecure white men to deal with; and corporate cultures to navigate that often compromised our values and sometimes our dignity.

I was especially struck by the double-edged sword that sales seemed to represent for Clarence Smith, clearly the most successful one of the group when he joined the partnership. A gifted salesman and perennial top producer at Prudential, Clarence was the only one who had a car, which back then made him a major domo among us young guys. But he always acted like sales embarrassed him. He never wanted to be identified as a salesman. He wanted to be considered more than that—better than that. It was as if selling represented some second-rate art of the flimflam and not a sophisticated higher art of the deal. He may have had the dark-skinned, chiseled good looks of an Ashanti warrior, but his troubled, conflicted spirit seemed more like that of blustery Willy Loman in the classic American tragedy, *Death of a Salesman*.

Black American tragedy is of a specific order, however, bringing a particular death to the spirit. "I don't think I can take any more of this bullshit," Clarence was ranting one evening in early 1969, sitting at the bar at Cheers, downing his usual apple martini with a dash of bourbon. "If I have to sell one more overpriced policy to one more poor black bastard who doesn't need it, can't afford it, and is getting a shitty investment to boot, I'm going to shoot the next white motherfucker who tells me what a great job I'm doing."

And there it was: Clarence was at the top of his game at one of the biggest insurance companies in the country, outselling even the top white guys, yet he continually seemed to feel like a shyster. He was not only selling insurance, a notoriously poor investment as far as return on the dollar goes, to a largely black customer base, but felt he was also somehow complicit in helping Prudential take that money from blacks and invest it in much more lucrative products that blacks had no participation in whatsoever.

The idea of being part of a new black partnership that wanted to start a magazine catering to a black female market was a concept that would stir the passions of Clarence Smith for the next thirty years. At last, he had something to sell he could believe in: the value of the black woman in the American marketplace. In the beginning, though, when there was no market research to confirm such value, no focus groups or advertising figures, Clarence had to sell what indeed often appeared to be flim and flam. Of course, he was great at it. But as a salesman he would prove to be much more than that—much better than that. He and I would remain partners long after the others who joined us in the beginning had fallen on their swords, done in by fear or greed or emotional instability.

Though none of us had any experience in running a magazine or even working in a partnership, we knew we had to organize—legally establish the partnership, elect officers, secure an office, brand ourselves with a name, and raise money. In some ways, it almost didn't matter what the business was. All of us viewed entrepreneurship as a way to not just own something, but to provide jobs to black people, which we felt was key to reducing poverty in our community. That was the very powerful subtext in starting the business.

Cecil Hollingsworth was the partner who gave us the visible trappings of being in business. Already a small entrepreneur, he not only had an office and diverse business contacts, but impressive embossed letterhead that read THE HOLLINGSWORTH GROUP. He was the group of one who quickly became part of the group of five. We took The Hollingsworth Group as the name of our partnership and began meeting after work in Cecil's office at 102 East 30th Street, in which we added a couple of secondhand desks and a small conference table. The office was really a one-bedroom apartment on the second floor of a six-story brownstone townhouse on Manhattan's East Side. A few of the apartments in the building had been converted into professional office spaces on the first two levels, while residential apartments remained on the other floors. It seemed a perfect setting for five young professional men going into business for themselves.

Once we had settled on a name for the partnership, each of us took a business title to establish lines of command and demarcate areas of expertise. I was executive vice president in charge of finance; Clarence was executive vice president in charge of advertising; Cecil, executive vice president in charge of circulation; Jonathan, a vice president in advertising, and Tony

Janniere was made president of The Hollingsworth Group, largely because he was so handsome we thought he had the most presidential aura.

"Okay, if we're going to make a go of this we've got to give it our full commitment right *now*," Clarence said as we were sitting around the conference table in the office one night. We had been meeting practically every night, going over the procedures for establishing a legal partnership, talking about meeting with the investors that a top partner at the Shearson, Hammill and Co. investment banking firm was lining up, thinking about a name for a Negro women's magazine, and wondering about what kind of Negro woman to hire on the editorial side who could actually run the magazine.

It was apparent that if we were going to commit, we'd have to leave our day jobs and devote ourselves full-time to getting the magazine off the ground. I would have to give up my graduate school studies at New York University, where I was a PhD student in public administration. There would be no salary in the beginning, no health benefits or job security of any other kind. It was a gamble, pure and simple. A huge risk. We knew *zip* about running a magazine, or any other business enterprise, for that matter. We knew a little more than *zip* about Negro women and the consumer market we believed they comprised. Tony and Jonathan and I were single. We would manage. I still lived at home, so I knew I could take the chance. Cecil and Clarence, though, had families to support. Could they really afford to give up their livelihoods for a venture that was totally unknown?

Apparently so, because here was Clarence now throwing down the gauntlet, demanding that we put our careers on the line, our futures in question—and go for it. "All right, guys," he said, "are we going to do this? You ready to leave your jobs? Let's have a show of hands." We went around the table.

"I'm in," Jonathan said quickly.

"Me, too," said Cecil just as quickly.

"Yes, yes," I said.

"You know I'm down," Clarence added.

Tony said nothing. He had not raised his hand. He finally let out a small sigh and said, "You know, guys, I don't think I can go with you on this one. The *Times* is pretty comfortable. I got a nice paycheck. This idea is just a little too risky for my blood. I'm sorry. I really am."

In a first vote of the partnership, Tony, our president, had abdicated, an early casualty who was too fearful of an uncertain future to take on the present challenge. It was a decision he would regret many times for many years, he would tell me many times over the years. Yet for all entrepreneurs, there is that moment just before you jump off the cliff into the abyss of pure risk that you hesitate for just a second, give in to self-doubt and second-guessing for just a minute, then finally, take a deep breath—and go for it.

In the case of the four of us who decided to go for it that night sitting around a small table in a small office, we were perhaps propelled by the arrogance of youth or the frustration that comes from careers that feel limited, and therefore unsatisfying. But the real wind beneath our wings as we took the plunge that night would be the courage that comes from faith, and an instinctive belief in self, which led to a certain conviction that we would somehow land still standing.

CHAPTER 3

Sapphire? Seriously?

"Damn, she's fine," whistled one of the partners under his breath. It wasn't as if we didn't all think this. Clarence, Cecil, and I were seated around the small conference table in our office on East 30th Street, openly staring at the young lady Jonathan had just ushered in.

Jonathan Blount quickly stepped up as president of The Hollingsworth Group following Tony Janniere's hasty, risk-averse exit, and was clearly relishing his new title. He had taken it upon himself to personally seek out women who could run a magazine for Negro women as its editor-in-chief. A magazine that had no name as yet, no advertising as yet, and no editorial content as yet.

By April of 1969, The Hollingsworth Group was a legal business partnership, and we now needed to hire an editor-in-chief to help develop a first issue of our fledgling magazine. We had managed to secure early seed money in the form of a loan from four partners at Shearson, Hammill and Co., which allowed us to hire our first top editor and pay the partners a small stipend.

Unfortunately, there was no large pool of editorial talent from which to choose an editor-in-chief, considering how few—if any—black women worked for major white magazines in the late 1960s. Nor did we partners know what to even look for in an editor-in-chief—beyond the obvious. Which meant being good-looking—or fine—was a good enough start.

Bernadette Carey, the young lady Jonathan had brought in to be interviewed for the editor-in-chief's position, was definitely fine. Light-skinned with long hair, she looked to be in her early thirties, currently worked at the *Washington Post*, and before that worked at the *New York Times*. She had graduated from Smith College and came recommended by Clay Felker, the editor of *New York* magazine, then a hot new publication that was already generating buzz in media circles. Felker was one of the many white men and women in the magazine business who would give us partners advice and help as we tried to start our own hot new publication.

Jonathan pulled out a chair for our lovely guest, took the seat next to her, and then hurriedly went around the table introducing the rest of us. "My dear sister," he said after the introductions, oozing charm and leveling those green eyes into hers with laser-like intensity, "I understand you might be interested in working with us. You know we're about to launch a magazine for Negro women."

"Oh, yes," Bernadette said casually. "I've been thinking about doing a women's magazine myself."

"That's interesting," Jonathan said quickly. "What were some of the ideas you were thinking about?"

Bernadette said she had been collecting some editorial and advertising information, though she didn't mention anything specific about editorial content for her purported magazine.

"What do you do down there at the *Washington Post*?" Cecil asked. None of us had ever heard of this woman, which didn't really mean anything, since we didn't know *any* black women in publishing at the time. I admit it, though, we were all mesmerized by the one seated before us.

Bernadette was a beauty, but more than that she had style, class, and the tinge of sophistication young men like us found so appealing in slightly older women. She worked for a major newspaper, which was not a magazine exactly, but close enough. We would later learn that she was also dating David Frost, the British TV talk show host who was then the biggest thing on nighttime television next to Johnny Carson.

Bernadette told us she wrote features for the paper—a lot of women's general interest articles. Okay, that was promising.

Jonathan tried to steer the interview back to the magazine with no name as yet. "We don't have a name for our magazine yet," he said, "but we're kind of thinking about calling it *Sapphire*. You know, like sapphire the jewel. It's strong and beautiful, like Negro women. What do you think of that?"

"*Sapphire?*" The question was as blank as the look Bernadette was now giving us. "Why would you call it that? I don't understand."

This did not keep us from hiring her as editor-in-chief, though Bernadette would say years later that she really thought of herself as "editor-in-formation."

Now, as clueless as we may have been about what to look for in an editor-in-chief—beyond the obvious—it quickly became apparent that we had made the wrong hire with this first one. First of all, Bernadette's editorial ideas didn't fly with the little ad-hoc focus group of black women we had asked to review them. Cecil's wife, Pat Hollingsworth, and Maphis Williams and Cydya Smith, who I believe were friends of Pat's, all thought Bernadette's ideas were fluff, as did Jonathan.

Secondly, Bernadette said she would only come on board if she got a 5 percent stake in The Hollingsworth Group, which was ridiculous, considering she had no track record of any kind with magazines. We didn't either, but The Hollingsworth Group was *our* partnership—us four guys—and we were not about to cede any of it to this woman we didn't know, and weren't sure could even do a magazine for Negro women. Besides, I was beginning to have some reservations of my own about Bernadette Carey.

"I don't know if the woman even likes being a Negro," I commented in the office one day when she wasn't there. We had all been grousing about how Bernadette was starting to come off as a tiresome prima donna. Half the time she wasn't in the office, and we didn't know if she had even made the move yet from Washington, DC, to New York.

"Well, it's not like she exactly *looks* colored," one of the partners observed.

"Jesus Christ!" another one blurted out. "You don't think she's trying to *pass* in color-struck DC, do you?" The question stunned us into silence. But it did all make a certain amount of sense. Her general wariness around us four assertive Negro guys. Her lack of interest in anything pertaining to civil rights or Negro news of any kind. And why hadn't any of us met David Frost yet, her reported boyfriend? On the other hand, we knew that Clay Felker certainly must have thought Bernadette was a Negro. Why else would he recommend her to be editor-in-chief of a magazine for Negro women?

The question became moot, though, since the partners refused to give

Bernadette the 5 percent stake in The Hollingsworth Group that she wanted. So she quit. Which may have been just as well. It was bad enough that we were catching hell from every Negro woman we knew for coming up with the name *Sapphire* for the magazine. It was unthinkable that we might have hired a woman to run the magazine who may not have even wanted to identify as Negro.

The issue of what to name the magazine loomed large, and to say the partners all came under fire for thinking we could call it *Sapphire* was an understatement beyond reckoning.

"You're joking, right?" said the young lady I was having dinner with at Rust Brown's restaurant on a cool Friday evening in the summer of 1969. It had been a rough week of pitching the magazine to venture capitalists, and I was sharing with my date the ongoing frustration of trying to raise money for the publication. *Sapphire* just was not catching on among the white boys who were supposedly interested in financing new and novel black business ventures.

"Well, of course it's not catching on," said my date with some impatience. "Don't you guys know who Sapphire is, what she represents?"

Well, yes, we knew Sapphire was the name of the black female character on the old television comedy show *Amos 'n' Andy*. She was the wife of George "Kingfish" Stevens, the loud, boorish lead character who always had a silly business scheme going that always ended in disaster. Sapphire, his mate, was just as loud, bossy, and raunchy as her husband—and a hoot to watch. Hands on her hips and a shriek on her lips, she took no tea for the fever with Kingfish and his cohorts, Amos, Andy, Lightnin', and Calhoun. The characters were viewed by many if not most blacks as negative stereotypes. But *that's* not the Sapphire we had in mind in naming the magazine. No, we were thinking of sapphire the jewel—hard as steel, but of enduring quality.

"You mean a jewel like your mother?" my date asked with sarcasm. My mother's name, in fact, was Jewell, with two l's. And the answer to the question was yes, women like our mothers, and the black women we were married to and dating, whether dark or light or copper-colored, like the pretty actress and model having dinner with me were the women we had in mind when we pictured the magazine's readers. They represented the audience we hoped to reach. And they were outraged about the proposed name. It was a stereotype that represented the *worst* in black women. "I'm going to tell you right now, I'll never spend a *dime* on a magazine named *Sapphire*," my date said.

The partners' wives were even more outraged. Pat Hollingsworth, Cecil's wife, said she had run the name past several of her married girlfriends, including Clarence's wife, Elaine. The feeling was unanimous: *Sapphire* was a dreadful name. It had to go. Easier said than done, however, since all of the pitch materials we were giving out at our investor meetings had the name emblazoned on practically every sheet. Redoing the materials would be a considerable cost.

Naming the magazine turned out to be the first big fight of the business venture, and perhaps an inevitable one, since the four black men starting the magazine had made the bigger mistake of not including any black women in the early planning stages. Sure, we talked with our wives and girlfriends about the magazine in general terms, but never really solicited their input in a professional, business way.

Clarence, always something of a ladies' man, would chat up black women he knew whenever he ran into them on the subway or in popular bars and restaurants, such as Rust Brown's or the Cellar, both on Manhattan's Upper West Side, and both of which catered to an up-and-coming black professional crowd. The young black women in this crowd comprised the very demographic the magazine wanted to reach.

Passionate, earnest, and eager for information, Clarence always explained to the women whose advice he was soliciting how he and his three partners were starting a magazine for Negro women and needed input. "Would you read such a magazine," he'd ask. And if so, "What would you like to see in it?" Invariably, a woman would point out that perhaps the "brothers" should hire some "sisters" during the planning stage to help them put together a magazine for Negro women. Just a thought, but one that didn't really occur to us partners in a substantial way at the very beginning. That proved to be an unfortunate oversight.

The next woman we interviewed for the editor-in-chief position was Ruth Ross, whom Jonathan told us he had called. She came highly recommended by Osborn Elliott, editor of *Newsweek* magazine, where she worked as a general interest writer. Elliott told Jonathan that Ruth was the "leading journalist" at *Newsweek.* By that I'm sure he meant the leading *black* journalist, since we partners had not heard of her any more than we had heard of Bernadette Carey from the *Washington Post.* Ruth Ross did, however, possess the darker-skinned good looks, manner, and sensibility we thought more appropriately reflected the kind of Negro woman we wanted to head the magazine editorially.

She was in her late thirties and tall—about five foot eight—had a short curly natural, spoke in a deep husky voice, and carried herself with great pride. She was outspoken, professional, smart, something of a militant politically, and worked for a real magazine. We hired her immediately. Good thing we did, too, because Ruth Ross is the one who came up with a name for the magazine that resonated immediately

We were all in the office late one evening, kicking around magazine names with Ruth, who was barefoot and lying stretched out on the floor, hands clasped across her chest, gazing at the ceiling as if it were an oracle. After the *Sapphire* fiasco, we knew we had better have our editor-in-chief involved in any future magazine name discussions. By now we had even engaged a marketing firm that specialized in coming up with business names. As name after name was being kicked around and falling flat, Ruth suddenly blurted out in what we would later think of as a moment of divine inspiration two little syllables: *Essence.*

That stopped us cold. "Hmm," we said collectively. That was it: a name, a spirit, a power, all conveyed in one short, pithy word that would define a new market, a new audience, and a new black business. We all grinned and looked at Ruth. Thank you, baby. Thank you.

———

Jonathan did not bother to introduce us to our next editorial hire. He simply announced one day that he had talked the venerable Gordon Parks, already a legendary photographer for *Life* magazine, into joining our magazine venture. It was not clear what Parks would do just yet, other than take on the title of editorial director and lend his considerable stature and credibility to four black men who had neither. We did not think anything of bringing a *man* into the magazine who would have a leading role on the editorial side. After all, white men ran most of the big "Seven

Sisters" white women's service magazines in 1969. There was John Mack Carter, editor of *Good Housekeeping*; Sey Chassler, top editor at *Redbook;* Bob Stein, editor-in-chief at *McCalls*. Still, hiring a black man to have a major say in editorial content for a black women's magazine was one of those politically incorrect moves almost as disastrous as trying to name the magazine *Sapphire*.

Jonathan was turning into something of a loose cannon. Independently hiring staff without consulting the partners, reaching out to possible editors without our knowledge, he operated as if the magazine was his personal fiefdom and the other partners his serfs-in-waiting. We did have to admit, though, that landing Gordon Parks was a major coup. He was the one black person in publishing we had all heard of.

Tall, courtly, with a full, rakish mustache and wavy slicked-back hair, Parks exuded the confident air of the urbane, intellectual gentleman. He was highly respected among whites as well as blacks in media, having made history by becoming the first black hired as a photographer for *Life*, the largest general interest pictorial magazine at the time. He would go on to be an award-winning filmmaker, author of several books, accomplished artist, and renowned playboy admired by men and women alike for dating and marrying some of the most beautiful women in the world—black, white, and Asian.

Many years later, on the occasion of his seventieth birthday celebration in a ballroom at the Waldorf-Astoria Hotel, I had the honor of sitting next to Gordon on the dais, watching as woman after woman approached him to hug and kiss him, wish him happy birthday, some of them slipping him her phone number. He turned to me with a knowing look and said, "Ed, I'm 70 years old. When you get to be my age, don't worry about a thing. It just gets better."

The fact that the esteemed Gordon Parks would give up his affiliation with *Life* and *Time* magazine, where he also worked, to join a fledgling magazine with no money, no track record, and until recently no name, gave the four of us partners instant, enormous credibility in the publishing community. But Gordon also got something in return: star power affiliation with a black venture, which seemed to speak to his spirit in a way that none of his "firsts" at white companies ever had.

Like other successful professional blacks working in mainstream corporate America, even Gordon Parks had his frustrations and challenges dealing with ever-present racism. He once told a woman he'd met at a party that he had flown into New York just the day before and was to be picked up by a chauffeur-driven limousine hired by the book publisher he was in town to meet with. When the white limo driver saw that it was a black man he was picking up, he quickly sped off, leaving Gordon standing dumbfounded at the curb. The driver was subsequently fired, but the racial slight remained.

There would be no such slights at a black magazine venture. There would, however, be other challenges. The first one, not surprisingly, came as a result of having a black man with the title of editorial director positioned higher than the black woman with the title of editor-in-chief. Gordon Parks may have been something of a legend by the time he joined the magazine called *Essence,* but he soon enough became the 800-pound gorilla in the room as he and our tall, outspoken editor-in-chief started butting heads over what editorial direction the magazine should take and who would have final authority in making editorial decisions.

This was not a fight the partners paid much attention to initially. We had a much bigger battle on our hands—trying to raise capital, for without money, there would be no magazine. The struggle to secure financing for *Essence* was ongoing and relentless, and would consume us from the day we quit our corporate jobs to go into business, to the day two partners and five years later that the magazine became fully capitalized at $2 million and finally turned the corner, looking as if it might actually become a Thoroughbred and start running in the black.

CHAPTER 4

Show Us the Money

"Hold it right there!" snapped the security guard as the five of us were hauling typewriters and boxes of supplies through the lobby of Shearson, Hammill's Wall Street headquarters late one night in 1969. "Just what do you think you're doing?"

"It's all right! They're with me. I work here!" Michael snapped back. He flashed the guard his employee badge, showing he was not just any employee. He was Michael Victory, a Shearson, Hammill and Co. partner and executive vice president—one of Shearson's ruling class. "They have my permission to take these things," Michael added with the imperial air of entitlement the British have historically used to take things. The guard did a double take, looking suspiciously from the good-looking white man with the slight trace of a British accent to the four black men who were with him, before finally letting us out the door.

I can't say I blamed the guard. The four of us partners, dressed in jeans and leather jackets and me sporting my big Afro and full beard, must have looked like thugs from another 'hood as we carted boxes through the marbled lobby of 14 Wall Street to the waiting van parked outside. The compact, broad-shouldered white guy leading the way was the one among us that the guard couldn't quite figure out.

Fourteen Wall Street is directly across the street from the New York Stock Exchange, and though Shearson, Hammill, as we once knew it, is long gone—the basement of the building is now a T.J. Maxx department store—in the spring of 1969, Shearson, Hammill and Co. was one of the leading investment banking houses firing the engine of American capitalism. By the early 1970s, however, the venerable house, like many Wall Street firms, had been hobbled by the stock market crash of 1973–74, and would be merged in 1974 into a brokerage house controlled by the mighty Sanford Weill.

But in 1969 when Black Capitalism was the name of the game, Shearson, Hammill and Co. was proving to be the lifeline to four black men who wanted to be winners in that game. One of the men working hardest to make sure we had a shot at that was Michael Victory, the Shearson executive vice president who was with Russell Goings at the meeting Russ had called back in November to talk about black men going into business for themselves. Russ Goings had Michael Victory's ear, and Michael Victory had the ear of Shearson, Hammill.

At 34, Michael was already a rising star at the firm, an executive VP, partner, and the number two guy slated to become number one. As a British immigrant who never quite got over growing up poor, Michael was the one white guy at Shearson who could relate to the brothers. He'd been a minority in his adopted homeland, an outsider who "talked funny," didn't come from money, and had to compete on merit, not pass through on privilege, to get where he was today: at the very top of the Shearson, Hammill food chain.

Born in London, Michael came to North America at age 13 with his mother after his father was killed in World War II during the Battle of Dunkirk. Mother and son first arrived in Canada in 1947, then came to America two years later, settling in Providence, Rhode Island. Michael's mother was an Irish nurse who quickly found work. Still, the family was relatively poor, and Michael would tell me the only real ambition he had growing up as a tough and scrappy little immigrant kid was to make money. He joined the U.S. Army after finishing Providence College, then went to Harvard Business School on the G.I. Bill, graduating with distinction in the top 5 percent of his class. By the age of 26 he had joined Shearson as one of the bright hot shots and quickly found himself on the company fast track.

Michael and I came together around the idea of a magazine for Negro women, but we became lifelong friends around our common ground and shared values. Like me, he was an only child who grew up poor, raised by a single mother. Like me, he recognized the value of making money in order to make life better. Like me, he could be tough and stubborn, but also proper and soft-spoken. He admired my calm. I admired his forthrightness. He liked to dress well. So did I.

Perhaps because he was himself an immigrant with an outsider's view of American culture, Michael acknowledged the reality of white privilege, and was quick to exercise it whenever it benefited a situation, as it did when we four partners had to get past a hostile white security guard. I think there was something about the idea of four black men trying to get a toehold in American business that resonated with Michael, maybe even spiritually. He was an immigrant who had done well because he was smart, had some opportunities—and was white. He recognized this. Just as he recognized that there were others who were equally as smart and American-born, but had not done so well because they were not white—and therefore did not have some opportunities. Maybe liberal guilt was a factor, but I think he may have been stirred by the real sense of injustice.

Whatever it was driving him, Michael was tirelessly committing Shearson resources, big and small, to ensure that his firm take the lead in helping four young black men launch a magazine. Which is how the four partners happened to be hauling boxes and typewriters through Shearson's lobby one late night in 1969. Michael had accompanied us to the mailroom earlier that day, saying, "Take whatever you need."

By this time we had expanded our offices on 30th Street to a maze of little cubicles on the lower level of the townhouse and started to take on staff, Ruth Ross and Gordon Parks being our latest hires. While they were squaring off over what the editorial direction of the new magazine should be—a feud we didn't pay much attention to initially—the partners were in the throes of trying to raise capital to publish the magazine.

We needed seed money at the outset just to keep body and soul together as we worked on a business plan, solicited advice and support from professionals in the magazine business on *how* to run a magazine, and held endless pitch meetings with potential lenders and investors trying to raise money. Michael flexed his muscle in securing our initial seed money by persuading four Shearson partners to pony up their own money. Each made a personal loan of $3,000 to The Hollingsworth Group to get us out of the starting gate once we had incorporated.

To the four Shearson partners—Donald Cecil, Charles Knapp, Walter

Maynard, and Robert Thul—I'm sure a loan of $3,000 apiece represented the ultimate in good faith, as well as hard proof of Shearson's commitment to promoting black entrepreneurship. To us black partners, though, $12,000 from four white men running a multimillion-dollar investment bank represented "liberal guilt money," pure and simple—scarcely a drop in the bucket, given the $1.5 million we had calculated we needed to fully capitalize the magazine.

Admittedly, though, we were happy to take the money and run. That $12,000 allowed us to pay the rent on the expanded office space, pay Clarence and Cecil a little stipend, since they had families to support, buy office equipment, and hire our first editor-in-chief. Since Jonathan and I were single, we elected to take no salary in the beginning.

But it seemed that no sooner had we taken the money than we needed an additional $13,000 to pay the bills necessary to keep the business running. This time I used my own muscle to convince Michael to arrange a meeting between me and William Hudgins, the CEO of Freedom National Bank. The bank was the black-owned institution located on Harlem's famed 125th Street commercial strip that had been founded in 1964 by the baseball great Jackie Robinson and his partners, Rose Morgan and Dunbar McLaren. It was the one place I figured I could go to secure a loan, representing nothing more than four black men who were starting a magazine.

Jackie Robinson has always been a personal hero of mine—not just because he integrated Major League Baseball with grace and class when he started playing for the Brooklyn Dodgers in 1947, but because he helped start Freedom National Bank seventeen years later with the specific agenda of helping black businesses obtain capital. To me his greatness as an athlete has always been matched by his astuteness as a businessman who recognized that if we are going to have viable black businesses in our community, we must have access to money. Furthermore, Robinson understood that in the perverse catch-22 of American racism, most black businesses never got off the ground because white banks historically denied them loans. He started Freedom National Bank as a direct challenge to racist lending practices. This is why he is such a hero to me.

But I wasn't sure how far hero worship was going to get me with Bill Hudgins as I now waited in the reception area outside his office, hoping to get a $13,000 loan. I did know that the only reason he had agreed to see me in the first place was that Michael Victory had asked him to. Before becoming a banker, Bill Hudgins had already made his name and no doubt his fortune in Harlem real estate as a shrewd investor and speculator. He was known to be a tough negotiator, but as an up-by-his-bootstraps, risk-taking kind of guy, surely he could relate to me and my partners.

"Mr. Hudgins will see you now," his secretary said, eyeing me with interest. She showed me into a large, comfortable office dominated by a large, impressive desk positioned in the middle of the room. Seated behind it was an impeccably dressed older black man whose wavy black hair, angular cheekbones, and reddish skin coloring hinted at Native American genes mixed in the blood line. Hudgins stood up to greet me, shaking my hand.

"Have a seat, Ed," he said warmly, gesturing to the chair in the front of his desk, before sitting back down in his swivel chair. "You know I'm a pretty busy man and don't usually take the time to personally hear why a customer wants a loan. I leave that to the loan officers. But Michael said I should meet you. So we're meeting. How can I help you?"

I quickly outlined the *Essence* business plan, giving our advertising and circulation projections, the demographics of the black female market, and why it represented an untapped gold mine. I mentioned the $12,000 initial seed money we had received from the four Shearson partners, which was quickly spent. We now needed an infusion of $13,000 as soon as possible to pay ongoing bills.

"Hold it a minute, Ed," Hudgins cut in. "I know you come out of banking—worked for a while at First National City Bank. Is that right?"

"Yes, sir," I replied.

"And your partners come out of sales. Okay, tell me this," Hudgins said, tilting back his chair and staring at me with his arms folded. "Do any of you have any *actual experience* in the magazine business?

"No, sir."

"And you want my bank to lend you guys *$13,000*? That's why you're here, right?"

"Yes, sir."

For a second there I thought Hudgins was about to laugh. He suddenly tilted the chair upright and leaned toward me, elbows on the desk, pressing his fingertips together in a steeple position. "Why would I do that, Ed?" he finally asked, still staring at me as you would a child who has just asked for $13,000. "Why would I lend you and your partners money when you don't have any money and have no way to pay me back? Four men I don't know, who have no track record in the business you're trying to start and nothing to put up for collateral. Why would I lend you $13,000?"

"Because we're good for it," I said. I told him the partners all had good credit, strong work ethics, and good intentions.

Hudgins let out a deep laugh, settled back in his chair, and gave me a look that now resembled admiration. "You know something, young man, you probably *are* good for it," he said. "Otherwise I don't think Michael would have asked me to see you. Even though I don't know you, I do know Michael Victory, and if he is vouching for you, that's good enough for me."

We got the $13,000 loan. I've often thought if we had not received that money from Freedom National Bank just when we did, exactly when we needed it, I probably wouldn't be where I am now, talking about *Essence* at all. In that brief meeting with William Hudgins I learned an enormous lesson about the value of relationships in doing business. In business interactions it is not just who you know, but who you have taking that extra step to vouch for you that can make all the difference between success and failure.

Just because I was a black man representing a black venture did not mean a black-owned bank was going to automatically give the venture a loan if it appeared to be a bad risk. This is the reality of business, which has nothing to do with race or racism. It was my relationship with Michael Victory—a man who had vouched for me—that made me a good risk to William Hudgins, who had his own valued relationship with Michael Victory.

Nearly twenty years later, I served on the board of Freedom National Bank as its chairman, and *Essence*'s executive editor had just left the magazine to start her own real estate brokerage business. She went into contract to purchase a Brooklyn commercial office space, but with no job, no business history and no large cash reserves, there was not one majority-owned bank that would give her a risky commercial mortgage, despite her own good credit. In danger of losing her contract deposit, she came to see me. I vouched for her, and persuaded Freedom National Bank to give her the mortgage. I knew she was good for it.

———

For most of 1969 no matter how many times Michael Victory may have told investors The Hollingsworth Group was "good for it," we scarcely made a dent in raising money beyond the $25,000 in total received from the $12,000 loan that four of the Shearson, Hammill partners put up, and the $13,000 loan from Freedom National Bank. True to his word, Michael had lined up meeting after meeting for the partners to do pitches to investors, lenders, venture capitalists—the very people we thought would be savvy enough to recognize the profit potential in a magazine geared to black women. The general market of women's service magazines constituted a $2 billion industry in 1970. Black women in the 18-to-34 age category, our magazine's target group, totaled 4.2 million. This was the giant sleeping beauty that Madison Avenue had been ignoring—a potentially huge consumer market niche just waiting to be tapped.

We had done variations on the details of this spiel more than a hundred times over the course of 1969, the year before the magazine launched. Each partner had his script for what was starting to feel like a little dog-and-pony show as we took our assigned places, waiting to hit our marks. This evening we are in a small meeting room at the Shearson, Hammill Wall Street headquarters, where most of our pitches take place. Five white men, including Michael, are seated around a rectangular conference table, while the four Hollingsworth partners are seated in a row of chairs at the head of the table, a little distance from the investors.

Among the other white men present are Louis Allen, from Chase Manhattan bank, and Bob Gutwillig, a vice president at Playboy Enterprises. The others I didn't recognize. But they all look pretty much the same to me—a pool of white faces that we're here to convince to invest some green in our magazine.

Jonathan, the good-looking, fast-talking president of the group, is first up. Passionate about the magazine—the idea was his, after all, he liked to brag—he was always articulate and persuasive, and a charmer to even the most hard-nosed businessmen when doing his part of the pitch:

"Good evening, gentlemen," he began. "Thank you so much for coming out tonight to meet with me and my partners. I know you're busy men, so let me get right to the point. We're here to talk to you about why Black is Beautiful in the American marketplace; why black women today represent Black Power with enormous profit potential; and why *you* should view a magazine catering to this powerful market as a terrific investment opportunity."

The rest of his spiel was excerpted from the script written in the business plan, which was in the pitch package given to the investors before the meeting: "It isn't easy being a Black woman in American society," Jonathan said, downshifting his voice to a plaintive blues note. "Throughout most of her history in this country, she has had no realistic, complimentary images of herself either as a woman, or as a member of the community. Nevertheless, in the past decade she has undergone a transformation of self—a psychic and socioeconomic revolution. Today she is beautiful because Black is beautiful. Black is beautiful because she is beautiful. She has in the truest sense come of age."

Jonathan now leveled his piercing green eyes at each of the white men, looking as if he is about to either cry or cut somebody. This always had the intended highly dramatic effect he was so good at conveying.

By the time we started raising capital for the magazine, a race and a gender had indeed been transformed. We were on the cusp of the revolutionary seventies, a decade in which Negro became black; Black became uppercased; women publicly burned their bras; sex became liberated; and Black is Beautiful became the new anthem of a race that seemed to be on the verge of winning the struggle for civil rights. The civil rights movement was cresting just as the women's movement was gaining momentum, empowering a new generation of black women to ride on the tide of both, and a new magazine to be in the vanguard of marketing to them.

"These women control the purse strings of a market worth more than $30 billion," said Clarence, next up on the pitch. "And the best way to reach this, America's fastest growing consumer market, is through Black-oriented media, namely, a women's service magazine aimed directly at them." As the advertising guy, Clarence came to the pitches armed with stats and bottom-line reasoning. He could quote facts and figures on black women's purchasing habits, a particular advertiser's market penetration, who increased market share by focused ads directed to a particular ethnic group. Clarence wasn't a tall guy, but he presented tall, standing military regal, speaking in a deep, crisply even voice that was at once soothing and urgent. When Clarence Smith spoke, everybody listened, captivated.

Cecil did the circulation pitch, outlining the specific demographics of the black female market we were going after and how it was expected to grow. "There are 12 million Black women in America," he said. "Census data shows that 56 percent of them live in urban areas. This is a concentrated market, and by 1970, fifty U.S. cities will have Black populations of 25 percent or more. Furthermore, the Black population is increasing at a rate 35 percent greater than whites."

I was last up, the money guy who came with the financial projections on what it was going to cost to publish the magazine the first year, and what we could expect to make in revenues if we hit all of our advertising and circulation targets. Bottom line: To fully capitalize the magazine at a level that would be comfortable and self-sustaining during the critical first year of operation, we needed to raise $1.5 million.

The investors listened politely, even intently at times, asked questions, and seemed impressed. Yet at the end of the year, not one dime had been raised beyond that initial $25,000. I had even cut my Afro and beard at the suggestion of Michael. "Ed, it's time to cut the hair," he told me bluntly after one pitch meeting that seemed to quickly go south. "You look too bloody threatening. Nobody is going to give a bloke who looks like a Black Panther five cents, let alone a million dollars." He may have had a point. So I cut my hair. Still *nada*. So I grew it back. What the hell. With or without hair, no one was giving us any money. That was the *real* bottom line.

To be fair, while the idea of four young black men starting a magazine for black women may have had a sexy, seductive kind of appeal, it also resulted in an understandable "You gotta be kidding me" kind of skepticism on Wall Street. We partners were too naive to recognize that investors really didn't give a damn about the "new" black woman, or any other black woman, for that matter, and certainly were not going to throw good money at four black men who had never published anything in their lives.

Even Michael had his bouts of doubt and exasperation with us. The day we showed him a draft of the business plan we intended to distribute at investor pitch meetings with the magazine name *Sapphire* emblazoned across its cover he practically threw us out of his office. "What is this shit?" he barked, losing his usual cool. "It's a piece of garbage, that's what it is. Makes no sense whatsoever. You must be out of your bloody minds thinking of calling the magazine *Sapphire*. My God! Are you all daft?"

Michael had already been called on the carpet following that night we took supplies out of the Shearson, Hammill building. "Michael, I hear you and four black guys were seen stealing supplies from the mailroom," one of the Shearson partners had called to tell him. "Care to explain that?" Michael smoothed over the concerns of the questioning partner. But he now seemed to be having his own concerns. Yet to his credit our little missteps seemed to just strengthen his resolve to ensure that his four protégés get enough start-up capital to publish at least one issue of the magazine. He ended up writing most of the revised business plan himself, as well as helping to draft the funding proposals that finally netted us $130,000 in financing by mid-March of 1970.

We planned on publishing the first issue of *Essence* in May 1970. Though $130,000 didn't come close to the $1.5 million we needed to be fully capitalized, it would get us launched. We could manage to publish at least a first issue of the magazine, which would bring in the revenue needed to keeping the magazine going. That was the projection anyway. And the hope.

———

"Look at this one, Ed," Russ is saying, pointing to a favorite collage by Romare Bearden as he gives me another tour through what I've come to think of as his Harlem mansion. We are viewing the Bearden piece hanging on the wall in a hallway landing between the second and third floors, and Russ is giving me yet another lesson on art appreciation, especially for the works of such African-American masters as Romare Bearden and Jacob Lawrence. Over the years these lessons will lead to my own passion for art collecting, but tonight I'm only half listening to Russ's musings.

"See how he [Bearden] uses what we usually think of as drab colors— brown and beige, dark green and deep blue—to create this dramatic effect?" Russ gushes. "I *love* that!" Romare Bearden is a good, personal friend of Russ Goings's, which Russ loves to point out, and Russ Goings is a devoted patron of Romare Bearden's, which his art collection bears out.

Russ loved showing off the magnificent art in his elegant four-story townhouse on Manhattan Avenue, a six-block sliver of tree-lined street wedged between Central Park West to the south and Central Harlem to the north. I've arrived early for the dinner party that Russ and his wife, Maddie, are hosting this evening, giving Russ time to once more show me the house and the art. I love coming to these parties. Russ and Maddie started them as a way to give us partners a place to unwind, eat some of Maddie's good home-cooked meals, and have an informal setting in which to do fund-raising pitches with some of the financiers Russ always invited.

Tonight is different, however. It has been a full year since the partners quit their respective jobs, incorporated, and set out to launch a magazine. Tonight's fete is a gathering of friends and supporters to celebrate the closing that happened earlier in the week when The Hollingsworth Group secured $130,000 in financing, enabling a magazine called *Essence* to finally become a reality. Maddie, for one, couldn't be happier.

Barely five feet tall, Maddie Goings is a lovely lady as short as Russ is tall, but someone who can go toe-to-toe with him any day. Feisty and fearless, she was the other half to a brash and bold mate, and as committed to helping four black men start a magazine for Negro women as her husband was. She became a second mama to the four of us—feeding us, encouraging us, affirming our partnership. After all, the magazine was intended to be for her and women like her, so she couldn't help but embrace the nice, hardworking young men who had conceived the idea and now had the money to make it happen.

"Is that you, Jonathan?" Maddie said, opening the door. "Get in here, boy!" Maddie took Jonathan by the arm and led him through the vestibule into the dining room where most of her guests were already seated. "Look at you, all skin and bones," she said, now rubbing her hand along Jonathan's slender arm. She directed him to the chair next to hers at the table. "You better let me fatten you up," she said, grinning. "Ain't no woman gonna want you if you lookin' frailer and prettier than she is."

"Now, Miss Madeline, you know I'm holding myself out for you," Jonathan bantered back, sounding a bit manic, as he often did. "I don't know why you want to keep on keepin' on with old Russ over there. Come away with me and I'll treat you like the queen you are. Wouldn't you like to be on the cover of my new magazine?"

Maddie beamed. Her guests laughed, and the party was on.

There was an even dozen people present for tonight's dinner, seated at a long table in the stately old world dining room accented with rich oak wainscoting. Besides Russ, Maddie, and the four partners, Michael Victory was present, along with Suzanne Warshavsky and Benito Lopez, two young attorneys from the law firm representing Shearson, Hammill and Co., who represented us pro bono at the closing, and Phil Smith, a vice president at First National City Bank and my former boss. Clarence and Cecil have also brought their wives, Elaine and Pat.

Russ is the first to make a toast: "To The Hollingsworth Group," he says from his place at the head of the table, holding up a champagne flute. "Congratulations, gentlemen. You did it. Of course, it did take a little help from some of your well-placed friends to make it happen," he added with a self-satisfied chuckle.

He was right about that. We were scheduled to go to press with the first issue of *Essence* in April, yet had just secured the financing needed to get us launched on March 11, 1970. At the zero hour Michael had persuaded Chase Manhattan Bank to invest $50,000 in *Essence;* First National City Bank and Morgan Guaranty had signed on for $30,000 loans; and Pioneer Capital and Franklin Capital Investment made the smaller MESBIC loans that brought the total capitalization to $130,000. We had five years to pay back the money at a 9.5 percent annual interest rate. Michael had called in some chips to get that $50,000 investment from Chase, and thanks to my relationship with my former boss Phil Smith, the senior vice president heading up City Bank's venture capital division, the bank loaned us an initial $30,000. We would return to the First National City Bank coffers several more times for money, securing a total of $100,000 in financing over a three-month period from March to May 1970.

At the March 11, 1970, closing, however, the day the partners were to collect the $130,000, Louis Allen, head of Chase's venture capital arm, is a no-show. He was to bring $50,000 to the table, the largest of the pledged investments, and he wasn't even present! We stopped the closing, and

Phil and I left the room to call him. "Why the hell aren't you here?" Phil demanded to know.

Allen explained that he didn't think the closing was really going to happen, so he didn't feel it was necessary to bother to come. Phil Smith, who was Louis Allen's counterpart at City Bank, used a few choice words to persuade Allen to walk the couple of blocks from Chase's headquarters in lower Manhattan to Dewey Ballantine's law office—and to bring the check for $50,000. Allen did so, no doubt stirred by the white guilt Phil managed to elicit. Michael Victory, our steadfast white knight, was also a no-show at the closing. What was up with *that*? Michael said he had a scheduling conflict, but we partners were wondering if he, too, was beginning to have a crisis of faith in the venture.

Yet as time went on both Michael Victory and Louis Allen would prove to be stand-up guys exactly when we needed them to be. *Essence* was severely undercapitalized from the very beginning, and within a year we were almost out of money. We needed to raise $50,000 immediately, otherwise we wouldn't be able to publish the next issue. I called Michael, who suggested I call Louis Allen. I did. His secretary, who happened to be a black woman familiar with The Hollingsworth Group, told me Allen was out of town, but that he would be getting back that afternoon. She gave me his airline, his flight number, the time his plane would be arriving, and where—Newark Airport.

I rushed to the Port Authority bus station across town and jumped on the first bus going to Newark, New Jersey's international airport 30 minutes away. Allen was coming down the plane's arrival ramp when he spotted me waiting for him near the gate's door. "Ed Lewis!" he said, surprised. "What are you doing here?" Clearly I hadn't been on his flight, and I certainly wasn't dressed for business success that particular day. But I was all about doing business. I told Allen we needed more money—like yesterday—otherwise there would be no magazine come next month. I then explained again, as I had so many times before, the importance of the magazine, what we were trying to achieve, and why we needed $50,000 to keep publishing.

Allen looked at me and shook his head. "Ed, I'll swing with you one more time," he said. He made a call from a nearby phone booth, and by the time we got back to his office, a check had been drawn for $50,000.

From that initial capitalization of $130,000 in 1970, to 1974 when *Essence* was fully capitalized at $2 million, Chase Manhattan Bank, led by Louis Allen, would turn out to be the magazine's largest investor, continuing to put up money as needed. The man who didn't bother to come to that first closing ended up committing $450,000 of Chase's money to *Essence* over the years. As he told me, "When I saw you that day at the airport waiting for me, I knew you guys were serious."

My seriousness as a businessman would be tested many more times during the coming years as The Hollingsworth Group grew from a partnership of four young men who started an undercapitalized magazine to a privately held, multimillion-dollar media corporation known as Essence Communications Inc. I turned 30 the year *Essence* launched, and while I would spend more than half my life working for the business I helped to start, it was those first thirty years leading up to the magazine's launch that would irrevocably shape me as the serious man still standing.

PART II

Getting Ready

(1940–1968)

CHAPTER 5

1314 Brook Avenue

The undercapitalization of *Essence* magazine could be a metaphor for an entire race of people. It certainly was for my own early life, growing up an American Negro in the Bronx with a father who worked all his life at menial jobs beneath both his abilities and his aspirations, and with a mother whose labor as a domestic, a beautician, and a factory worker never got us out of that category sociologists like to label "the working poor." I was a decade baby, born on May 15, 1940, to parents who were both 23.

My mother was pregnant with me when she married my father, she would tell me when I was almost grown. My father, as was characteristic of men trying to be honorable back in those days, "did the right thing" by marrying the woman who was carrying his child. This made me feel a little better about him.

Like many men for whom a few moments of sweet passion result in an unwanted complication that dashes hopes, dreams, and opportunities, my father lived most of his 54 years in the shadow of regret, becoming one of those BAD (bitter, angry, disappointed) men who define a pathology. He drank too much. Fought with my mother too much. Neglected me too much. It wasn't until I went to college and took up the study of political science, trying to get a handle on how things work and why things work the way they do, that I began to understand how issues of race and class affected me.

When I was growing up in a basement apartment with my parents and paternal grandparents on 1314 Brook Avenue in the Bronx, it was just the Bronx, not the dangerous South Bronx, an area known some thirty years later as the urban badlands of drugs and crime. The Bronx I grew up in was a mixed working-class community of Negroes, Italians, Jews, and a few Puerto Ricans. The majority of the Negroes and Italians lived in tenement walk-up buildings behind the stately boulevard of the Grand Concourse with its luxury Art Deco apartment buildings where most of the Jews that I knew lived. I belonged to a little gang of young boys that would sometimes venture farther north to fight the tough Italian kids known as the Fordham Baldies.

In our world of gang fights, dance shows, and numbers running, nobody had dreams of being anything as incomprehensible as a magazine publisher. I considered myself lucky to have a job working at the neighborhood grocery store owned by Mr. Zachary Weinstal and his mother. I must have been about 10 years old, and this was my first real paying job. People would come in to buy groceries and I had to give them change. At first I didn't think I was good enough to have the job, but I must have been doing something right because Mr. Weinstal kept me. My mother shopped here too, and this is where I realized the extent of my father's drinking. Like most of the shoppers, my mother often bought on credit, and there were always two Lewis tabs, one for the family's shopping bills, and one for my father's beer.

I may not have had a clear sense then of what I wanted to be when I grew up—though I dreamed of one day living on the Grand Concourse—I did know that I did not want to be like my father, a drinker who was always angry and abusive to women the way he was to my mother. He actually hit my mother when I was about 7 years old, and I remember running over to him in a rage and saying, "If you ever hit my mother again, I will kill you!"

My father raised his hand to strike me, but my mother quickly stepped between us. "Don't you *dare* hit this child," she hissed at him, gently pushing me out of the way. My father dropped his hand. He never hit me. Nor did he ever strike my mother again. I believe that was the moment my mother knew for certain that as soon as she could, she would leave him. As for me, my father's behavior led to two vows that I've never broken. The first is that I would never drink to the extent that I lost control. The other is that I would never be abusive to women, or anybody else, for that matter. Some children are eager to follow in a parent's footsteps. Others swear they will not repeat a parent's dysfunctional behavior.

I was my parents' only child whom everybody called "Sonny," and I inherited my father's name, looks, beautiful smile, and his love of and talent for dancing. My early love of jazz was also developed during the years my father worked as a janitor at City College, a job he held for twenty-five years.

As a teenager, years after my mother had left him, I would often help my father clean the toilets and scrub the floors at the college. Lewisohn Stadium, which was a part of the college, would have these wonderful jazz concerts, most of them produced by George Wein, the legendary producer of the Newport Jazz Festival and the man who would help me launch the Essence Music Festival almost fifty years later.

My father, who also loved jazz, could not afford to take me to the concerts, but as the janitor who had keys to many of the college's facilities, he would open the gate at Lewisohn Stadium and let me slip through before a concert started. These venues introduced me to such giants as Miles Davis, Duke Ellington, and Charlie Parker, leading to the great love for jazz that I have to this day.

It would be nice to think that those times my father and I worked together or those times he gave me free entry to a jazz concert represented true bonding moments. They didn't. These occasions were the result of court-ordered visitations mandated after my mother divorced my father in 1951 when I was 11. By then we had moved from the basement apartment of my grandparents to an apartment at 1376 Washington Avenue. But once my parents divorced, I was sent to live with relatives in Brooklyn, while my mother, who had met another man, moved in with him. She didn't want me to see her as a newly single mother living with a man so soon after leaving my father, especially without knowing where this new relationship might be going. My father moved into a small room in a building near Yankee Stadium owned by Lloyd Dickens, a reknown Harlem real estate developer.

The family I lived with in Brooklyn included two of my mother's second cousins. They were sisters, Mozelle Taylor and Hazel Abel, who along with their mother owned a two-family brownstone on Bainbridge Avenue. The house happened to be right across the street from the family of Floyd Patterson, who was then a teenager, but would later be a heavy-weight boxing champion. Mozelle and Hazel were both married, and each had a son, ages 5 and 7, respectively. I essentially became the free live-in babysitter to the boys, the house cleaner, the gofer, and in my mind the little slave who was worked practically to death. My mother came to see me every week, promising that as soon as she was settled she would bring me back home to the Bronx.

I suppose my mother's cousins and their families were prosperous compared to my poorer working-class family. The cousins were home-owners, owned a car, and held what were considered good jobs. One of the sisters was a teacher, and their mother was a Pentecostal preacher who ran her church on the ground-floor level of the house. I remember the place always being filled with shouting, holy-rolling church members. Which is why when Hazel did something so un-Christian to my mother, I never forgave her.

My mother would often travel by bus to Virginia to visit her mother, and on one such trip her cousin Hazel was also visiting. Hazel gave my mother a ride back to New York in her car, but once they had entered New York City through the Holland Tunnel, instead of driving my mother home to the Bronx, Hazel dropped her off on a street outside the tunnel near no public transportation of any kind, leaving her to fend for herself getting home. I couldn't believe she would treat my mother—her family—so callously, especially since she was supposedly a Christian. Absolutely unforgivable, as far as I was concerned.

The cousins did feed and care for me, however, and I was always a very responsible child, dutifully taking care of my cousins' own children, and keeping the two sisters' respective apartments neat and clean. I was so responsible that Cousin Mozelle told my mother she was going to adopt me. "Oh, no, you're not!" my mother informed her. She quickly moved up her timetable for bringing me back to the Bronx.

During the two years I lived in Brooklyn, my mother pushed my father to pay some child support. He refused, so she took him to court. I'll never forget standing with my parents before the judge in that big courthouse on the Grand Concourse while the judge reviewed my mother's petition. He looked at my father, then at me, and said to my father, "You seem to have a very nice young boy here. You don't want to pay anything for his care?"

"No, I don't," my father said coldly. "I don't want to pay anything."

I can't begin to describe how that made me feel. My own father telling the judge he did not want to provide for my care. The judge was just annoyed. "Well, sir," he told my father, "I'm ordering to you to pay forty dollars dollars a week in child support."

"He can't afford that," my mother piped up. The amount was knocked down to twenty dollars a week. The judge also stipulated that I have Sunday visitations with my father. So I would take the subway every Sunday for an hourlong ride from Brooklyn to the Bronx to spend some time with my dad in his little room. We mostly watched baseball games on TV that were being played live at Yankee Stadium right down the street. But I was a Dodgers fan, and while living in Brooklyn, I would go to Ebbets Field to watch them play. My dream was to be the next Jackie Robinson, a man I just idolized. I would spend hours standing in front of the mirror, holding a bat, trying to emulate his pigeon-toed stance. I knew baseball statistics inside and out, not just Jackie Robinson's, but all of the Dodgers players.

I don't recall my father and I talking much during those times we'd watch baseball games or those times I worked with him at City College. He turned into a defeated, lonely man who eventually moved back into that basement apartment with his mother, who was widowed at that point. He remained there until he died at age 54. My father never got over my mother leaving him. I think he thought she never would. But given my mother's own fearless, take-no-tea-for-the-fever temperament, I could never figure out why it took her so long to go. She told me she thought it was important to try to make the marriage work, probably for my sake.

I could certainly see why my father was so taken with my mother when they first met at a dance at the Savoy Ballroom in Harlem in 1938. A short, brown-skinned woman with curves in all the right places, my mother was a real head turner, with great legs and a great fashion sense who loved to dress well, a trait she passed on to me. She also talked a mile a minute—a trait she did *not* pass on to me. In fact, I'm convinced the reason I'm so quiet is that I had a mother who talked constantly, never letting me—or anybody else, for that matter—get a word in edgewise. I would sometimes cut in and say things like, "Mom, *please*. Let someone else talk for a minute!"

While my father's people were city folks—his parents having migrated to New York from Virginia before my father was born, the youngest of three children—my mother's people remained rooted in the land of the South. My grandmother's first husband, Charles Spencer—my mother's father—died on May 20, 1927, exactly thirty years after the date on which he was born, May 20, 1897. Some say he was killed working in the steel mills of Ohio; others say he was murdered. In any event, my grandmother, Mary Spencer, who had had nine children with this man before she was 30, also owned 110 acres of farmland with him in Farmville, Virginia, not far from where my paternal grandparents were born.

People said my grandfather was working in the steel mills of Ohio in order to keep up payments on the land. Following his death, my grandmother was given $5,000 as part of an insurance settlement, which she used to pay off the Farmville property. It remains in the family to this day, divided equally among my grandmother's nine children and their offspring.

The idea of empowering black women took root with a grandmother who understood the importance of holding on to the land and passing it on to her heirs. This was a concept I would repeat when I sold a magazine and shared the wealth from the sale with the mostly black women who were its shareholders.

My grandmother subsequently married a widower named Robert Croner, who had five children of his own, making a total of fourteen children growing up on the farm. I would grow up living between the two worlds of city life with its daring, fast-paced rhythms, and the slower-paced country life of a tobacco farm and logging business crawling with children and livestock.

My mother sent me to Farmville every summer from the time I was 5 until I was 15. This is where I got to know my numerous other cousins who were also spending their summers with our grandparents—our parents' own version of a free summer camp program. There could be ten to twenty children at any given time in the summer, all staying in the big fourteen-room house that my grandmother and her second husband owned.

We had no electricity or indoor plumbing. We used kerosene lamps for light at night, drew water from a well, and went to an outhouse to use the toilet. We kids also learned to do everything from chop wood for the fire that was used to heat the house and cook our meals, to churn buttermilk, change a baby's diapers, help my uncle Tracy log trees, pick worms off tobacco leaves, milk the cows, and feed the pigs. I even occasionally rode a pig, which was quite a feat: to get on the back of a pig and ride it around the pen the way a cowboy rides a bull, though with much less bucking, but slimy to hold on to.

My mother and grandparents were of the mind-set that hard work was a good thing and likely to keep us kids out of trouble. I initially hated going south for the summer. I had a cousin from Washington, DC, whom I would hang out with, and we used to say coming down south was like going to the bottom of the earth—the place could be eerily quiet and still at night, with air as pure as anything I've ever breathed in my life. As I got older I viewed it as one of the best places to cool out and just relax.

City life, by contrast, was always jumping, and my father's side of the family loved to jump to dance music. His only two siblings, my uncle Freddy and aunt Madeline, were exhibition dancers, a brother-and-sister team who were featured performers for the Paul Whiteman big swing band popular in the 1950s. I loved watching Uncle Freddy and Aunt Madeline rehearse, and I would occasionally sneak into one of the dance halls where they were performing to watch their shows. My uncle, with his hair conked back, dressed in his natty tuxedo, and my aunt, glamorous in her floor-length white gown, were the high-stepping black Fred Astaire and Ginger Rogers of ballroom dancing in the Bronx. They were fabulous—had to be, since you rarely saw Negro dance couples performing with big white swing bands. Even my father was a skilled dancer, a talent he passed on to me. He would occasionally even moonlight after his janitor's job by giving dance lessons to people in the building where we lived.

When Uncle Freddy wasn't waltzing or lindy-hopping on the dance floor, he reigned as the neighborhood numbers king. He had a reputation for being a tough, mean man who always packed a knife or a razor, and was ready to use them both in a New York minute. For some reason he took a liking to me—maybe because he had no sons, just a daughter—and was always nice to me. We lived in the same apartment building, and he and his wife would often watch me after school until my mother got home from work to pick me up. In those days, most extended families lived in the same neighborhood, if not the same apartment buildings, and usually watched each other's children while parents were working.

I must have been about 9 or 10 when Uncle Freddy gave me a job running numbers for him. Everybody in the neighborhood played their numbers with my uncle, and he had me running up and down Brook and Washington Avenues, taking numbers and collecting money. I guess I was pretty good at it, since I never got any complaints from either the customers or my uncle. I had been doing this four or five months, maybe more, when I happened to be waiting for my mother in the apartment of another uncle, one of my mother's brothers, who also lived in the same building we did. When my mother came to pick me up, my uncle's wife said offhandedly, "Sonny, I saw you running up and down the street today. Why were you doing that?" As if she didn't know, I would realize years later.

"I was running numbers for Uncle Freddy," I answered.

"You were doing *what?*" my mother said, her eyes widening.

"I said I was running numbers for Uncle Freddy," I repeated, clueless that I was getting myself and him in trouble.

"How long you been doing that?" my mother asked, her voice now growing shrill. I told her. She practically dragged me down to the basement apartment of our building to tell my father when he got home that his brother was using me to run numbers. I'll never forget what happened next. My father took me by the hand, marched upstairs to his brother's apartment, and pounded on the door. When Uncle Freddy opened it, my father glared at him and said, "If you ever use my son again to do your business, you will no longer be in this world." This was one of the few times I remember my father doing something that suggested he might have cared about me after all.

My uncle, though not exactly a father figure, seemed to take a more genuine interest in me than my own dad did, and once even stood up for me to the father of the neighborhood bully. Samuel Grey was the terror of the neighborhood who beat up us smaller kids with a regularity we were almost getting used to. He was a big guy like his father and everybody was scared to death of him. He used to chase me when I was living in that basement apartment, and I'd jump down ten steps just to get away from him. I was about 8 years old.

One day I'm throwing around a football with a buddy of mine when Samuel Grey comes along on his bicycle and tries to ram the bike right between my legs from behind. I was so stunned he would try something that crazy that I went momentarily berserk. Before I knew it, I had beaten the crap out of him. I just started punching and didn't stop. I wasn't even sure of what had happened until I heard people cheering, saw windows fly open, saw Samuel Grey lying bloodied on the ground. Then I saw Samuel's father about to throw a punch at me himself for whipping his son.

Uncle Freddy suddenly appeared, and stepped to Mr. Grey. "Don't even think about putting your hands on my nephew," he said, "because if you do, you're going to have to deal with me." Mr. Grey backed off. He knew he was looking at the one man on the block meaner than he was. I became something of a neighborhood hero after that, and was never again bullied by Mr. Grey or his son.

My uncle was married to a very light-skinned woman, and they, too, like my parents, had only one child, a daughter. My cousin Vernell Lewis was a very pretty light-skinned girl that my grandparents just doted on. It seemed to me that Vernell could get anything she wanted just because of her light skin. I used to look in the mirror and think there must have been something wrong with me because I was dark-skinned. Maybe that explained my father's indifference toward me, I would sometimes think.

Issues surrounding skin color, self-esteem, class and money, relationships between men and women, father hunger, and power in the family and the neighborhood were recurring themes that played out in my community as I was growing up Negro in America during the 1940s and '50s. They would continue to play out in articles in the pages of *Essence* many years later as a magazine that was started for Negro women had evolved into a publication for black women that would hold up a mirror to an entire race, reflecting not just its beauty, triumphs, and achievements, but all the good, the bad, and the ugly that make us all fragilely human.

CHAPTER 6

"Why Are We So Poor?"

I am screaming at my mother, tears streaming down my face. It is 1959 and I have completed my freshman year at the University of New Mexico. Back home in the Bronx for the summer, I get the official notice saying I have lost the four-year football scholarship that got me to the university. No explanation. Just a curt letter from the athletic department saying that I am not being invited back to play football. I had heard before I left for summer break that this might happen, and now here it is. I can't believe it.

Worse, I know my mother cannot afford to send me back to the university. We are now living in the St. Mary's housing projects on Brook Avenue in the Bronx with George Clarke, the man my mother met at a Horn & Hardart automat and moved in with shortly after divorcing my father. Our economic situation had not improved much.

"Why are we so poor?" I cry, showing my mother the letter that is shattering my dreams. Yet as soon as I hurl that awful question, I regret it. Uncharacteristically, my mother, always known for her incessant talking, says absolutely nothing. She just gives me a steely-eyed withering look that haunts me even now. A look of hurt and disappointment, shame and anger. The very emotions I am feeling as I cry tears of frustration.

The late, great actor and playwright Ossie Davis once said the trouble with poverty is not that poor people have no money; it's that poor people have no power. And this is exactly how I feel. Powerless. Without money I cannot continue my higher education, which will make me powerless to change my economic condition or that of my family. This is not my mother's fault. Jewell Spencer Lewis, the woman to whom I have lashed out, is the very woman who has loved and nurtured me for all of my 19 years. The one who instilled in me the importance of education and the certainty that I would go to college.

Though my mother had barely completed high school, her reverence for learning came from her own insatiable curiosity and great native intelligence. She loved to read and travel, and was a huge movie buff. One of the things I felt best about during my later business success is that I was able to provide my mother with travel opportunities—trips to Asia, the Caribbean, and much of the United States.

My mother worked all of her life in lower-level jobs as a factory worker, a hotel housekeeper, and for quite a while as a beautician assisting Rose Morgan, the famed Harlem hair salon owner who had been married to boxing champion Joe Louis. Rose Morgan became the richest black woman in Harlem during the 1940s and '50s with her black beauty shops and hair care and beauty products, and used some of her wealth to help Jackie Robinson finance Freedom National Bank.

Like many working-class families, my mother came from people whose real wealth was a sense of sharing, caring for one another, looking out for each other. With the nine children my grandmother had with her first husband and the five children that her second husband came into the marriage with, my mother grew up with thirteen siblings. Her natural siblings, five brothers and three sisters, were all strong and well built, with the boys having a powerful muscularity and the girls growing into good-looking, well-endowed women.

Their physicality was developed during all those years they worked on the farm in Virginia. Those who didn't come north, like my mother did, stayed and worked the land. Some of them worked other people's farms. My uncle Tracy was making 50 cents a day farming for other people before he had his logging business, and he would bring that money back to the family to help pay for food and other necessities. What was always most remarkable to me is how all the siblings worked together and stuck together, as evidenced in something just as remarkable: the continuing tradition of family reunions that the Spencer clan still celebrates. For nearly sixty consecutive years my mother's family has gathered at the original Farmville home of my grandparents to bless the ties that bind with annual family reunions. We haven't missed one since 1955.

All of my mother's people had a high regard for education, though my grandmother could no more afford to send any of her children to college than my own mother could afford to send me back to the University of New Mexico. Yet in a most astounding display of family unity, my mother's brothers and sisters recognized that the brightest one in the family was a sister named Matilene, who showed a great aptitude for math and physics. The siblings decided she was the one who should go to college, so they all pooled their money and sent her to a local college where she majored in both math and physics. My aunt Matilene S. Berryman married a taxi driver and became an oceanographer working at the Department of the Navy for many years. She also wrote books and scholarly papers on the subject of the oceans.

Like many of my mother's other siblings and extended family members, Aunt Matilene was much better off financially than we were. The relatives owned houses in places like Brooklyn and Washington, DC, while my own family rented New York City apartments all of our lives. But whatever we had and wherever we lived, Jewell Lewis made it clear that family was always welcome. When any of my cousins from Washington came to New York, they had a place to stay in our home and would be well fed. It was the same when I went to visit them.

But the goodness exhibited in my mother's generous spirit, her devotion to church and family, her fine intellect and innate sense of style, and her unconditional love for me all seemed to count for nothing that day I had the gall to ask, "Why are we so poor?" The question didn't even deserve a comment, much less an answer, as my mother's withering look quickly told me. I had yet to learn the real meaning of wealth.

———————

It was quite unexpected for me to end up at the University of New Mexico. I started DeWitt Clinton High School in 1954, the year I moved back to the Bronx from Brooklyn, and turned out to have both an aptitude and an affinity for the game of football. I wasn't especially tall, but years of spending summers in Virginia doing hard physical labor, like helping Uncle Tracy lift all those logs, had left me strong and well built.

DeWitt Clinton High School was a predominantly white, all-boys school back in the 1950s, with a student population of 5,000. It wasn't as academically elite as the Bronx High School of Science, Stuyvesant High School, or Brooklyn Technical High School, all premier New York City schools with national reputations. But Clinton had its own cachet. As the only high school in the city not restricted to neighborhood students, it was open to and attracted students from all across the Bronx and Harlem, and would graduate such notables as Langston Hughes, James Baldwin, Neil Simon, Burt Lancaster, Richard Rodgers, Ralph Lauren, and *Saturday Night Live* comedian Tracy Morgan.

The school also had a first-rate football team, also predominantly white. While I may have dreamed of being the next Jackie Robinson, football was the game I took to naturally. I started playing for Clinton in 1956 as a fullback, playing my best two years during the 1957 and 1958 seasons. During the last game of the 1957 season against Evander Childs High School, I intercepted a pass in the final seconds of the game that would have meant a win for Childs if the pass was completed. Instead, Clinton won, and my teammates went wild, hugging me and carrying me off the field in victory. That was quite a feeling, I must say.

Though I was quiet and easygoing, I was tough, tenacious, and fast on the football field. I was also a diligent student—not brilliant, but studious and serious about going to class and staying out of trouble. All of this evidently made me more popular than I realized, because I was elected captain of the DeWitt Clinton football team in 1958, my senior year. I guess my teammates saw leadership qualities in me that I didn't recognize in myself yet.

Being popular enough with my white teammates to become team captain was no small achievement, but that didn't translate into my being popular with the girls in high school. I was shy, for one thing, and too nervous about talking to girls because I never knew exactly what to say. I did go out with one girl, Carolyn Clark, for most of my high school years, but we were really more like good friends than a heavily romantic girlfriend/boyfriend. She came from a family of seventeen kids, and was a whiz in math and science. She was the smartest girl I'd ever known. And ever since knowing her, I've always been attracted to a woman's intelligence.

I admit a lot of the girls I liked didn't always like me back. I also admit I was hung up on the light-skinned Negro girls who attended Clinton's all-girls sister school, Walton High, which was practically next door. Since

I had always thought my own dark skin made me unattractive, I suppose I thought others with dark skin were unattractive too.

Plus, I'm sure seeing how my cousin Vernell, Uncle Freddy's light-skinned daughter, an only child like me, got all the fawning attention from family members, particularly my paternal grandmother, made me think it was better to be light. I was surprised to learn that some light-skinned girls didn't necessarily share or even like that particular line of thinking. I'll never forget Francine Miller, a gorgeous girl whom I was madly in love with, writing in my high school yearbook, "Remember, Ed Lewis, beauty is only skin deep." She knew I was more "madly in love" with her skin color than the content of her character, and that turned her off.

My misguided perception of beauty would change over the years as I dated and came to appreciate women of all skin colors, finding that I could also be as turned on by a woman's intellect, personality, and talents. As a teenager, though, when hormones were raging and wet dreams erupting, shy, socially awkward guys like me really just spent most of our time going steady with that old reliable partner, our right or left hand.

Without girls as an ongoing distraction, I continued to excel in football and came to the attention of a scout from Virginia who had seen me play a few games. He happened to be the trusted eyes and ears of Marvin Levy, the new head football coach at the University of New Mexico who was recruiting senior-year high school football players from around the country. The scout told Levy he should definitely add me to the list of recruits.

Based on nothing more than the word and judgment of the scout, Levy called my coach at Clinton and told him he would be coming to New York and wanted to take me and my mother to dinner at the Waldorf-Astoria Hotel. Oh, my. I'd never even seen the famed Waldorf-Astoria on Park Avenue, with its gilded lobby and Edwardian-coated doormen, and here was this perfect stranger inviting me and my mother to have dinner with him there.

The day he arrived in town my mother and I were at the hotel promptly at seven that evening to meet Marvin Levy in the elegant Peacock Alley restaurant. The maître d' led us to a corner table where the coach was already waiting. He rose to greet my mother, pulling out a chair for her, shook my hand, introducing himself to us both, and then gestured for me to sit next to him. He quickly got down to business. "Ed, I've been hearing some really good things about you," he began. "Your game against Stuyvesant last week was very impressive, I understand. Very impressive, indeed."

Yes, it was, if I did say so myself. Stuyvesant High School was an elite school with a top-notch football team, and was Clinton's archenemy. I had played one of my best games ever the week before when I scored the winning touchdown. That game helped earn me an All-City Fullback title in 1958. It was near the end of the season, my senior year, and I had already received offers to play football from a few colleges—Michigan State, Hofstra, even Columbia—but none of them were offering any money. I couldn't even think about going to a private college or a university outside of New York City without financial aid of some kind. Coach Levy was clearly here to make me an offer I wouldn't refuse.

"The University of New Mexico is committed to building one of the strongest football teams in the Western Athletic Conference," the coach continued, "and I'd like you to think about being a part of that effort, Ed. We're recruiting from all over the country, and are prepared to offer you a full, four-year scholarship if you come to Albuquerque. How does that sound?"

"That sounds real good," my mother interjected. "Doesn't it, Sonny?" she said with a smile, looking at me expectantly. "A *scholarship*! Now isn't that something?"

Truthfully, I didn't quite know where New Mexico was, and couldn't even spell Albuquerque, but a four-year scholarship? Coach Levy, it turned out, wasn't just a jock coach. He'd graduated from Coe College, a well-regarded liberal arts school in Cedar Rapids, Iowa, and had also attended Harvard University. He told my mother he was committed to his athletes getting a real education, and not majoring in some useless subject like basket weaving just so they could play football. That was all she needed to hear.

What we didn't see, however, was something in writing guaranteeing a four-year anything. This would be my first early and painful business lesson. Always, always, get the deal in writing. Coach Levy was right about one thing. The University of New Mexico was building a solid football team, and seemed to be going after good Negro players in particular. Just two years before, when the UNM football team was headed by Coach Dick Clausen, Levy was part of the staff that brought in Charles Roberts, a Negro quarterback from Davenport, Iowa, and Don Perkins, also Negro, a halfback from Waterloo, Iowa. Having gone to college in Iowa, Levy apparently knew where the bodies were when it came to recruiting top Iowa high school football players. Don Perkins would go on after college to play for the Dallas Cowboys for eight seasons and be inducted to the Texas Sports Hall of Fame in 2006. There was also another Negro quarterback on the team, Joe Gayle, out of Chicago, who had transferred from a junior college.

Marvin Levy himself would earn the dubious distinction many years later of coaching the Buffalo Bills professional football team and taking the team to the Super Bowl four times—and losing at the Super Bowl four times. But the year he recruited me, the University of New Mexico was the only predominantly white college that had two Negro starting quarterbacks, something downright historic in 1958.

Levy recruited another New Yorker the year I went to New Mexico, a big white quarterback named Phil Steinberg, who came out of Lafayette High School in Brooklyn. Though I was a mostly B and C+ student, I was very proud to have passed the rigorous New York State Regents exam required of all high school graduates going on to college. Phil Steinberg and I would be flying out to Albuquerque together.

My mother and her boyfriend, George Clarke, saw me off the day I was scheduled to take my first plane ride—to Albuquerque, home of the University of New Mexico Lobos. By my senior year of high school my mother and Mr. Clarke had been living together for nearly seven years. They were unable to marry back then because of an antiquated New York law that stated unless a divorce was uncontested, the only grounds for legally parting ways was adultery. Mr. Clarke had a wife who apparently didn't want to give him a divorce, even though they had been separated for many years—and even though he was committing open adultery by living with my mother.

Mr. Clarke, who, like my father, was a menial laborer and worked most of his life as a messenger in the garment district, was a good man who treated my mother very well. That was all I really cared about. He was also nice to me. In fact, he often treated me more like a son than my own father did, and some people even thought I looked like him. He and my mother came to a few of my football games, for instance, something I don't recall my father ever doing. I knew my mother was in good hands with this kind man, so I could head off to a college hundreds of miles away without worrying about her. My mother, for her part, sent me off with a Bible, a care package of food goodies, and her proud blessings.

Little did I realize how quickly I'd be clutching the Bible and holding on to the blessings. Phil and I boarded our TWA flight at New York International Airport with the giddy excitement of two college-bound kids flying off to a new adventure clear across the country. Then, as now, there were no nonstop flights to Albuquerque from New York. The plane's first stop was St. Louis, with a layover of about an hour. Then it was up in the air again for the final leg of the trip.

As the plane was on its ascent, we heard a loud bang, and the aircraft suddenly rumbled and shook violently from side to side. Phil and I looked out the window and saw *flames* spewing from the rear of the engine right outside our window. "Holy shit!" Phil said. "The plane is on fire!" We looked at each other, then instinctively grabbed each other's hand and held on tight. I gripped the Bible my mother had given me in the other hand and closed my eyes, thinking that in any minute, I was literally going to crash and burn.

The pilot's voice suddenly boomed across the loudspeaker, calmly telling us, "Ladies and gentlemen, we've experienced a fire in our number three engine, but there is nothing to be alarmed about. We've stopped the fuel flow to that engine and activated a fire extinguisher to put out the fire. We will be landing in Albuquerque shortly. By then any residual fire will be blown out by the air flowing around the engine." He was right. The flames disappeared, though the smoke lingered. Phil and I relaxed. We were going to live.

The next sight we saw as the plane flew into New Mexico airspace were patches of barren, desolate brown earth stretching to what seemed like infinity. It looked as if some scorched earth policy were under way. *Oh my,* I thought, staring out the window at the desert-like terrain growing larger as the plane glided onto the runway. *Where are we?*

———

Albuquerque in 1958 was unlike anything I have ever seen geographically. Mostly dry and flat, occasionally dotted with a sprinkle of thorny cactus and wild sagebrush, the city is divided north and south by the mighty Rio Grande, and lies at the base of the low-range Sandia Mountains flanking it to the east. The most I had seen of the United States prior to my first plane ride to the state of New Mexico was the state of Virginia every summer, and the District of Columbia occasionally. Both of those were only a few hundred miles from New York City by car, bus, or train—and still on the East Coast, with little physical change in the landscape.

New Mexico, on the other hand, may as well have been on the other side of a brand-new world. The sweeping expanse of America lying between the desert and the Bronx encompassed the low-lying Great Plains of the Midwest, the desolate, starkly beautiful Dakota Badlands, the stunning, wide-open vistas of Big Sky, the majestic Rocky Mountains, the awesome Grand Canyon. Rising along a trajectory heading west and south were the great urban cities of Chicago and Detroit, the grain capitals of Omaha and Des Moines, the cattle meccas of Denver and Kansas City, the oil-rich metropolises of Houston and Dallas. This is where vast Middle America spread out, supplying the country with its food and fuel and automobiles.

It was on this first plane ride that I got my first sense of just how huge and beautiful America really is as we flew over geography and cities that stretch "from sea to shining sea." Years later as the publisher of *Essence,* a magazine geared to reaching black women who populate America's East and West Coasts, the North and South, as well as the enormous heartland in between, I would recognize the tremendous value in having our editors travel America's vast territories, getting to know readers who are as different, diverse, and complex as the country is.

But first I had to get over the culture shock of being Negro in the land of the Navajo, the Latino, and the Anglo.

Coming from a city of eight million people, I was used to what we would one day call "ethnic diversity." In my Bronx neighborhood of Negroes, Italians, Jews, and a sprinkling of Puerto Ricans, each ethnic group had its own community large enough to ensure comfort and a measure of protection. Albuquerque also had its diversity, but the Anglos and Native Americans and Mexican Americans who made up the majority of the city's 250,000 residents were completely new for me. So, too, was the idea of being a tiny minority. There were only 5,000 Negroes in Albuquerque, most of them affiliated with the surrounding military bases. So, unlike the Bronx, I did not have the comfort of refuge in a large black community.

My entering class at the University of New Mexico in 1958 had seven Negro students, which, believe it or not, was two more than the school had when we arrived: five. And out of the dozen of us, there were only two Negro women. On the total scale of things, the entire student body enrollment of 8,000 at the University of New Mexico wasn't much greater, relatively speaking, than DeWitt Clinton High School's enrollment of 5,000, which didn't even include girls in the count.

Clearly, I was not in the Bronx anymore. Albuquerque initially felt desolate and lonely. It was basically a college town, and the beer-swilling college kids, the *Anglos,* as whites are called in this part of the world, seemed as foreign to me as the brown- and red-skinned people whose culture defined the state's food and architecture and fashion. Because there were so few of us, we Negro students would bond together out of our sheer primal need to be among that which was known and familiar.

––––––

"Hey, man, how you doin'?" said the tall, muscular, light-brown-skinned guy with gray eyes who has just entered my dorm room without knocking. I've just arrived in the room myself from the airport, and am unpacking, trying to get my bearings. "I'm Charles Roberts, but everybody calls me Chuck," the guy continues, an easy smile lighting up his open, handsome face as he extends his hand.

"Oh, Chuck Roberts from Iowa," I say, impressed, shaking his hand. "You're one of the starting quarterbacks, right? A junior?"

"Yep, that's me," Chuck answers affably. "And I know you're Ed Lewis out of New York. You're a long way from home, man. How'd the coach hear about *you?*"

I tell Chuck how Marvin Levy recruited me, which pretty much matched his own story of coming to the university, except that the coach had actually seen Chuck Roberts play.

"I'll tell you one thing, these folks in New Mexico sure know how to court a ball player," Chuck says, laughing. "I'd never felt so *wanted* in my whole life when Coach came after me two years ago!" He laughs again, and I like him immediately. We will still be friends more than fifty years later. I'd never met anybody from Iowa before, and certainly never thought any Negroes lived in that part of the country. Just goes to show how much of a world there is beyond a city of eight million people—and just who occupies it. Like me, Chuck knew he would go to college, but definitely wouldn't be in Albuquerque if he wasn't on a sports scholarship.

Most of the Negroes at the university were on scholarship, whether they played football or ran track and field, the two sports the school's athletic department was investing money in heavily. As a freshman, I didn't play varsity football, though we first-year players did do some scrimmaging with other freshman college teams in the conference.

Nor was my social life much to speak of that first year. The dorm didn't serve meals on the weekends, so there were regular Friday night parties in town, usually at the house of a former Negro student named Roy Griffin. We would play cards, listen to Ray Charles records, and eat a good home-cooked meal. I occasionally dated one of the Hispanic college girls, but for the most part I stuck to the books and studying. I chose political science as a major because I had always had this great curiosity about how the political process works, and how it can used to bring about social change.

The Montgomery, Alabama, bus boycott had captured my imagination three years before when a daring Negro seamstress named Rosa Parks refused to give her seat on the bus to a white man. After she was arrested, all of the Negroes in the city, led by a young minister named Martin Luther King, Jr., boycotted the bus company, refusing to ride a bus anywhere. Within a year the city's bus company went broke, effectively breaking the back of segregation in public transportation in Montgomery. This single act would ignite the American civil rights movement.

It's amazing what can happen when people work together, I remember thinking. I'm not sure when my own political activism was sparked, but by the end of my freshman year in Albuquerque, I understood that injustice is global, racism is not just white against black, and we all have more in common than any differences separating us by skin color, language, or religion.

By then I had also come to appreciate the desert beauty that was Albuquerque. The pink adobe clay that defines the city's pueblo-style architecture, the brilliant sunrises and exquisite sunsets, the near perfect weather that cools down even after the hottest day, and the wonderful culture of the brown- and red-skinned peoples whose history of oppression often intersected my own, all led to a love and respect for the Southwest that I hold to this day.

It was unthinkable that I might have to leave it all after my first year.

Though I didn't play varsity football my freshmen year, everyone on of the football team went to the big out-of-state games. Our final game of the 1958–59 season was against the Air Force Academy on its home turf of Colorado Springs, Colorado. By half time Air Force was seriously beating our ass. The score was 21–7. At the start of the third quarter, Air Force kicked off, and Don Perkins caught the ball at the twenty-yard line. Though he wasn't a big guy—he couldn't have weighed 200 pounds—Perkins had incredible strength, with speed to match. He started running the ball up the field with the force of a locomotive, and trying to bring him down was like trying to take down a mountain. He was finally toppled at our twenty-yard line. But the team was so galvanized by this stunning run that we would leap from behind to beat Air Force 28–27. Chuck Roberts threw the winning touchdown pass, making him the leading passer in the Western Athletic Conference that year.

It was an incredible victory for the New Mexico Lobos. We had lost a heartbreaker game to Wyoming just the week before, and morale had been low. Now here we were taking out Air Force in an upset victory—the number two college football team in the nation! I was thrilled to be one of the cub rookies among the fierce Lobos. When we arrived back in Albuquerque, there were 5,000 cheering fans waiting at the airport to greet us. So this is what college football is like. I could hardly wait to be in the mix next year.

My spring training sessions were good—though there was that one day during a scrimmaging session that I tried to tackle Don Perkins and a linebacker who was blocking for him hit me so hard I was knocked out flat and actually saw stars. Through blurred vision I next saw Coach Levy standing over me and heard him say, "Ed Lewis, are you going to get up anytime soon?" But even with this little mishap there was no question that I would be a part of the team the next year. Everybody said so.

Then Coach Levy accepted a coaching position in California before the school year was over and he was gone. So, too, I later learned, were my prospects for playing football my sophomore year or any other year. I had overheard a disturbing conversation that implied I might be cut from the team, and I was concerned enough to seek out Chuck Roberts for advice. I found him playing cards in one of the dorm rooms.

"Hey, Chuck, I need to speak with you a minute," I called to him, sticking my head in the room, trying to sound nonchalant.

"Sure, Ed," he replied pleasantly, turning his cards over to a buddy to play out his hand. "What's up?" he asked out in the hallway, closing the door.

"I'm not sure," I said a little uneasily, "but I've heard that I might be cut from the team. Have you heard anything?"

"What?" Chuck said, sounding genuinely surprised. "Naw, man. That's not even possible. Why would they do that? You've played well. Where'd you hear something like that?"

Who knows where rumors really start. Being a quiet type, I would overhear things when nobody knew I was even around. I'd heard a couple of Anglo guys on the team in the locker room one day saying something about "that stuck-up Negro from New York."

"Yeah, he better watch out," one of them was saying. "After Coach Levy is gone, he probably will be too, though I guess the university will find a way to give him a job or something if he wants to stay."

I didn't share all that I had overheard with Chuck, just the part about my possibly getting financial help if I was to be cut from the team.

"Well, I'd take them up on that," Chuck said. "But I'd be really shocked if you got cut," he added. "They don't take a scholarship away without a reason. I mean, you would have to do something really awful for that to happen." Chuck looked as horrified as I was feeling over the thought that any of us could ever be kicked off the team.

But I *was* kicked off the team. And that summer day in 1959 when I got the letter saying I would not be invited back to play football my sophomore year, I felt like I'd been knocked to the ground again by that linebacker blocking for Don Perkins. I didn't see stars this time. I just started crying. If Chuck was right, I must have done something really awful.

And the only awful thing I could think of was being born poor. It would be almost thirty years before I finally found out why I had really been kicked off the team.

CHAPTER 7

BMOC

It's true. What doesn't kill you makes you stronger. Losing my football scholarship seemed to be the end of my world as I knew it. I was filled with self-doubt and self-recrimination, felt like a failure, and still didn't know exactly *why* I had been cut from the team. A few other players were let go too, but that was not my problem. My problem was being kicked off the team even though I had been told I played well during the scrimmage sessions. That's what was eating me. What the hell *happened*?

Did Coach Levy's departure mean I no longer had a "rabbi" to look out for me, making it easier for the athletic department to give me the boot? Maybe they were pissed that Coach Levy had left after only one year as head coach and were taking this resentment out on me, his colored Yankee recruit, in which a year's worth of tuition and food and lodging had been invested. Maybe because I was quiet and shy, people thought I was a stuck-up "uppity" Negro, like those guys I'd overheard in the locker room say about me.

Maybe . . . maybe . . . I could have gone crazy with all the maybes and why-mes? But I didn't have time to stew in my own pity juices for long, because no sooner had I received that letter saying I was not being asked to come back to play football than I learned people at the University of New Mexico were working to get me back—not to play sports but to finish my college education.

"Mrs. Lewis, Ed is much too bright a young man to forfeit a college education due to a lack of money," Howard Mathany, the dean of men at the university, had called to tell my mother, assuring her that a way would be found to keep me in school.

I met Dean Mathany as a freshman and quickly came to see him as a mentor. I would sometimes drop by his office to just talk. Like most whites, Dean Mathany didn't know a lot of Negroes—not that there were many of us in Albuquerque to know!—and I think he liked the idea that one of the university's young Negro jocks thought he was worth seeking out for advice. In any event, the dean became one of my biggest advocates. And he was the first person I called when I got the letter basically firing me from the football team. I told him I couldn't afford to return to the university without financial help. "Don't worry, Ed," the dean said calmly. "We'll figure something out."

Before I knew it, I was offered a job on campus for the coming year as a resident adviser in Mesa Vista and Coronado Halls, two of the male dormitories. The pay? Free dormitory room and board for the school year. Dean Mathany also facilitated my getting an Eleanor Roosevelt scholarship and a National Defense Student Loan, which covered tuition. And just like that, I was back at the university in the fall of 1959 to begin my sophomore year.

Nothing, of course, is ever "just like that." My relationship with Dean Mathany and other professors and administrators at the university would be my introduction to the politics of networking and developing allies across all lines of age, race, gender, and professions among people who could help me. This was not something I did consciously as a college student. This is something I have done naturally all of my life. Be it a dean or a professor, a football player, black, white, brown or red, if I genuinely like and respect someone, I am down with the friendship, typically for the long haul. Some people are good at keeping confidences. I am good at making and keeping friends, something that would prove to be invaluable to me in business.

One fortunate outcome resulting from the loss of my football scholarship is that I now had the time to pursue other campus activities besides sports, and this opened up a whole new world to me of student politics and political activism. As a dorm counselor, I was the go-to person for advice, guidance, and an occasional shoulder to lean on. It didn't matter that the guys being counseled were white, or that I was black. What mattered is that they trusted me, respected my counsel, and saw me as a leader, something I still did not recognize in myself.

My Negro football teammates were as surprised as I was about my dismissal from the team, but we continued to hang out, playing cards, going to Friday night parties. We remained a tiny minority in the larger campus universe, so sticking together was something we did naturally. But once sports was no longer my primary focus, my universe of activities and interests expanded across racial and even global lines. I started hanging out at International House, a student facility catering to the university's foreign exchange students, where I would meet people from other parts of the world, some of whom became lifelong friends.

One of the people who would become a best friend was Enrique Cortez, a graduate assistant in the language and history department, who was from Monterrey, Mexico. Enrique, a slim, handsome man, and natty dresser, came from a prominent Mexican family, but had such a down-to-earth, engaging personality that he put everyone at ease. He was one of the first people who actually started to make me feel good about my looks. It amazed him that I thought being dark skinned made me unattractive. "*Mi amigo*," he would say, laughing. "You *loco* or something? You see how all these *chiquitas* around here are giving you the eye?"

I certainly didn't see what he saw—in me. Nor did I see all the girls he claimed to see who were supposedly looking my way with interest. I did date a cute Mexican American student named Patsy Apodaca during my freshman year. We would study together, go to the movies, and hang out at some of the off-campus Friday night parties. But nothing more serious. My dating life had always been limited, even in high school. I was never good at "rapping" to girls the way my buddies were. And going to the University of New Mexico at age 18 where you didn't even see any Negro girls only made my shyness worse. I felt about as cool as I did back in the Bronx when I was 9 and a fast 14-year-old girl tried to seduce me and nothing happened. My social life at UNM that first year was pretty much like that sexual encounter—a dud.

Patsy Apodaca was the first girl outside my race whom I dated. New Mexico is a racial buffer state bordered to the east by Texas, Colorado to the north, and Arizona to the west, where interracial interactions were pretty much accepted in the late 1950s. The state had a fair-housing law on its books as early as 1949, ten years before I returned to UNM as a sophomore, so the idea of "race mingling" was not considered an unconscionable offense. Nevertheless, coming from New York, where some parts of the city and some attitudes were as segregated and racially perverse as parts of the Deep South, I had it my head that I could somehow "get back at white men" by dating "their women."

Which meant that by my sophomore year I started to openly date white girls on campus, thinking, *This will show those guys in the athletic department who kicked me off the football team.* What it actually showed *me* is that dating to make a political statement or to exact some ill-conceived notion of revenge is the worst reason and the worst way to have a relationship. It is virtually impossible to establish real bonds of intimacy or be authentic if you're relating to someone as a political abstraction to be used as a weapon, rather than as a flesh-and-blood human being with whom you can have honest interactions.

I said I'd never abuse women the way my father abused my mother, but I realize I dated many white girls with a kind of callous indifference that was its own form of emotional abuse. And that I do regret. It would be two more years before I met a white girl at the university whom I actually fell in love with.

Since I had always had an interest in politics, student government and campus political activism turned out to be healthier outlets for my passions. I was majoring in political science, and would choose Russian and Chinese history as subjects to minor in. I loved Russian history, and I especially loved the Russian writers who wrote about this history: Fyodor Dostoyevsky, Leo Tolstoy, Alexander Pushkin. I was fascinated by these writers, whose works typically examined the Russian caste system of serfs—the category of people who were "slaves to the land," just like my people had been. How do serfs politically overcome their caste status and rise above their conditions? It seemed to me as an American Negro there was something I could learn from people who had overthrown their own monarchy less than fifty years before and taken power.

I think I've always instinctively understood that politics is the most effective mechanism for activating social change, which is why becoming active in student politics appealed to both my natural inclinations and my competitive spirit honed as a football player. As a dorm resident adviser

I was already known to a fair number of students, and had become pretty popular on campus. A few of the students urged me to think about running for a student council position.

"You'd be great on the student council, Ed," one of the guys in Mesa Vista Hall told me one evening after I'd helped him figure out how to get a professor to let him drop a class after the deadline. "You're so cool and calm and good at looking out for us underclassmen," he said. "I'm sick of these frat boys always running for office like they're the only people worth voting for. They need somebody to give them a damn run for their money." I was surprised to learn how many other students felt the same way. A number of them offered to make campaign flyers for me and canvass the dorms. Even my football buddies were on board with support, offering to do whatever I needed if I decided to run for student office.

I may have been shy, but getting involved in student government was appealing enough to force me out of my introverted comfort zone. So I filed the required petition declaring my candidacy for a seat on the student council—and launched my campaign. I debated my opponents in public forums; educated myself on the issues most pressing to students by listening to what students told me; got to know the workings of the Board of Regents in Santa Fe, the governing body of the state university system; and became quite forceful in articulating why I thought I was the best candidate to serve the needs of my classmates.

Unbelievably, I *won.* This turned out to be just as thrilling as that upset victory over the Air Force Academy during my freshman year when I was still on the football team. Only now I was the winner heading my own team of student political supporters who had helped get me elected in my first run for office. I would be returning to school in the fall as a junior and a member of the UNM Student Council, the first and only Negro to hold a student government position in the university's history. I had suddenly become a real BMOC—an authentic Big Man on Campus.

The student council meeting was turning ugly. "This is outrageous," I said. "I don't care what the Regents are saying. We're not supporting any policy dictating who can and who can't be hired based on political affiliations.

Didn't we learn anything from the McCarthy hearings? Tell me we're not going down *that* path, for Christ's sake."

"Oh, hold up a minute, Ed. Don't even try to equate this with the McCarthy hearings," said a sophomore student council member, a blond, Aryan-looking frat dude oozing smug superiority. "You people always think . . ."

"*You people!*" I sputtered, ready to jump across the table and choke the smugness right out of him. "*You're* the people who think you should rule the world. Well, I'm here to tell you, you *don't,* and you *won't* as long as I have breath and have a seat on this council . . ."

"All right. Let's all simmer down," the student body president cut in. "We're just here to review what the Regents are proposing. You know we have no authority to accept or reject anything. We can only make our feelings known."

"Well, then, my feeling is that the Regents should all take a flying leap to where the sun don't shine," I said, furious. "This is unbelievable."

The first controversy in my first year as a member of student government involved the Board of Regents trying to push through an edict that would prevent UNM from hiring any faculty member deemed to be "leftist." *Leftist?* I knew this was just a code word for *Communist.* To me the Regents' proposal reeked of the same odious travesty that had occurred a few years before when Joseph McCarthy, a Republican senator from Wisconsin, started hauling hundreds of Americans in front of the congressional hearings held by the House Un-American Activities Committee to ascertain whether or not they were "loyal" Americans. Being loyal meant they had to prove they were not a Communist or a Communist sympathizer, which at the time was all but synonymous with treason.

Those deplorable "red scare" hearings went on for years, and were tantamount to a national witch hunt. Now the New Mexico Board of Regents was raising this ugly specter again with talk of blacklisting any "leftist" faculty person.

"And just what does leftist *mean* anyway?" I demanded to know. "And who's going to determine who's a leftist, and who isn't?" The student council members were silent, including Blond Aryan Dude.

As the lone Negro on the student council, I knew there were ethnic implications in this attempted move by the Regents, because I knew the word *leftist* was also code for something else: Jew. My outrage was rooted in the specific fear that one of my favorite professors, Henry Tobias, a Jew who taught Russian and Chinese history, represented the very kind of independent, freethinking, intellectual "leftist" spirit that the Regents wanted to discriminate against in hiring. This was not going to happen while I was on the student council. Not if I could help it, anyway.

Shortly after the raucous student council meeting, Enrique Cortez and I were hanging out in the lounge at International House with Roland Ajayi, a buddy of mine from Nigeria, and Steve Maurer, a Hungarian friend who had fought in the 1956 Hungarian revolution. Enrique could barely contain himself. "Ooh, I hear you got some big *cojones, Señor* Ed," he said, grinning. "You walk soft but carry the big stick, eh, *amigo*? Watch how the *chiquitas* love you now," he cracked with a chuckle.

Word of my outburst at the student council meeting had quickly spread across campus, as had the protest action I took part in when a group of students marched on the university administration building, calling out the Regents on their veiled racist proposal. They dropped the idea of trying to dictate hiring policy. By the late 1950s nobody wanted to be accused of anything associated with another McCarthy-like witch hunt.

Enrique and Roland and Steve were impressed that the Regents had caved behind the protest action, and carried on as if I had single-handedly brought them down. "Ah, yes, you know when and how to get angry, Ed," Roland said with admiration. "Africans must learn how and when to get angry. That is how one becomes effective in the fight for freedom." He was referring to the liberation movements gaining momentum all across Africa as colonialism was taking its last gasps of power. His own country of Nigeria had just won its independence from Great Britain that year, 1960.

My friendships with students like Roland and Enrique and Steve gave me a global perspective on politics, on understanding how the forces of oppression are worldwide and insidious, and require coalitions between all races and classes of people if these forces are to be defeated. Unfortunately, Roland did not live to see a fully independent Africa. He died in 1961 from complications after open heart surgery, done to correct a congenital heart defect. I still treasure and wear the suit he gave me—his country's national dress—shortly after we met and became fast friends at the university more than fifty years ago.

The longest-running friendship I developed at UNM was with a professor—Dr. Henry Tobias, the Jewish teacher who I felt represented the very sort of academic free thinker the Regents wanted to prevent the university from hiring. Like me, Henry was originally from the Northeast—Paterson, New Jersey—and his parents had immigrated to America from Russia before he was born. A tallish, wiry man with a thick head of hair that gave him a distinguished look, Henry was 35 when he came to the university my sophomore year, and taught both Russian and Chinese history, two subjects that had always fascinated me.

My love of Russian history had to do with how a people had overcome. My love of Chinese history had to do with respect for a culture that is ancient, having survived pretty much intact for more than 5,000 years. I figured the Chinese had probably seen it all, and as a result had developed a philosophy of life that was worth studying.

While Henry was a skillful teacher, I doubt if we would have become good friends were it not for the day I ran into him as I was going into the student union building to get a cup of coffee. He was coming out and stopped me, saying, "Hey, there, Ed, where're you going?" I told him. "Mind if I join you?" he asked. I was a bit surprised that a professor wanted to have coffee with me, but flattered enough to let him. I learned later that Henry regularly did this with his students in order to get to know them.

We spent the next three hours over several cups of coffee just talking—about everything: politics, philosophy, civil rights, the coming election. He couldn't believe I was supporting Richard Nixon in the presidential race over the good-looking, charismatic Democrat John F. Kennedy. I suppose he thought all Negroes followed the party of FDR and voted Democrat. At 20, I couldn't vote yet, but I told Henry there was something about Kennedy that I just didn't like. Maybe he was too handsome, too charismatic, too pretty an image to be real. I said I didn't think he could relate to my people when it came to civil rights.

"I'll be so glad when we finally have a Negro president," I said.

"Really?" Henry asked, looking surprised. "You think there will be an American Negro president someday?"

"Yeah. Well, sure. Why shouldn't we have a Negro president?" I don't know where that idea came from, nor do I remember even having it before I made the statement. It was Henry who would remind me of my prescient remark when a good-looking, charismatic Democrat named Barack Obama ran for president of the United States some forty-eight years later.

Henry was one of those professors who do what all good professors do: make you think. And he had a way of connecting the dots that often left me spinning.

"Quick. What did Abraham Lincoln, Benjamin Disraeli, and Franklin D. Roosevelt all have in common?" he asked the class one day.

Uh . . . They were all white men?

"They were all *tall*," Henry answered in response to the class's blank stares. He then launched into his "commanding heights" lecture, explaining that in terms of strategy on a battlefield the commanding officer always wants to be positioned on a high point—at the top of a slope or hilltop—looking down, because that's the best way to see what's going on in the field. So, too, with leaders, he continued. The great ones are often tall, and because of their height, tend to have a commanding way of viewing things, frequently bringing bigger ideas and larger perspectives to their decision making.

I know I wasn't Henry's most brilliant student, but I may have been his most curious and passionately engaged. I loved the reading assignments, the lectures, the probing Socratic method he used to get us students to think outside the box. What started out as a typical professor-student relationship turned into a deep, personal friendship that I still cherish. I think Henry always appreciated the outspoken stance I took on the student council opposing the Regents' attempt to discriminate in hiring.

My political activism only continued to grow, both on and off the student council. I became fast friends with a leftist liberal named Mark Acuff, editor of the school newspaper. Mark and I got to be known around campus as being "on the fringe," meaning we marched together, partied together, and got down with anything that had to do with liberalizing the university. By now, 1963, the American civil rights moment was gaining steam, along with the liberation movements in Africa, and students, black and white alike, were in the forefront of both.

Mark happened to be good friends with Allard Lowenstein, a former student radical living in Washington, DC, who was active in the National Student Association. NSA had its roots in the late 1940s, and had started as a national college organization to enhance student government, increase civil liberties on American campuses, and expand access to higher education. Mark had told Lowenstein about my political activities at UNM, which prompted Lowenstein to invite me to be part of a summer training program NSA was conducting at Bryn Mawr College in Pennsylvania, preparing college kids to go to work in Africa. It was nearing the end of my junior year and I was preparing to make another run for student office—this time for president of the University of New Mexico student body.

Once again I had my supporters, and I campaigned as hard as I had the first time I ran for office—maybe even harder, since this election would truly be historic if I won. This time, however, I also had my detractors. Several of the fraternity houses launched a smear campaign, spreading rumors that I was running for student body president only so I could date white girls. It was a vicious tactic, but it worked. I lost to my opponent by a mere 100 votes! Henry told me to view that as a victory, considering how few Negroes there were on campus to even vote, and one of them—me—almost beat his white frat opponent.

Still, losing the election hurt. Licking my wounds from the defeat, I took Lowenstein up on his offer to join NSA's training program at the end of my junior year. For two weeks in bucolic Bryn Mawr, I studied the politics of communism and the revolutionary tactics of freedom fighters. NSA was supplying anticolonial organizations in Africa with as many young people as it could train in a summer, although that summer I almost drowned.

A group of us had taken off one Sunday and headed to the resort community of Wildwood, New Jersey, where we went swimming in the Atlantic Ocean. I've never been a particularly good swimmer, and this day I swam a ways out from shore, got caught in an undertow, and when I turned around and saw just how far out I was, I started to panic. What saved me was me. *If you don't relax, you're not going to make it back,* I said to myself. So I relaxed and just took my time swimming back in. It was not my time to go. I would use this "just relax" strategy many times in business during the coming years, and just as it saved my life, it saved many a business deal.

At the end of the training, NSA held its national conference at Indiana University in Bloomington. I went to the conference representing the University of New Mexico, and had my first encounter with other young

Negro student activists, among them Jesse Jackson, representing North Carolina A&T College, and Stokely Carmichael, representing Howard University. Stokely was also head of the Student Nonviolent Coordinating Committee (SNCC). Jesse was a tall, good-looking guy, and we hit it off immediately. Not so much me and Stokely. He was a fiery talker, speaking with the rapid, lilting staccato of his native Trinidad, and seemed to equate my shy quietness with timidity. I overheard him call me an Uncle Tom during one of the plenary sessions, and wondered where *that* came from. But he was to soon do an about-face on that comment.

Lowenstein wanted to run for president of NSA, a position he had held in the past, and asked if I'd give an endorsement speech for him at the conference. I told him I would, but that he might not like what I had to say beforehand. He didn't seem to care. He just wanted my endorsement. The March on Washington had just taken place, and it killed me that I didn't have the financial means to attend that historic event. But that didn't keep me from giving my own assessment of where I thought things now stood with the civil rights movement.

Here is part of the speech I gave at the general session before endorsing Lowenstein:

No doubt about it, the recent March on Washington will go down as one of the finest moments in American history. The great Martin Luther King, Jr., in the spirit of the great Mahatma Gandhi, has shown that nonviolence as a political strategy is as powerful a force in defeating oppression as any military weapon. But the tide is turning. Yes it is. The nonviolence of the current civil rights movement is being replaced by a growing militancy. Young, northern black men like myself are choosing to march to a different beat: The beat of Malcolm X. The beat of Che Guevara. The beat of all men who strike back when hit. The beat of all revolutionary men who dare to pick up the sword or the gun or the machete—and in the words of Malcolm, "seize power by any means necessary!"

The applause was thunderous. Stokely jumped up from his seat and ran up to hug me. "My brother," he said, looking shocked, "your words were powerful. So powerful. I had misjudged you."

Stokely, Jesse, and I represented the new breed of political activists who by the early 1960s were making the transition from Negro to Black. By the early '70s, when *Essence* magazine launched, "Black Power!" would be the roaring anthem.

Two weeks after the conference, a church firebombing in Birmingham, Alabama, killed four little black girls. "I can't stay here!" I yelled at Enrique and Paul, enraged. We were in my dorm room and I was furiously throwing books into one of the boxes I'd just hauled in. It was September 1963, my senior year, and I was dropping out of school to go down south and work for SNCC. The senseless death of four little innocent girls by racist, murdering whites left me reeling. I had to do *something*.

"*Mi amigo*," Enrique said with a stricken look. "You know you are not one to turn the cheek around if it is slapped. You will not do well in a place like Alabama. It is very dangerous. *Por favor!*"

"Enrique is right," Paul Amorin, my friend from Brazil, added. "Eduardo, your place is here at the university. This is where you will do the most good. Not the Congo. Not the south in America. You are a leader *here*. *Pleease*, stay and finish your education."

I knew they were right. I had decided not to go to Africa following the NSA training because I wanted to finish school. Plus, NSA wanted to send me to the Congo, the hottest political spot in Africa at the time. I probably wouldn't have made it out alive. The same with Alabama, which is what my friends were trying to tell me. I finally calmed down and listened to them.

My mother made the trip to Albuquerque to see me graduate in the spring of 1964. For the second time in my life that I can remember, she was speechless. This time with joy. She was a little disappointed, though, that I wasn't coming back home to the Bronx with my newly minted bachelor's degree. I had decided to stay at the university for another year and pursue a master's degree in political science, with a concentration in international relations.

I was also pursuing a relationship with a French assistant professor that had first sparked when I was a student in her class during my sophomore year. She was my first "older woman"—and the second European woman I had fallen for at the university.

Claude Book was by no means a beautiful woman—handsome

was more like it—but she turned my head more than a little bit. Very self-assured, very independent, she was maybe in her early thirties when I developed a crush on her in her French class. She had maturity and great presence. She also had a husband, an American southerner, and a professor, too. But Claude was no cheating cradle robber. Though she was older and my professor, we didn't really start seeing each other until I was in graduate school. She had left her husband by then, and I, 24 by then, had moved to off-campus housing, taking an apartment in Albuquerque's lovely historic Old Town.

Even so, we were discreet in our dating. Sometimes we would double date with Henry and his second wife, a younger woman who had once been a student of his as well. It all sounds pretty scandalous, I know, but Claude represented my first relationship rooted in real love and mutual respect. To this day, we are still dear friends.

Ingrid Iversen, on the other hand, was the blond Danish beauty I fell in love with before Claude, and it broke me up when she left me. "Ed, you knew I would not be staying," she told me with matter-of-fact briskness, sitting on the edge of my bed in the dorm a few days before she was scheduled to go back to Copenhagen.

"I know, I know," I said, trying not to sound pathetic. "I just thought maybe I could go back with you—you know, visit your country, get to meet your parents. I've never been to Denmark. I've never even been to Europe." I sound pathetic.

Ingrid was an exchange student I'd met at International House at the beginning of my senior year. I knew she was going to be in Albuquerque only a year. That was the reality from the beginning. But she was the first white girl I'd had an authentic relationship with—no trying-to-get-back-at-the-white-man bullshit with her. She was intellectually challenging, well read, well traveled. And all of this appealed to me in a way that I'd never experienced with other women. Maybe it was because she was European and didn't bring centuries of American race baggage to our interactions. She didn't view me as the exotic American Negro, good only for sex. Nor was she the blond goddess I put up on a pedestal to fantasize over. We could be real together, and that was surprisingly exciting. I couldn't believe she was leaving already.

Both Ingrid and Claude taught me to see beyond stereotypes of race and beauty when it comes to intimate relationships. A woman's intellect, her sense of style, her aura of confidence—regardless of race or looks—were all attributes I came to value and be turned on by. This appreciation was as much a part of my "higher education" during my college years as the development of my political consciousness. In fact, it helped inform my political consciousness.

And it would be indispensable in both my business and romantic dealings with black women when I helped launch a magazine expressly for them.

CHAPTER 8

Flunking Out

University Arena, affectionately called the Pit by University of New Mexico students and faculty, is filled to capacity: graduating students, their parents and friends, university alumni, distinguished guests. I am one of the distinguished guests, seated on stage with Denise Chávez, a New Mexico author, actress, director, and teacher who is to receive an honorary doctor of letters and be the commencement speaker for this year's graduating class of 2004. Stewart Udall, a political activist and scholar, will receive an honorary doctor of laws degree. I am to receive an honorary doctor of humane letters.

Enrique Cortez, my wonderful, affirming Mexican friend, is in the audience. So is Chuck Roberts, my good-natured college football running buddy. Dear Dr. Henry Tobias, still my favorite professor, is also present, along with my second wife, Carolyn, and a host of other friends, faculty, and admirers I don't even know. Claude Book isn't here, though I certainly intend to spend some time with her before I leave Albuquerque. I am happily married now to a beautiful black woman, but will be forever grateful for the lessons in life and love that I learned from Claude, my older, onetime French *chérie*.

It has been forty years since I sat where this year's university graduates are now sitting. That spring day in 1964 I was granted a bachelor of arts degree in political science with a minor in Russian and Chinese history. Today I have returned to what has become a beloved alma mater as a university favorite son. A distinguished alum and generous donor. A University of New Mexico Lobos graduate who became a respected magazine publisher and CEO, more successful than he ever dreamed he would be.

The thing about returning anywhere—be it home or an alma mater—is that the occasion usually calls for a recounting of sorts, a look at what went down to get us back to where it all started. I left the University of New Mexico in 1965, full of promise and possibilities, having spent another year after receiving my bachelor's degree earning a master's degree in political science, with a specialty in international relations. I continued to be fascinated by the potential for politics to change things, globally as well as domestically. It had taken two extra years to get an undergraduate degree because I took time off to work for the Albuquerque City Manager's Office, learning about city budgets, fair housing laws, and the mechanics and politics of municipal governments.

Work during my graduate school year, however, was spent as a teaching assistant. Though I did not support the candidacy of John F. Kennedy, I was just as horrified when he was assassinated on November 22, 1963, as I had been when a church bombing in Birmingham killed four little black girl two months before. Kennedy's enduring legacy would be the Peace Corps, a program he started that recruited mainly college-educated young people for volunteer social service work in underdeveloped countries around the world. Many of these countries were in Latin America, and given UNM's geographical proximity to Mexico and South America, it became one of the university sites used by Kennedy's administration to train Peace Corps volunteers. Much of Latin America was also under Socialist or Communist rule.

Henry Tobias, known to be an expert on the subject of communism because of his specialty in Russian and Chinese history, became the sought-after professor to help with the Peace Corps training. Since the volunteers who were being sent to Communist-ruled countries were expected to push democracy as part of their interactions with the locals, it was imperative that they have a working knowledge of communism in order to effectively counter it with democracy's ideology.

"I really don't have the time to add the Peace Corps to my teaching schedule," Henry was telling me one day at the beginning of the school term as I was hanging out in his office, killing time before the start of a graduate seminar. "You know the material as well as I do, Ed," he added. "Why don't you teach the Peace Corps class?"

Me? Really? No doubt about it, I'd certainly taken enough of Henry's courses in both Russian and Chinese communism to be something of an expert on the subject. Teaching assistants weren't paid a lot, but I didn't really need a lot of money to get through this last graduate year. My old 1950 Oldsmobile was paid for, and my off-campus apartment in Old Town didn't cost much. It might be fun to teach students around my own age a subject I had both an expertise in and a passion for. Besides, it would count toward graduate school credit. With the blessing of Henry, the history department hired me.

There were about 150 Peace Corps trainees sitting in the lecture hall the first day of my course on World Affairs and Communism. Today's introductory session would be a basic overview on the varied philosophies of communism's heaviest hitters: Lenin and Stalin, Marx, Hegel, Trotsky, and Bakunin. We'd get into the specifics of each man's thinking later in the course, but for the next 45 minutes I would just touch on their theories as they related to the idea of a proletarian class and a middle class like that developed in American democracy.

I was pleased that the class seemed to be listening intently. A few of the trainees were even openly staring at me and smiling. Evidently, I was making an impression. At the end of the class, however, as the students were filing out, a young black man came up to me and gently said, "Sir, your fly is open."

Oh. My. God. I know it is possible to pass out and remain upright because that's exactly what I did. I was so mortified that I went faint for a minute, though I was still standing. Reeling from losing face, I was certain that I would next be losing my new job. I hurried over to Henry's office and quickly told him what had happened, fully expecting him to fire me on the spot. Instead, he just roared with laughter. "Well, Ed," he said, trying to catch his breath, "that's one way to hold a class's attention, though I doubt if any of those kids remember a damn word you said."

Fortunately, I kept my job, kept my zipper up, and got through the rest of the school year respectably enough. To my surprise, I was able to lecture during each of the hour-and-a-half class sessions for at least forty-five minutes before opening the floor for questions. As shy as I was, being prepared and knowing the subject matter was the surest antidote to stage fright. I also believe I really connected with the students, since I was not the kind of teacher to pretend to know something if I didn't. I would just say I didn't know and not try to fake it.

One person who constantly challenged what I knew, or thought I knew, was I. Gregory Newton, the older, distinguished black man in charge of Peace Corps training in the southwest region who was spending a year in Albuquerque overseeing the trainees. Newton, a lawyer out of Washington, DC, worked for Sargent Shriver, head of the Peace Corps, who also happened to be President Kennedy's brother-in-law. Dr. Newton was the most intellectually gifted black man I'd ever met, and he would sometimes make me think I must have been be dumbest black student he'd ever met.

At first I didn't think Dr. Newton even liked me. He had a way of always looking at me as if trying to size me up. Then he would pepper me with questions: Why was I so stuck on political science? Why the jones for Russian and Chinese history? "*What do you mean you don't know why you lost your football scholarship?*" he once asked incredulously. I had finally found out twenty-seven years after being kicked off the football team.

In 1986 I was in in Albuquerque to receive an award from the university, and stopped by the home of Dean Mathany, who was then in his eighties and retired as the university's dean of men. I'd heard he was ailing and thought this might be my last chance to see him. Dean Mathany, though frail, was still sharp as a tack. We talked of many things, and he told me he had learned long after I left the university that some coaches in the athletic department thought I was becoming too racially "militant" during my freshman year, and weren't comfortable keeping me on the football team.

There it was. Even before I became what could be considered a campus militant, the coaches had picked up on something in me I myself wasn't even aware of at that point.

Dr. Newton, it turned out, was actually impressed with my undergraduate militancy. He knew about my involvement with student government as a junior, my summer training with the National Student Association, my radical little speech at the NSA conference in Indiana. He had even heard I planned to drop out of school my senior year and go work for SNCC following the church bombing that killed those four little black girls in Birmingham. One day he caught up with me outside the hall where I lectured and accompanied me to a little makeshift lounge for teaching assistants in one of the other classroom buildings.

"So, Ed, have you given any thought to what you'd like to do when you've finished up your studies here?" he inquired while helping himself to a cup of coffee from the pot someone had left on a hot plate.

I'd been thinking a little bit about applying to law school. Nothing concrete. Just an idea. I shared it with Dr. Newton.

"That's quite interesting," Dr. Newton said thoughtfully, now seated at a wooden table across from where I was sitting eating a sandwich I'd brought from home. "I could probably help get you into Georgetown University's law school if you want," he said casually.

"You're kidding, right?" I asked, astonished.

"Not at all. One of my frat brothers is a professor in the law school, and we're always on the lookout for talented young people of our race to get into Georgetown."

I could barely contain my excitement. The idea of a career in law, especially civil rights law, had obvious appeal. Some of the biggest battles for civil rights were being won in American courtrooms. My own cousin, Barbara Johns, had led a student boycott of R. R. Moton High School when she was a 16-year-old junior in Farmville, Virginia. Segregated Moton High was woefully inferior to the white high school in town, and comprised one of the five cases tried in the historic lawsuit *Brown v. Board of Education.* Thurgood Marshall, the mighty lawyer who argued *Brown* all the way to the United States Supreme Court in 1954—and won—was as big a civil rights hero to me as Dr. Martin Luther King, Jr. To think I could be in this esteemed company with a law degree from prestigious Georgetown University was an idea beyond my wildest imagination.

So, too, was the idea that I would ever join a fraternity, especially a black one. The black ones admitted only light-skinned Negro men—stuck-up and pretentious guys who no doubt looked down on darker-skinned men like me. That was my feeling, anyway, until I met I. Gregory Newton, a member of the Omega Psi Phi Negro fraternity. He was neither light-skinned, stuck-up, nor pretentious. Dr. Newton was simply the most inquisitive, erudite, and amazing black man I'd ever met in my life, and if men like him were in a fraternity, then that's where I wanted to be too.

I later learned that Dr. Newton had just served a three-year term as the fraternity's Grand Basileus, its supreme leader.

A few Negro students had approached me about helping them to start a campus chapter of Omega Psi Phi while I was a senior at UNM, but I would never even entertain the idea. A chapter was approved anyway without my help. But now that Dr. Newton was suggesting a frat buddy of his could maybe get me into Georgetown, I thought twice about rejecting what could be so powerful an affiliation.

I ended up pledging the fraternity during my graduate school year. I certainly could not have done it as an undergraduate because I know my temperament would never have tolerated the whole hazing process. It was a pledge I have never regretted. The brotherhood I share with Que ("Q") men, as the Omega Psi Phi frat brothers are called, has been both enduring and sustaining. And in the case of my relationship with Dr. Newton, the ultimate Q man, the brotherhood would also prove to be life altering.

True to his word, Dr. Newton and his friend H. Carl Moultrie facilitated my admission to the Georgetown University School of Law in the fall of 1965. I passed the rigorous LSAT (Law School Admission Test) exam and arrived in Washington, DC, on a hot day in late August, heady with anticipation. I received a small scholarship, thanks to the help of Dr. Newton, and a settlement from a car accident I had had in Albuquerque, in which I was blindsided and suffered a back injury. The money would be enough to get me through my first year.

My future seemed unlimited. A career of service as a civil rights lawyer was an appealing possibility. So was corporate law with its potential for international influence. Nowhere in these equations did I factor in the possibility of failure. Or the likelihood of doing anything as woefully devastating as flunking out.

––––––––

Washington hadn't changed much in the six years I'd been living in the Southwest. Still predominantly black—"Chocolate City," as we blacks call it—it remained something of a college and political party town in which women outnumber men almost two to one. The cousins I used to visit and spend summers with down south when I was growing up in the Bronx were still living there, grown now, like me, following their own dreams of success. The city was familiar in the way family and habits are familiar.

Georgetown University School of Law, on the other hand, was as different culturally as the University of New Mexico had been when I first landed on its dry, barren terrain. But the Anglos at Georgetown were typically very mainstream upper-crust white: privileged, Ivy League–educated, moneyed, entitled, and highly competitive. Even so, I held my own that first semester.

I was living on 14th Street in a townhouse near the university that was overrun with cockroaches and testosterone. Dr. Newton had put me in touch with the three guys who were my roommates, all of us Q fraternity brothers who were in professional graduate schools. Two were dental students at Howard University, and the third, Kirk Smothers, was at Georgetown Law like me, though he was a second-year law student. Kirk was brilliant, and he would go on to have a distinguished career as a JAG attorney with the Navy.

That first law school semester was not especially onerous, though the work load could be heavy. Constitutional law. Torts. Contract law. All of them were required first-year courses. Lots of memorizing. Lots of late-night studying. Lots of coffee drinking. And lots of solitude. Unlike UNM where I was popular and had friends to study with, I was very much on my own at Georgetown. My Saturday nights were typically spent at the library alone, hitting the books. In some ways I was stunned to even be at Georgetown in the first place, and I certainly wasn't going to blow the opportunity by partying.

Oddly enough, I cannot recall one friend I made in law school. There was one black woman in my class, but we didn't make any connection; and there was Kirk, my housemate. He was a good enough guy, but as a second-year law student, he wasn't spending much time hanging with me. So even in a city filled with black women and the opportunity to date and party with as many of them as I probably wanted to, I was the loner passing on social opportunities. Not so much out of shyness, though that was still operating, but out of single-minded drive and the need to focus on succeeding in an elite law school.

I should have partied, for all the good it did me *not* partying.

By the middle of my second semester it was clear that I was in academic trouble. The first semester was all about learning, and studying what we were learning. There were no tests and no grades. The second semester we were tested on what we had learned, and expected to write cogent essays expounding on this knowledge. I didn't do well at either. Nor was I an active participant during the critical class discussion sessions where students got points for showing off by trying to one-up each other with their competitive legal sparring. Though I was able to pass both the rigorous New York State Regents exam in high school required for college, and the even more rigorous LSAT required for law school, I have always thought of myself as a poor tester when it comes to taking exams. Maybe I tense up. Go blank. Spend too much time on a question instead of moving on to the other questions.

But I was not about to say any of that to the dean of the law school who had asked me to come to his office near the end of the second semester when my final grades came out. They were not good. Sitting behind his large mahogany desk, the dean looked at me with the studied concern of a doctor who is about to give his patient a bad diagnosis. "Ed, I'm sorry, but I don't think you're going to be able to make it," he said, confirming my worst fear.

"Isn't there anything I can do?"

"I'm afraid not," he said curtly. "You're a fine young man, and there are other careers you are probably more suited for. The field of law is not for everyone."

The dean's words may as well have been a death sentence because I plunged into that pit of despair ringed with the seven stages of grief following a monstrous loss: shock, denial, bargaining, guilt, anger, depression, and finally, acceptance. Flunking out of law school represented a certain death to my spirit. I would be consumed with shock and guilt, shame and anger—all at the same time. I would try to bargain: *Isn't there anything I can do?* I had pleaded with the dean. I would feel guilty. *How could I let Dr. Newton down like this?* I would be filled with rage and self-loathing: *How could you let this happen, you dumb-ass idiot!*

I was grieving the loss of the ego-driven professional persona I had constructed of myself. In the language of therapy (which I certainly could have used during this awful time), becoming a lawyer formed the core identity of my superego, the higher self I envisioned myself to be one day. And for the longest time, after being told I might not be suited for the law profession, I remained stuck in the second stage of grief: denial, coming right after shock.

When the school term was over, I told no one I had washed out of Georgetown, except my roommates, who would have found out anyway with Kirk in the house. I gave up my room in the house, and moved in with my cousin Ernest, whose mother had died a couple of years before. My mother—his mother's sister—had stepped in to help following my aunt's death, and my cousins revered my mother like a second mother. So of course, Ernest and his siblings were happy to let me stay with them in their mom's house. My grandmother had instilled in all of us the importance of looking out and caring for one another, especially in times of need.

But there was nothing anyone could have done to restore my shattered ego. I took a summer job with an antipoverty program and moved from Ernest's house to my aunt Matilene's home, another one of my mother's sisters who also lived in Washington. This aunt was the whiz in math and science whom my mother and her siblings had sent to college. She now worked as an oceanographer for the Department of the Navy, and at age 60 would go back to school and get a law degree. Even my old auntie would prove to have the chops for law, something I didn't have!

As the summer was coming to an end, I had worked my way up on the rings of grief to the stage of depression, though I still had one foot stuck on the ring of denial. My aunt and cousins didn't know I had flunked out; neither did my mother, and this only fueled my depression. How could I ever face my mother? And what was I going to *do* now that my future as I had planned it was over?

I finally called Dean Mathany back at UNM to confess the terrible truth. "Dean Mathany, I flunked out of Georgetown," I blurted into the phone as soon as he picked up. I carried on about knowing I wasn't an intellectual heavyweight, but thought I could at least get through the first year of law school, but guessed I just didn't have what it took . . .

The dean cut me off, reminding me that I had a master's degree, varied interests, and a string of accomplishments. One failed situation did not mean *I* was a failure. He then mentioned that he had a friend heading the personnel department at First National City Bank in New York City who was recruiting talented minorities for an executive training program. Dean Mathany offered to make a call to his friend and put him in touch with me if I wanted. This kind gesture was the affirming life preserver I needed to pull me out of despair and into the light of grief's final stage: acceptance. I grabbed it.

————

This is the second time I've been at the Waldorf-Astoria Hotel. The first was when Coach Marvin Levy took me and my mother to dinner in the Peacock Alley restaurant downstairs, offering me a scholarship to play football for the University of New Mexico. There have been many highs, but some excruciating lows since then: Losing the football scholarship. Having my heart broken by a Danish girlfriend. Flunking out of law school. Now here I am trying to figure out my next move as a 25-year-old black man with prospects, but no game plan.

James Richards, Dean Mathany's buddy in personnel at First National City Bank, did get in touch with me about the bank's executive training program after the dean called him. That's why I'm here cooling my heels in one of the Waldorf's smaller hotel rooms before my interview at the bank tomorrow morning. Richards was apparently impressed enough during our phone conversation to offer to have the bank pay my way up to New York from Washington to meet with some City Bank officials. The bank's headquarters at 399 Park Avenue is right down the street from the Waldorf, hence my free overnight stay in a five-star hotel.

I don't know if Dean Mathany told Richards I had flunked out of Georgetown, but I sure the hell didn't intend to tell him, or anyone else, if I didn't have to. Accepting the reality of my failed law school experience was one thing. Announcing it on a résumé was out of the question. Truthfully, I was still in denial. The idea of becoming a banker at a place like City Bank wasn't bad. It just wasn't what I had in mind for myself at the beginning of my life's career run. But if football teaches you anything, it is how to back up on a play and make a better run when you spot another opening.

The interviews at the bank the next day felt like some sort of capitalist inquisition. No less than ten City Bank vice presidents, division managers, and department heads met with me to see where I might best fit in at the bank. I told all of them I didn't have a degree in finance. I was happy to learn that it didn't matter. "If you have intellectual curiosity and are willing to work, we will teach you finance," more than one of them would tell me in different ways over the course of the daylong interview sessions.

By the end of the grueling day, I had been offered a spot in the bank's highly touted executive training program. I was to start in a few weeks, giving me time to pack up in Washington and literally move back home to the Bronx.

My mother and Mr. Clarke had married in 1960 during my sophomore year at UNM, and were still living in the St. Mary's housing project. My room was pretty much as I'd left it. I can't say I felt one way or another about moving back home after seven years. I really didn't have any other choice. But I still had not told my mother I had flunked out of Georgetown. I just couldn't fix my mouth to say those words. Instead, I concocted the rather preposterous story of coming back to New York because I had transferred from Georgetown's law school to Columbia University's law school. What did my mother and stepfather know? I would even leave the apartment every day and take three subway trains to get to Columbia University's campus in upper Manhattan.

I strolled through the halls of the law school on Amsterdam Avenue, carrying my old Georgetown law books. Sat around the law school library, thumbing through law journals. Hung out at the West End bar, a popular spot on Broadway near the university. Sat chilling with *real* Columbia students on the steps in front of Low Library, the university's administration building. All of which was about as healthy as lying curled up on the grave site of a dearly departed loved one. Yes, I was still just a little crazy with grief and denial.

Sanity was restored when I finally told my mother I had flunked out. I was about to start working at First National City Bank, so I couldn't carry on the pretense much longer. My mother, bless her, took the news with soothing reassurances and her typical nonstop banter: *"Well, Sonny, I'm sure you did the best you could in that law school. That's all anybody can do. And you got a nice job now with that bank. I'm real proud of you, Sonny. Glad you're home, too. You got too skinny down there in DC. Didn't Matilene feed you? I have some money in that City Bank, by the way. Did you know that? Say, do you think the bank might like to contribute to my church's building fund? I know you're just starting out, and everything, but maybe you could put in a word with one of those bank officers because . . ."*

Yes. I'm home.

First National City Bank's executive training program was a rigorous six-month immersion course in every facet of banking: finance, accounting, corporate law, international banking. Professors from some of the best business schools in the country—Columbia, Harvard, Wharton, the University of Chicago—were brought in to teach us trainees in a few months what MBA students took two years to learn. After six months we were sent out to branch offices to get firsthand, on-the-ground knowledge of how banks operate day to day.

The work was interesting enough, but I noticed that trainees in the program who in fact had MBAs or undergraduate degrees from the top business schools were steered to City Bank's financial engineering division, the fast track to advancement. Financial engineering was a fancy name for credit analysis. This was the area where trainees were introduced to the computer, a relatively new technology in 1966 used in credit analysis to forecast how companies would be doing ten, fifteen, or twenty-five years out.

The thing is, there were no black trainees in the bank's financial engineering division, a fact that didn't escape me or two other black colleagues in the program, Preston Edwards and Cleveland Cristoff. If financial engineering was the fast-track division, this is where we wanted to be. I had told bank officers during my first round of interviews that I wasn't interested in being hired to be black window dressing at the bank—"the spook who sat by the door," as the black novelist Sam Greenlee put it in his newly published novel of the same name. I wanted to be where the action and the advancement were.

Preston was the first black trainee designated to go into the financial engineering division after he and I and Cleveland had gone to bank higher-ups to demand inclusion. Only three of us stepped up because other blacks in the program seemed fearful of rocking the boat. They were glad to just have a bank job.

I was tapped to follow Preston into financial engineering, and once I started I couldn't believe what I had gotten myself into. The nomenclature in this new business culture may as well have been Sanskrit. Understanding how to use the computer, extrapolate the numbers, make the assumptions, and run the forecasts had me spinning. I realized the other guys in the division all came from business school backgrounds, with degrees in finance or accounting. I had *two* degrees, both in *political science*. This definitely put me behind the eight ball in terms of understanding a business discipline.

Then I started to notice that these same guys with better school backgrounds were getting to the bank at six and six thirty in the morning and staying until seven or eight at night. It didn't occur to me that maybe this is what gave them another advantage—they simply *worked* hard. Well, I certainly knew how to work hard too. So I started getting to the bank at dawn and burning the midnight oil. I was still struggling, but my efforts to learn and get my arms around financial engineering didn't go unnoticed.

Phil Smith, the bank's senior vice president in the venture capital division, was looking for an up-and-coming black at the bank to work with him. My name got floated. We met, clicked, and he hired me. Neither of us could have ever imagined that in just another couple of years City Bank would be a major investor in the magazine I was to help start, or that Phil Smith would be the force leading the investment.

I became something of a force myself while working with Phil. He wanted a black in his division who could evaluate some of the black-owned companies that were seeking venture capital from City Bank. I was assigned to assess the viability of a company called All-Pro Fried Chicken, a restaurant franchise started by Brady Keys, Jr., who had been a professional football player with the Pittsburgh Steelers and Minnesota Vikings.

Brady and I would become friends as well as business associates. He had opened his first chicken restaurant in San Diego in 1967 after being turned down by about ten banks. Repeatedly, he was told: "You have an excellent franchising idea, but we're afraid to risk the money on Negro management." He finally secured seed money from the owner of the Steelers team, Art Rooney, Sr. A similar scenario was about to unfold in my own life.

I first met Brady in 1968 when he was operating an All-Pro restaurant in Pittsburgh, having already established the San Diego operation. I recommended that City Bank invest in the Pittsburgh venture, then I joined All-Pro's board to keep an eye on the bank's investment, which eventually grew to about $500,000. I would travel to Pittsburgh at least once a month and spend time in the Hill section of the city, where the restaurant was located. This was also the neighborhood the Pulitzer Prize–winning playwright August Wilson made famous with his series of ten plays depicting black working-class life in Pittsburgh during each decade of the twentieth century.

When I left First National City Bank in 1969 to launch *Essence* magazine with three other black men, I had learned enough about managing cash flow, structuring debt, projecting future earnings, and keeping a steady eye on the bottom line to recognize that if the magazine could survive those critical first five years of operation, I stood a better-than-even chance of keeping it profitable. At the outset, the magazine seemed as unlikely a venture as a chicken restaurant franchise started by a pro football player.

But as a former ballplayer myself, a former college activist, a banker, and even a flunked-out law student, I knew something about odds, risk and failure. Taking a chance on the venture would be the easy, successful part. Taking a chance with all of the people, personalities, and passions that would make *Essence* a winner turned out to be the less easy part.

PART III

Getting Through

(1970–1980)

CHAPTER 9

"Black Man, Do You Love Me?"

I couldn't believe the little townhouse on 30th Street had the space to accommodate the assorted crowd that was squeezing in: magazine editors, writers, publishers, models and fashion designers, photographers, investment bankers, corporate attorneys. Russ and Maddie Goings were there, so were Michael Victory and his wife, as well as the wives and girlfriends of The Hollingsworth Group partners. Gordon Parks arrived grand style in a limousine with a beautiful woman on his arm. Ditto Jonathan Blount, The Hollingsworth Group's irrepressible president. Ruth Ross, *Essence*'s editor-in-chief, came by taxi. I came by subway. The narrow street running in front of our offices at 102 East 30th Street between Lexington and Park Avenues was jammed with traffic, people, and an expectant air of excitement.

It had been a grueling year of pitching investors for money, coming up with a magazine name, looking for an editor-in-chief, hiring staff, lining up advertisers, negotiating printing and distribution contracts, and finally closing on $130,000 in initial capital. Now here we were holding forth on two floors of an East Side townhouse celebrating an accomplishment I considered nothing short of miraculous. Four black men with absolutely no experience in publishing had actually published *Essence*, a magazine for black women. The mood that night was both celebratory and cautiously optimistic. By whatever means we got there, the launch party for the first issue of *Essence* was considered *the* place to be in the spring of 1970. Whether you were invited or crashed, it didn't matter. Just be there.

I certainly didn't know many of the two to three hundred people who were streaming in and out of the townhouse's second-floor reception area. I thought I spotted the model Norma Jean Darden, who had done a provocative fashion spread for *Essence*'s first issue. Norma Jean would go on after a long career as a top model to become a best-selling cookbook author and restaurateur, and run a successful catering business.

I recognized Clay Felker, editor-in-chief of *New York* magazine, and George Hirsch, the magazine's publisher, who arrived at the party with Osborn Elliott, editor of *Newsweek*. John Mack Carter, editor-in-chief of *Ladies' Home Journal*, was also present. All these white men, along with other magazine editors and advertising honchos, had given advice or loaned some of their staff to our fledgling magazine, which was crucial in helping *Essence* set up its editorial and advertising departments.

Essence's first executive editor was also white, Barbara Kerr, who brought her boyfriend, Robert Wagner, the legendary former mayor of New York City, to the party, setting off the kind of celebrity buzz that is priceless for any new venture. Barbara, then 59, had worked in both broadcast and print media for more than thirty years, serving most recently as a managing editor at *Mademoiselle* magazine and an associate editor at *Seventeen* magazine. Ruth Ross met Barbara while at *Newsweek*, and she and Gordon talked Barbara into leaving *Seventeen* to come work for *Essence*. Like many of the whites who would work for or give technical assistance to *Essence*, Barbara seemed to relish the idea of helping a black-owned start-up. In the late 1960s, the idea of a magazine for black women captured the imagination of many whites in media.

Jonathan was about to speak and stood at the podium set up next to the display easel showing a blowup of *Essence*'s first cover. "Thank you, thank you, ladies and gentlemen, for joining my partners and myself this glorious evening to celebrate the launch of *Essence*, the premier magazine for black women." He sounded breathless, surrounded by a crush of people crowded on both the second floor and on the staircase leading up from the ground floor's editorial offices. "As many of you know, it has been a long and winding road to get the magazine whose cover you now see displayed before you to a physical reality. Without our mighty champions Russell Goings and Michael Victory at Shearson, Hammill, and our indispensable friends in the larger publishing community, the magazine would still be just an idea that my mother had." Jonathan was on a roll. He thanked a number of people by name, introduced the rest of us Hollingsworth Group partners, gushed over Gordon Parks and Ruth Ross, and pretty much did as he usually did—played lord of the manor to his partners-in-waiting.

Essence's coming out had been touted the month before in the February 11, 1970, issue of the *New York Times*, which contributed greatly to the launch party's cachet as the black event of the season. A long item by Philip H. Dougerty in his popular Tuesday advertising column gave the magazine its first seal of approval. "Some of the best brains in publishing and advertising have contributed to the creation of *Essence,* a magazine for Negro women due for publication April 28," the column began. "A dummy of it was unveiled yesterday, and a handsome piece of work it is. Few magazines in publishing history have had more going for them." Dougerty then noted that Jonathan, "the 24-year-old president of the Hollingsworth Group," had said the magazine was "capitalized for more than a million dollars through Shearson, Hammill and Co."

The partners were mortified when we read this. *Essence* was nowhere close to being capitalized for that kind of money, and no investment had ever been made by Shearson, Hammill, the corporate entity. It took a damn year to raise a paltry $130,000 from the investors we did secure. The truth was, we were in hock for $25,000 we had borrowed in combination from Freedom National Bank and four of Shearson, Hammill's partners, and for another $167,000 we borrowed from First National City Bank over the months leading up to *Essence*'s launch. What was Jonathan thinking? To say we had more than a million dollars in financing was not only a crazy lie, it made it appear that the publication was fully capitalized from the very beginning. Nothing could have been further from the truth. Our struggle to raise money was just beginning.

The first issue of *Essence* featured a cover showing a beautiful, sensually full-featured black woman crowned by a glistening Afro emerging from shadow into the light of a new day. The cover date was May 1970, the newsstand price was 60 cents, the subscription rate was $5.00 for a year, $9.00 for two years, and the magazine had 82 pages, 13 of them advertising. The next month's issue had 5 pages of advertising, a new editor-in-chief, an imperial editorial director, a president who was growing increasingly out of control, and three partners-in-waiting who would soon be waiting to revolt.

Ruth Ross, our outspoken editor-in-chief, bumped heads almost immediately with Gordon Parks, our esteemed editorial director. As editorial director, Gordon's name and title were positioned at the top of the magazine's masthead in larger typeface over both those of the editor-in-chief and the rest of the magazine staff, including The Hollingsworth Group partners, who were listed at the bottom of the masthead. Gordon's celebrity status carried clout and the final authority in most editorial matters. I happened to overhear him and Ruth going at it in the art department one day as they were reviewing layouts for the magazine's first issue.

"For God's sake, Gordon, every color page *can't* be devoted to fashion and beauty," Ruth was saying, her voice rising. "How about some color for the cover story? It is the *cover* story, after all, and it's a pretty hot story at that. Readers are going to eat it up. Can't they at least *see* the visuals with some color added? Black women are about more than head wraps and studded belts, you know."

"Ruth, my dear, you obviously don't read *Vogue*," Gordon said dismissively, "otherwise you'd know that Negro women are a very large segment of that magazine's market. I happen to know that *black* women, as you call them, are very much about head wraps and accessories. Style is very important to Negro women. They want to see beautiful models in beautiful clothes who look like them, so yes, *all* of the fashion and beauty pages in this first issue will be color."

End of discussion. Gordon was the man, and he had spoken. Who were we, the four partners and founders of the magazine, to question the one man who was giving our magazine venture its credibility? Even after Gordon left the magazine, his name would remain at the top of the masthead at the insistence of our investors, who felt his celebrity was important for getting advertising. So we let our male editorial director's edicts override the concerns of our female editor-in-chief's. The first issue of the magazine came out with 21 continuous pages of fashion and beauty photos in full vibrant color with very little text.

The cover story, on the other hand, titled "Black Man, Do You Love Me?" by the journalist and novelist Louise Meriwether, was an emotionally charged 3,000-word feature story on black men dating and marrying white women. Illustrated with a moody, full-page black-and-white photo of a darkly handsome black man having his face stroked by a female hand of indeterminate race, the message was explosively clear: Black men in 1970 had the growing option of choosing to love either black women or white women. The subject resonated loudly, as it still does, and *Essence* was the first magazine to sound the alert.

Other articles in the first issue included a feature titled "Five Shades of Militancy," by journalist Gilbert Moore, which profiled diverse activists Rosa Parks, Shirley Chisholm, Barbara Ann Teer (director of the National Black Theatre in Harlem), Kathleen Cleaver, and the women of the Nation of Islam. The black-and-white photos for this feature were all shot by Gordon and his son, Gordon Parks, Jr.

Fiction would become a staple in the magazine's initial editorial lineup, and in the premiere issue a haunting short story, "Mother's Day, 1970," by the respected author Alice Childress, depicted the pathos of a single mother trying to love her drug-addicted son. The magazine's first celebrity feature, by Charles Hobson, profiled the tempestuous blues and jazz singer Nina Simone, illustrated with a black-and-white photo tinged in a blue overlay showing her in a teary-eyed onstage performance. A travel feature on the Bahamas, a career piece on data processing, book and music reviews, poetry, an astrology column, food and home furnishing stories, a guest editorial, and a mental health column by the noted psychiatrist Dr. Alvin Poussaint of Harvard University rounded out the first issue. All of these first features were written by black authors, educators, and journalists.

On balance, the magazine's launch issue seemed pretty balanced, despite the warring sensibilities of its editor-in-chief and editorial director. Ruth was more political and more militant, and thought the magazine's editorial content should reflect the changing politics of the day. The civil rights and women's movements were in full swing, and black women were coming into their own on both fronts. Ruth saw the magazine as a platform for discussing politics: a creative think tank for provocative ideas and opinions by noted black journalists and commentators, as well as an artistic outlet for black literary writers and poets. Health and financial information, career advice, celebrity profiles, relationship articles about men, parenting tips, and food and home furnishing information were all part of the eclectic service mix Ruth envisioned.

Gordon's editorial vision had been shaped by his years photographing for *Vogue* and *Life* magazines. These were the big picture books, splashy and flashy, beautiful to look at, arbiters of taste and style in American culture. Gordon envisioned a similar mandate for *Essence* in *black* American culture. But in Gordon's photographer's eye, *Essence* should first and foremost be esthetically beautiful.

Indeed, the first issue of *Essence* showcased black women in fashion and beauty pages as they had never been seen before in American media: cute and coquettish, attired in colorful head wraps and jazzy sportswear; sexy and sensual in swimwear that exposed long, lean torsos stretching across a page; spreads that featured Norma Jean Darden with a male and female model—all three models wearing barely-there underwear in ménage à trois poses for an accessories story on jewelry, belts, and sunglasses.

A beauty feature on natural hair styles showcased full radiant Afros adorned with beaded rope. Another beauty feature on skin care displayed a full-page close-up of a model's flawless face, wearing a nose ring in partial profile. In the eye of a less skilled photographer many of the fashion and beauty shots might have bordered on the pornographic. But under the brilliant, artistic eye of Gordon Parks's editorial direction, they were all just breathtakingly beautiful.

This first issue of *Essence* set the bar for the kind of high-quality, rich, and diverse content a black women's magazine could deliver both editorially and visually, and it would become a collectors' item as the magazine grew in profitability and popularity over the years. But that first issue had only 13 pages of advertising out of a total of 82 pages. The magazine looked beautiful and read easily because there were practically no ads to interrupt its editorial and visual flow. This is every editor's idea of a dream book.

Yet without advertising there is no revenue with which to produce a book at all. This is the yin-and-yang reality of magazine publishing. And the reality for *Essence* during most of its independent thirty-five-year run would be the ongoing, uphill battle waged with advertisers to recognize, respect, and value the black female consumer market.

"Black Man, Do You Love Me?" struck a visceral, plaintive chord on the cover of that first issue of *Essence*. The black partners of The Hollingsworth Group certainly loved the black woman. We knew what she potentially represented in the American marketplace. White advertisers, however, did not. For The Hollingsworth Group this single truth would become the constant blues note running through our dealings with Madison Avenue.

———

Judging by the attitudes of advertisers in 1970, you would think that black women and their families did not eat cereal, use toothpaste, drive cars, have bank accounts, use makeup, sleep on sheets, take vacations, or consume any of the other myriad goods and services that typified American life. The black woman was all but invisible to the manufacturers of the products *Essence* had to depend on for advertising.

Turning around this perception of no perception would take a certain genius. It took the specific genius of our partner and consummate salesman, Clarence Smith, *Essence*'s advertising sales director. Clarence would craft a sales story so compelling, original, and authentic that it became real, and created a new niche in the American marketplace. The story he told introduced the Essence Woman, a *striver*, who in 1970 was now educated, worked in new careers, had discretionary income, had the ability to influence, and wanted information geared specifically to her and her needs in media that reflected *her*. In advertising parlance, Clarence Smith became the master of the "intelligent hard sell."

Advertisers, of course, knew black women existed. Black women just weren't a factor to be considered as a separate demographic to be marketed to in separate media. This was what is known as a "tag-along" market, meaning advertisers believed black women could be reached through other media. The big Goliath reaching her in 1970 was *Ebony* magazine, the Negro publication started twenty-five years before *Essence*. As far as advertisers were concerned, *Ebony* had the lock on the black consumer market. Then there were the big "Seven Sisters," the dominant women's magazines in the general market that black women also read. According to Dougherty's column in the *Times* announcing the launch of Essence, in 1970 *Redbook* magazine had 535,000 "non-white" readers, *Woman's Day* had 786,000, *Good Housekeeping* 1,300,000, *Ladies' Home Journal* 1,100,000. And *McCall's* had more than a million readers who were specifically black. Who needed *Essence* when you could reach black women through *Good Housekeeping* or *Ebony*?

Advertisers needed *Essence,* Clarence insisted. In his sales calls to advertising agencies he first sold the *universe* of black women as a viable market distinct from other markets. This constituted the "intelligent" part of the sell. He then sold the idea of *Essence* magazine as the only vehicle reaching this market (the actual "hard sell"). His pitch stories were smooth and masterful, and went something like this:

> Gentlemen, the Essence Woman is not reading *Ebony.* That's her parents' magazine. And she's not driving a Cadillac. That's her daddy's car. No, the Essence Woman is ahead of the old pack and shaping a new curve. She's smart and accomplished. She wants to drive a smart, efficient car like a Volkswagen or a Toyota. She's taking her vacations in Rome or Paris, experiencing adventures her parents and grandparents never dreamed of having. And while she may be reading *Glamour* or *Redbook,* they are not connecting to her the way a magazine geared specifically to her needs connects to her. The Essence Woman represents the hip, trendsetting market you want to connect to with your products. The only way to do that, gentlemen–the only way to reach this striving new woman—is to advertise in *Essence.*

Clarence invariably came to these sales pitches armed with market research showing how much of an advertiser's product black women were already using. He had data on how much of an advertiser's *competitor's* products black women were using. The battle for advertising would be long and constantly uphill, but in those early days of the magazine Clarence practically invented a market that was not yet real in 1970. Prophetically, the market became real as the magazine became increasingly popular with black women.

As a manager Clarence also had the foresight to recruit an *Essence* sales staff from the ranks of advertising agencies. Ad agencies work on behalf of their clients such as Procter & Gamble, General Foods, and Revlon, who rely on them to place advertising in publications with the kind of circulation and demographics the businesses want to reach. This is the world depicted by the hit television show *Mad Men.* And, by 1970 a handful of blacks had broken into the "mad men" world of big-firm advertising agencies.

A few more were also starting to open their own advertising firms. Burrell Advertising in Chicago, and Lockhart & Pettus, UniWorld, and Mingo-Jones in New York, were some of the big black-owned agencies that opened in the 1970s, working in sync with black media to sell Madison Avenue on the market power of the black consumer.

Shrewdly, Clarence looked to the small pool of black account executives working for the big-name agencies to hire as *Essence* salesmen. Who better to pitch for *Essence* than salespeople who had once worked on the agency side? *Essence* also pitched the black-owned advertising agencies to buy ads in *Essence* on behalf of both their black and white clients.

Yet in the total universe of advertising, ads placed in black media represented "token buys," for the most part. Whether it was *Ebony* or *Jet*, *Essence* or *Black Enterprise*, which, like *Essence*, launched in 1970, advertising in these publications usually just paid lip service to the idea of equal opportunity. General Foods' entire advertising budget for all black media in 1970 was $118,000. Unbelievable. A typical budget for the size and reach of this market should have been more like $1.2 million.

Driving the advertising in any magazine is the publication's editorial circulation. How many readers are actually buying the magazine on the newsstand or subscribing to it by mail? This determines your circulation, which in turn sets the page rate for what you can charge advertisers. At the start, *Essence* was not in a position to command high rates. With an initial guaranteed circulation of 150,000 readers in 145 cities in 25 top markets, the rate for a full-page four-color ad was $2,500. Yet in the first year circulation was less than 100,000. By the time the magazine was sold in 2005, circulation was 1.1 million, and the cost for a full-page four-color ad was $30,000.

During all of the thirty-two years that Clarence Smith ran the advertising sales side of *Essence*, securing advertising would remain a struggle—a struggle to prove the worth of the black female market; a struggle to break high-end advertisers such as Estée Lauder into the magazine; a struggle to overcome racist perceptions that advertising in a black publication somehow "cheapened" a manufacturer's product; a struggle to convince a marketplace that black women occupied a particular niche within the market that was profitable.

Yet Clarence remained unflagging in his passion to sell a market that he truly believed in and obviously loved. Dynamic, persuasive, charming, and driven, his answer to the haunting question, "Black man, do you love me?" was always an emphatic *yes.*

Clarence Smith's early sales staff consisted entirely of black men—no women, no whites—though this was certainly not the case with other departments of the magazine, where key positions such as art director, executive editor, and production manager were held by white men and women. The Hollingsworth Group's mission as a black-owned enterprise had always been to hire, as well as showcase, black talent. We felt this deeply. But we soon realized this was not always going to be possible.

Like blacks working for ad agencies, only a smattering of blacks were working for major magazines in 1970, and none of them in management. Just as race discrimination was an obstacle to the partners raising capital and securing ads, race discrimination had historically kept blacks out of the very magazine positions now needed to run *Essence.* This catch-22 would put *Essence* between a rock and a hard place of publishing black while often being forced to hire white. Inevitably, this raised some sticky, sobering questions.

How do you reconcile employing whites when the expectation (both yours and your larger black community's) is that a black-owned business will provide jobs for black people? How do you fix your mouth to say a white applicant is more qualified than a black one if your black-owned business is not giving blacks a chance to become qualified? How do you provide equal opportunities to a people who have not had the opportunity to become equal? These are the questions that can try the soul and the bottom line of a black-owned business.

As corporate treasurer of The Hollingsworth Group, I knew that in order to "do good work" in the black community we first had to "do good business" as an enterprise. That meant we had to make money. Our ability to hire, train, give back, and be of public service to a larger black community would always be in direct proportion to our ability to become and remain profitable. And that meant, like any other business, we had to first hire the best people we could find to work for *Essence*, regardless of race or nationality. Money may be green, but talent is the color of water—clear.

No doubt about it, though, *Essence* would catch hell and be accused of everything from practicing black-on-black race discrimination in hiring to being under white control as it struggled in the early days to simply stay up and running.

————

I couldn't help but overhear the brewing catfight coming from one of the editorial offices on the ground floor of the townhouse as I was heading to Ruth's office. Although the second-floor reception area separated the editorial and art departments on the lower level from the third-floor sales, circulation, and promotion departments, staff was frequently up and down the staircase that connected the three floors, going in and out of each other's offices. By the time of the *Essence* launch, The Hollingsworth Group had taken over three floors of the house, though our art and editorial "offices" on the ground floor were really just cubicles separated by low, freestanding partitions. These may have given the illusion of privacy, but snatches of heated conversations could often be heard loud and clear.

The one I heard now was between Barbara Kerr, our white executive editor, and Louise Meriwether, the black freelance writer discussing a revised version of her cover story "Black Man, Do You Love Me?" Both women, facing off across Barbara's desk, were in snarl mode as Barbara leafed through the manuscript.

"My God, you took out one of the most interesting profiles," I heard Barbara say, sounding exasperated. "The one where the black woman ends up marrying a white man after getting fed up with all the black men she knew who were dating white."

"Well, you told me the story was running too long, so I cut it," Louise snapped. "Yeah, I know that profile was interesting, but it was also really beside the point, since the article is about black men and white women."

"I told you we could run the piece in two parts," Barbara snapped back.

"And I told you if we ran the story in two parts it would come off sounding like black women were bashing black men one month, and black men were bashing black women the next month. I'm not doing that. I don't care what you say."

Barbara was furious. Clearly not used to having her authority challenged, especially by a feisty, fearless black woman, she nevertheless backed off. The edited-down version of Louise's story stood, and would run in just the first issue of *Essence*.

Now, there is a world of difference between being in charge and being in control. From the beginning I was always clear that while The Hollingsworth Group may have had to hire whites for their expertise, the partners and the top editors had to maintain control over the images and content of the magazine—and most important, over the financial stake of the enterprise. Until *Essence* was sold in 2005, black financial ownership of the publication never fell below 50 percent, no matter how much money may have been invested by other people or other nonblack entities. This was the one thing our stalwart champion Michael Victory could never understand as a white man. And it was the very thing he accused me of being most stubborn about. "Ed, what difference does it make who has financial control of the magazine?" he would repeatedly ask. "Money is green."

Yes, it is. But power is black—at least it was at *Essence,* on both the business side and the editorial side. As the media theorist Marshall McLuhan famously observed, "The medium is the message." And in the black-owned medium of *Essence,* the message had to reflect a black culture, esthetic, and sensibility.

So when Louise Meriwether butted heads with Barbara Kerr, it never occurred to me or any of the other partners to challenge the black writer or to side with the white editor. Barbara may have known editing, but Louise knew her people and her culture. Even Barbara had to concede on that one.

The partners had actually approached Louise about being editor-in-chief for *Essence* before hiring Ruth. Tall, elegant, and spirited, Louise lived in Los Angeles at the time and had the distinction of being the first black woman hired as a story editor in Hollywood. A talented writer who worked with the Watts Writers Workshop, her first novel, *Daddy Was a Number Runner,* had been published in 1970, the same year *Essence* launched. But Louise was more interested in pursuing writing than being an editor. "No, I don't want to be an editor," she told us during our meeting with her when she came to New York to promote her book. "But I'd love to write for your new magazine."

I later learned that Louise had been bumped from a scheduled appearance on the *Today* show with Hugh Downs to promote *Daddy Was a Number Runner* so that Gordon Parks could appear to promote a new magazine called *Essence.* The partners were, of course, delighted at the coup that our black promotion director, Cathy Aldridge, had pulled off. And Gordon's illustrious reputation had sealed the deal.

Gordon's air of superiority, however, was continuing to create problems with Ruth as he repeatedly challenged her authority, rejected her ideas, and practiced his own snobbish reverse discrimination. He flat-out refused, for instance, to hire black freelance photographers to shoot for the magazine, taking the imperial position that there were none who met the high standards he had set for photography in *Essence*'s fashion and beauty pages. "I'm sorry," he would say during those rare times he met with a black photographer to review his portfolio, "but this just isn't what we're looking for. The lighting is too harsh in this photograph, for example. And this one is just a tad out of focus. You don't see that?"

We partners certainly didn't know enough about the creative side of the magazine process to butt in or even have an opinion on photography or any other editorial matters. That would cost us. As one art director after another, black and white alike, followed Gordon's lead over the years by seldom using black photographers, *Essence* lost respect and goodwill among black photographers, which would take a decade to restore. And suspicious questions over who really owned and controlled *Essence* would soon loom large.

Restoring respect and goodwill between Ruth and Gordon proved to be impossible, and this would cost us our editor-in-chief. While we partners may have understood that control of the magazine had to remain black, we didn't understand the gender politics involved in a magazine for black women, which dictated that the editorial side of the business had to be controlled by a woman. Maybe the big white women's magazines could get away with their editors-in-chief being men (and even that tradition began dying out in the seventies), but a black man running a magazine for black women was never going to really fly on the editorial side. We had no way of knowing this at the time we made the decision to fire Ruth Ross in order to keep Gordon Parks.

Black man, do you love me? This could easily have been the question Ruth put to the four of us partners in The Hollingsworth Group. The answer turned out to be *no*. And that would prove to be a very big mistake.

CHAPTER 10

Playboy in the House

If I had it do all over again, would I have sided with Gordon Parks in ousting Ruth Ross, our second editor-in-chief—the smart, committed black woman who gave *Essence* its name? Probably not. Hindsight, of course, is always 20/20. Looking back, the decision did turn out to be a mistake, especially given that we gave Ruth the boot almost as soon as *Essence* came off its first print run. She believed in the concept of the magazine as much as the partners did. She came from a magazine background, knew how to edit, write, meet deadlines, and manage a staff. She also had the respect and cooperation of not only those who worked with her in the editorial department, but of her peers in the larger publishing community.

Ruth's best friend at the time was a new writer named Toni Morrison, a young editor at Random House whose first novel, *The Bluest Eye,* had just come out to great reviews, coincidentally, the same year that *Essence* launched. Ruth took the four of us partners to Toni's for dinner one evening, saying she wanted us to meet some of the writers who were in her circle of friends—writers she wanted to feature in our new magazine. What I remember most about that dinner is the homemade German chocolate cake Toni served for dessert. It was the best cake I'd ever tasted in my life.

Toni Morrison would go on to become a Pulitzer Prize and Nobel Prize winner for her searing novels, and would indeed grace the pages of *Essence* many years later, writing a powerful essay for the fifteenth-anniversary issue of the magazine. But her friend Ruth Ross would not make it past the first editorial she wrote for a mock-up issue of *Essence* that was unveiled at a special preview in April, just before the magazine's launch. Unabashed in her militant stance, Ruth's editorial, a column titled "Dig It," minced no words on where she thought black women found themselves at the dawn of the 1970s. Here is how she put forth the mission of *Essence* as she envisioned it:

> ESSENCE magazine is not solely for the involved woman who has already come to grips with her differentness; who is actively engaged in protest tactics, community organization, voter registration and the call for unity among all Black people. It is also for the woman who is still struggling to identify herself willingly, happily and totally with her Blackness. And there is not a single Black woman on the face of the earth who has not wrestled or is not wrestling—consciously or subconsciously—with her special problem of identity and undergoing a process of change. This very fact is the central, spiritual reason why ESSENCE magazine will fill an absolute editorial need.

This vision did not exactly match that of either Gordon Parks or the partners. We did not conceive *Essence* to be some crucible on which black women could work out existential issues around identity, race, and gender. We men had a much simpler (Ruth would no doubt say "simpleminded") view of the magazine. It should look beautiful and have a fashion and beauty focus like that of *Vogue* or *Harper's Bazaar*.

Ruth did not eschew fashion and beauty in the magazine. In her editorial she acknowledged that "ESSENCE . . . will serve as a fashion and beauty authority, presenting the clothes, cosmetics, and hair styles that are adaptable to our particular good looks, taste, and many varied skin tones." She also noted that the magazine would do articles on food, home decorating, health, and family living.

The problem between Ruth and Gordon, then, was not so much what the magazine should cover but what the magazine should emphasize. Gordon was clear on wanting an emphasis on fashion and beauty; Ruth was just as clear on wanting to emphasize political issues, race dynamics, and gender conflicts. Truthfully, we were all flying blind. With no precedence for a black women's magazine, we had to create a model as we went along. And for the partners, what we thought we needed to create was often dictated by the ongoing pursuit of advertising.

A beautiful magazine emphasizing lifestyle as well as fashion and beauty was simply an easier fit for the advertisers Clarence Smith and his sales staff were going after. Black women looked good, used makeup, raised children, prepared meals, traveled, and decorated their homes. This was the black consumer market the sales staff was trying to sell.

Which is why Clarence was spitting fire after reading Ruth's first editorial, a column that never saw the light of day since we pulled it from the first issue of *Essence* and ran a message from The Hollingsworth Group partners instead. "How the hell am I supposed to sell advertisers on the idea of a *striving* Essence Woman," Clarence bellowed at Ruth in her office, "when our editor-in-chief is saying black women are trying to come to grips with their *differentness,* and wrestling with their special *problem* of identity? Jesus Christ! Are you fucking kidding me?"

Yet, while we partners may have started out wanting to publish a fashion and beauty oriented magazine, we soon realized that black women are not that one-dimensional in their interests, tastes, or concerns. Being black and being female were political issues in the 1970s, and the magazine would have to take on the bigger topics of race and gender in equal measure to fashion and beauty if it was going to be relevant. Unfortunately, by the time we understood this, Ruth was gone.

"All right, we all know Ruth is not working out," Jonathan was saying one evening in late March after the first issue of the magazine had gone to press. We partners were sitting around the conference table in our office on the second floor of the townhouse, where we regularly met after work hours to discuss company matters. Ruth was at the top of tonight's agenda.

"I'm sick of her always being up in my face telling me us guys don't know what we're talking about when it comes to black women," Jonathan went on. "Like *I* don't know black women. Come on! Besides, I'm not even sure *she* knows black women. She acts like they're all a cross between Rosa Parks and Harriet Tubman. And you know Gordon isn't standing for that. Some of their fights have been so bad I've had to step in between them. How are we supposed to put out a magazine with that kind of dissension going on? It's bad for morale, and me and Gordon are sick of it."

"Now, hold on," Clarence interrupted. "I don't know if it's such a good idea to get rid of our editor-in-chief at this juncture. I've had some problems with Ruth too, but she *did* get out the first issue of the magazine—yeah, Gordon helped—but it was Ruth who knew where the bodies were when it came to hiring staff and assigning features. Maybe we should talk to her first, explain how we feel, give her a chance to straighten up. I'm trying to sell ads here, guys, and the last thing I need is for the magazine to be perceived as being shaky in its editorial leadership."

Clarence had a point. Not only did we need to establish editorial continuity and consistency, we partners couldn't really afford to be perceived as some patriarchal cabal dictating to black women—and then firing black women if they didn't listen. At least not at a black women's magazine. But Jonathan and Gordon also had a point. Ruth *could* be contentious. I didn't dislike her. But her outspoken stubbornness and abrasive style did tend to rub me the wrong way. I had to admit I wouldn't be too sorry to see her go. But the looming question was, who would replace her?

"Oh, I don't think we'll have any problem finding another editor-in-chief," Jonathan said, as if reading my mind. "I've already been given a couple of names."

So after all was said and done, the partners threw down on the side of the patriarchy and voted to fire Ruth, right in the middle of trying to get out the second issue of the magazine. Jonathan and Gordon would carry out the deed of telling her.

By this time Jonathan and Gordon had developed a rather symbiotic relationship that would take an unexpected turn a few years later. Jonathan revered Gordon as the elegant, courtly father figure he wanted to emulate, while Gordon relished the admiration of a young and handsome black man who was smart and articulate, and as popular with the ladies as Gordon was. I later learned that Jonathan, originally from North Carolina, had been adopted as an infant by a middle-class black family, and his mother, a teacher, would continue to inspire his commitment to publishing a magazine for black women, which he always insisted had been his mother's idea.

I was not present to witness the hell that broke loose when Ruth Ross was given the ax the day after the partners met and voted her out—effective immediately. That's because Phil Smith and I were on a plane headed to Chicago in the ongoing quest to obtain financing for *Essence*. Phil, my former boss at City Bank, had become a true champion for *Essence* during its early start-up days and would continue to commit bank resources as well as his personal time to helping *Essence* raise capital. Although a staunch conservative politically, Phil truly believed that helping blacks start their own businesses was the way to provide equal opportunity. It was something he felt the entire country should get behind.

Standing about six foot two, Ivy League educated at Yale and Harvard, and Brooks Brothers buttoned down to the hilt, Phil was handsome, *looked* like a banker, and proved to be indispensable in helping me raise capital. He was the one at the closing on that initial $130,000 in financing who made the phone call to Louis Allen at Chase Manhattan ordering him to come to the closing with the $50,000 Chase had pledged. During the call Allen admitted he was thinking about *not* coming—that is, until Phil straightened him out. Now here Phil was, once again at my side, accompanying me on a highly anticipated trip to Chicago.

We were flying to a meeting with two executives at Playboy Enterprises—the number two and the number three guys at the company—the men considered to be the right hand and the left hand to the number one guy, Hugh Hefner, chairman of Playboy Enterprises and publisher of *Playboy* magazine. Playboy Enterprises was about to make the single largest investment by a private entity to our fledgling magazine, and that fateful act would lead to a firestorm in the coming months that would make the firing of Ruth Ross look like a little slap on the hand for stealing Oreos out of the cookie jar.

———

Getting out of the taxi at 919 North Michigan Avenue in Chicago's Lake Shore Drive area, I was a bit startled by the thirty-seven-story Art Deco building that rose before me. The word PLAYBOY, spelled out in nine-foot-high illuminated letters, stretched across the front of the building's stone facade like a bold, in-your-face challenge. The Playboy "bunny" icon was displayed just below the lettering. I wasn't expecting the Playboy Mansion, but neither was I quite expecting *this*. By 1970, Playboy Enterprises, like black-owned Johnson Publishing, located two miles south, had carved out a lucrative media niche in a windy city known for tough urban gangs and even tougher ward bosses. The Playboy name emblazoned across a whole building sitting on prime Chicago real estate was pretty much tantamount to flying your colors.

Phil and I were in town to meet with two vice presidents at Playboy. One of them, Robert Gutwillig, senior vice president, had been at an early investor meeting in 1969 when we partners were pitching for money, trying to raise a million and a half dollars to finance *Essence*. Gutwillig seemed interested in the venture at the time, and told us Playboy might consider making an investment. But he would have to run the idea by his bosses back in Chicago, Hugh Hefner and Robert Preuss (pronounced *pruce*), executive vice president. At the invitation of Preuss and Gutwillig, Phil and I were now in Chicago to make yet another pitch and go over the proposal one more time, hoping to quickly close a deal.

We had closed on that $130,000 initial financing in mid-March, and here it was late March—and we were still in a scramble for money. The first issue of *Essence* came out on time by the skin of its undercapitalized teeth, and we owed everybody from our freelance writers and photographers to our printer and distribution vendors. Getting out a second issue was going to take a miracle if we didn't get money—and get it soon.

"Gentlemen, we've reviewed the proposal you sent," Robert Preuss said, sitting relaxed, one leg crossed over the other, in a high-backed leather easy chair, looking impassively at me and Phil. We were in the wood-paneled executive suite on the thirty-seventh floor of the Playboy Building. Phil and I, less relaxed, are sitting next to each other, also in high-backed easy chairs, facing Preuss. Gutwilling sits to his right. A little table stocked with coffee, sugar and cream, cups, saucers, and spoons is between us. "Of course, we've shared the proposal with Mr. Hefner," Preuss continued. "I must say, it looks quite impressive. If your projections are correct, you just may be onto something with this venture."

"I'll tell you the truth," Gutwillig cut in. "Hef couldn't believe you guys got big guns like Chase Manhattan and Morgan Stanley to put up money for this little magazine. That's what got his attention."

Okay, Hefner is impressed, so can we cut to the chase here? I thought to myself. *Is he going to invest any money or not?* I shot a look at Phil, who stepped up.

"Gentlemen . . . Bob—may I call you Bob?" he said, as he leaned forward, looking at Preuss.

"Of course," Preuss said.

"Well, Bob, here's the thing. I wouldn't be sitting here with Ed if I didn't think he and his partners were onto something. My own bank is in to this 'little magazine,' as the other Bob here called it, for close to two hundred grand. The other 'big guns' he mentioned are in for $130,000. Now, of course, none of this is my personal money we're talking about. But it is my personal time that I'm taking to come here and meet with you guys. I'm busy. You're busy. Ed's busy. We're all busy. But we all want to make money, right? If you're willing to take a chance—which, as you know, is all any investment really is—then I think you have a chance to invest in a winner here. You've read the proposal, reviewed the numbers. The projections make sense."

The two Bobs were quiet for a moment, then shot their own looks at each other. Preuss finally spoke. "Okay, gentlemen, this is what Mr. Hefner is prepared to offer. He is willing to make an initial investment of $250,000 in your magazine—we'll get to the specific details in a minute. We also want one seat on your board of directors to keep an eye on our investment. That seat will be filled by Bob here," Preuss added, looking at Gutwillig.

Two hundred and fifty thousand dollars! It represented the largest infusion of capital to *Essence* to date. All we had to do was give a seat on our board of directors to Hefner's number three guy? We could do that. What we could *not* do was foresee the hell that would soon break loose by agreeing to that little condition.

If the partners were clueless over the implications of a black man, Gordon Parks, heading the editorial side of a black women's magazine, we were downright idiotic in failing to recognize the implications of Hugh Hefner, the white publisher of a skin magazine, investing in *Essence*. What could you say about a man who had made a fortune running pictures of naked women every month—mostly white and blond—in *Playboy*, the hugely successful magazine he'd started in 1953? That he made an ideal investor for a black women's magazine? Well, yes, he actually did.

Hugh Hefner was the one white man in publishing who recognized and valued the importance of the black consumer market. Black men represented almost 25 percent of *Playboy*'s readership in 1970, a fact that Hefner was quite aware of and respected with editorial content that often catered to the interests of black men. The very first *Playboy* Interview was with the great jazz trumpeter Miles Davis, written by Alex Haley, the black journalist who would later write a blockbuster called *Roots*. The *Playboy* Interview became one of the most popular and influential features in *Playboy* magazine, and Haley became a regular contributor, doing interviews with Jim Brown, Jesse Jackson, and Malcolm X, which led to his writing *The Autobiography of Malcolm X*, his first blockbuster.

It was *Playboy* that published Dr. Martin Luther King Jr.'s last speech following his assassination in 1968. It was *Playboy After Dark*, the late-night television show produced by Playboy Enterprises and hosted by Hugh Hefner in 1969 and 1970, that regularly showcased blacks such as Sammy Davis, Jr. and Bill Cosby, while television shows starring blacks like Nat King Cole and Richard Pryor were being yanked from the air by networks afraid of offending their southern white viewers. It was Hugh Hefner who would be on the right side of history as an early and vocal champion of the civil rights movement.

For a man who recognized the value of the black *male* market, it didn't take much of a stretch for Hugh Hefner to recognize and value the potential of a black *female* market. He may not have been politically correct in his sexual views of women, but he knew a good business idea when he saw it, and *Essence* represented potentially good business. The intent, however, was never for Hefner or Playboy Enterprises to assume any control over *Essence* with its investment. Hugh Hefner didn't want to *own* the magazine any more than I wanted to give back the money he had just invested.

But The Hollingsworth Group never successfully conveyed that message to the larger black public. And in our failure to get in front of a loaded issue and push back with facts rather than get trampled on, we allowed the $250,000 investment in *Essence* by Playboy Enterprises to turn into a horrific public relations disaster. Worse yet, it would be one of the partners and a new editor-in-chief fueling the disaster.

———

I returned to New York from Chicago floating on cloud nine. With Playboy's infusion of $250,000 in new financing, I gave all the partners a raise to $25,000 a year from the $10,000 a year we had been making. In the early months of getting the business up and running, Jonathan and I took no salary at all, since we were not married and did not have families to support. But now that the company was flush, I was happy to more than double the salaries of all the partners. I had always managed to pay the other *Essence* staffers a better salary than the partners out of proceeds from the earlier loans and financing the company had received. But nobody was getting rich working for *Essence*, beginning with the magazine's founders.

Two weeks after giving the raise, I rescinded it. "I'm sorry, guys," I said at one of our after-work partners meetings. "We just can't afford a raise now. We're still bleeding money, even with a $250,000 investment. I've got vendors to pay, loan payments to make, and a new editor-in-chief to hire. I don't know what I was thinking—$250,000 isn't all that much money when you've got bill collectors beating down your door." In another few months I'd be racing to Newark Airport to chase down Louis Allen of Chase Manhattan Bank for a quick infusion of $50,000 to keep operating. That's how fast the magazine went through money.

We didn't even have to put the decision to rescind our raises to a vote. I was the money guy, and the partners trusted me to keep an eye on the bottom line. If I said we couldn't afford a raise, they knew we couldn't afford a raise. We'd manage to keep on keeping on with our $10,000-a-year paychecks.

In setting up our partnership model, The Hollingsworth Group operated as a privately held company with publicly held corporate sensibilities. The four of us—Jonathan Blount, Clarence Smith, Cecil Hollingsworth, and me, Edward Lewis—had incorporated as an *equal* partnership. No one of us carried more authority or power than the others. We each had one vote, which would cause problems only if a vote was tied, in which case our board of directors would cast the deciding vote. Each of us could make decisions individually on behalf of The Hollingsworth Group, as well as jointly as a partnership.

As a corporation we also had to issue stock, which we did, again *equally*. Each partner was given 45,000 shares of Essence Common Stock, valued at one cent a share. To compensate for lower salaries in the beginning, The Hollingsworth Group would also set up a stock plan in 1973 for our employees who had been with the company at least two years. Under no circumstances, however, would any person or corporate investor ever be allowed to acquire more stock than the partners held either individually or in total. This would keep the ownership black.

Finally, The Hollingsworth Group was governed by a board of directors that approved or rejected any major decisions by the partners as it related to the magazine or other company matters. Our first board of directors consisted of the four Hollingsworth Group partners, along with Russell Goings and Michael Victory, our mentors from Shearson, Hammill, and Lewis Zurcher, a vice president at J.P. Morgan Chase, one of our largest investors. Now with the Playboy investment, Robert Gutwillig, the senior vice president at Playboy Enterprises, would be replacing Zurcher on the board as the seventh director.

The Hollingsworth Group business model up was a bit remarkable, even sophisticated, considering that most small black businesses neither issued stock, offered an employee stock plan, nor answered to a board of directors. They tended to be either sole proprietorships or mom-and-pop family-run businesses with decisions consolidated in the thinking and the ego of the business's founder. An equal partnership was not without its drawbacks, however, as our own partner interactions with each other would start to reveal.

In setting up the partnership and establishing corporate officers, titles were assigned based on professional skills and strengths. Clarence was named vice president and advertising sales director, given his talent as a salesman. Cecil was made vice president and circulation director because of his wide contacts in magazine distribution. I became executive vice president and treasurer because of my banking background and ability to raise money. And Jonathan . . . well, Jonathan possessed what we in business refer to as "soft sell" talents. He was handsome, smart, charming, more articulate than even Clarence, and therefore seemed ideal as the public face to put forth as the spokesman for The Hollingsworth Group. He was elected president following the early exit of a fifth partner, Phillip Janniere.

It was agreed at the outset that the partners would make decisions jointly, and Jonathan would be the one who spoke on behalf of the partnership. He truly relished the role and title of president, which in his mind apparently meant having carte blanche to hobnob with luminaries like Gordon Parks, while rarely deigning to speak to *Essence*'s "lower-level" staff; to hire limos on company money we couldn't really afford in order to squire beautiful women about town; and, of course, to constantly brag that *Essence* was *his*—his idea, his vision, his company.

We partners might have suffered indefinitely through all of this foolishness were it not for the fact that increasingly, whenever we made a corporate partners' decision, Jonathan executed something else. We'd vote to say X, and he would say Z. We would vote to give some corporate business to Company A and he would turn around and give it to Company B.

"What the hell is up with this guy?" Cecil Hollingsworth said exasperatedly one evening as he and I were having drinks after work. "I think he's a crazy nut job, that's what I think," Cecil then added, answering his own question. "We can't trust him to do *anything* we vote on. And what's with all his sneaking off to the bathroom every other second? Have you ever taken a good look at those beady little glazed eyes of his? I'm telling you, Ed, the guy is lit up on *something*."

I wasn't about to touch that one. But I could personally attest to the night I had to carry a drunken Jonathan out of the CBS Building on 52nd Street. We had just come from a meeting with one of our advisers at Holt, Rinehart and Winston publishers, which at the time was a CBS subsidiary and one of Cecil's invaluable contacts. The four of us partners stopped off at the little bar in the building's lobby where we usually went for drinks after a meeting with Holt. Within an hour or so, Jonathan got so drunk he passed out. I lifted him over my shoulder and carried him from the bar, across the lobby, and out to a waiting cab that Cecil and Clarence had run out ahead of me to flag down. Oh, my. It was *so* embarrassing. I still can't believe we got the cabdriver to even take him.

Jonathan would remain the most uninhibited man I'd ever met. I remember him arriving for an event in a limo one winter night wearing a full-length fur coat, and absolutely nothing underneath the coat. That's correct. He was buck naked! But we three other partners had to admit it, the ladies *loved* them some Jonathan Blount. He dated fabulous women from bestselling writers to beautiful models, and would often tell us that his purple silk sheets were the secret to successful seduction. Hell, the guy even had me thinking maybe *I* should invest in some purple silk sheets.

Playboy Enterprises may have been the biggest investor in the magazine, but Jonathan Blount and Gordon Parks were the bona fide playboys in the house on 30th Street. Gordon, though, always had class. I remember the kick I got out of seeing him striding down Fifth Avenue one morning, tall, dark, handsome, and distinguished, a cashmere overcoat thrown around his shoulders, a wide-brimmed hat tilted rakishly to the side, and every head turning to look with admiration as he passed by. No wonder Jonathan idolized him. He had it going on.

But Gordon would soon be going on to pursue other interests, for a small black women's magazine struggling for money and respect did not engage the passions of this renaissance man for very long. By the end of *Essence*'s first year of operation, Gordon Parks, like Ruth Ross, was gone, though his name remained on the masthead another year because investors felt his celebrity cachet would be a plus in attracting advertising. This left The Hollingsworth Group looking for a third new editor-in-chief in less than year, a president still acting like he was lord of the manor, and three partners-in-waiting soon ready and willing to take him down.

CHAPTER 11

The Reign Came Falling Down

No doubt about it, Jonathan Blount had become a recurring and escalating problem for the partnership. But dealing with him would have to wait. The Hollingsworth Group had a much more pressing matter to confront. We had to get out the second issue of *Essence,* while trying to replace Ruth Ross, the editor-in-chief we had just fired. Barbara Kerr, our white executive editor, carried on valiantly running the editorial department in the interim, though she wasn't too happy about her friend Ruth being let go.

Gordon Parks was also still at the helm, yet once his nemesis Ruth was out of the way he seemed to be distracted by other interests. Plus, he spent most of his time in the art department conferring with Uli Boege, our young German art director, on such things as how to photograph Grace Jones, then a fledgling model who would regularly stop by the office to see Gordon. Managing the nuts and bolts of the editorial process was not one of his renaissance talents.

Barbara, however, was a consummate editor and professional, but unfortunately would not be at the magazine much more than a year. She had come on board more as a consultant and friend to Ruth and mentor to the young black women who had been hired. Her primary job was to teach them editing skills so they could go on to run the editorial side of the magazine. Like Clarence, who was able to pull together a sales team from among the few blacks working for white advertising agencies, Ruth and Barbara were able to hire talented black women from the very small pool that had started working at white women's magazines in the late 1960s.

Annette Samuels, for instance, *Essence*'s first fashion editor, came from

Mademoiselle magazine, where she worked in the fashion department with the magazine's merchandising editor. She in turn persuaded Sharyn Skeeter, also at *Mademoiselle,* to join *Essence* as an editorial assistant, a position she had held at *Mademoiselle.* Barbara promoted Sharyn fairly quickly to fiction and poetry editor.

By this time Clarence had made contact with a young black woman named Marcia Ann Gillespie, who had crashed a party Time-Life had hosted for *Essence* before the magazine's launch. Marcia got the janitor to let her in a side door leading to the auditorium where the party was being held, since she didn't have an invitation to admit her through the front door. Marcia, who had heard about the party from Gordon Parks, worked as a researcher for Time-Life Books, and was someone my friend Calvin Swinson, an accountant at Time-Life, told me the magazine should think about hiring. In 1969, before *Essence* even launched, Clarence was doing informal type surveys every chance he could among some of the black women he knew, getting their opinion on what they thought of a magazine geared to black women. Clarence was the first of the partners to solicit Marcia's input by inviting her to lunch.

Clarence confirmed Calvin's view of Marcia. She was sharp as a razor, he said—knowledgeable, opinionated, a bit hard charging, but passionate in her beliefs. I would later take Marcia out for drinks myself, and was impressed by the depth of her intellect. Most impressive of all, however, was that she possessed a rock-solid certainty about what she thought *Essence* magazine should be. *That* captured my attention.

Peripatetic Jonathan, meanwhile, ever on the move to play queen maker to the next chief editor, wanted to pursue a possible editor-in-chief recommended by Richard Clurman, the number two man at Time-Life. Clurman knew where the bodies were throughout publishing, including those of the few blacks sprinkled in the Time-Life empire. And Jonathan, as president of The Hollingsworth Group, loved nothing better than being the one to bring in the black "talent" approved by one of our white advisers.

But considering Jonathan's poor track record in spotting potential trouble with this talent—beginning with Bernadette Carey, the first editor-in-chief, who quickly left; then Ruth Ross and Gordon Parks, the second editor-in-chief and the editorial director who were just as quickly at each other's throats—perhaps we three other partners should have thought twice about so quickly hiring editor-in-chief number three. On the other hand, we didn't know what to look for in an editor-in-chief any more than Jonathan did. And frankly, we now didn't have much choice in making this third hire for chief editor. We had a magazine to get out.

The interview with Ida Lewis, whom Clurman had recommended, took place in the home where she still lives, a small one-bedroom apartment on Manhattan's West Side filled with books, magazines, art pieces, and family photographs. Ida had been back in New York less than a year, having spent the previous five years living in Africa and Europe as a freelance journalist. A long-term assignment for *Life* magazine first took her to East Africa, where she spent a year writing about that part of the continent. She was based in Paris, a city she fell in love with, so she remained in France for another four years, writing freelance articles for *Jeune Afrique* magazine. When she returned to the States in late 1969 at age 36, her family begged her to stay, which meant she needed a job. And that's what brought her to us.

"My, what an impressive and handsome group of men you are," Ida told the partners once we had settled on a couch and chairs in her cramped living room. "You know when *Life* hired me, I was one of the first women to be sent on an overseas assignment, and I said then that I wish I was going to Africa for a black man or a black company." We guys grinned at that idea.

Ida is a short, gold-colored woman who wore a natural, eyeglasses, and had a cute gap-toothed smile that gave her an impish-looking charm. She was genuinely sweet, and seemed eager to work for *Essence*. "I like you young men," she said. "You're all so bright and good-looking, and the idea of learning to run a magazine really appeals to me."

Learning to run a magazine?

Now, here was an up-front, potential-for-trouble comment that none of the partners picked up on. The interview lasted an hour, we hired Ida Lewis on the spot, and she started as *Essence's* third editor-in-chief on April 15, 1970, two weeks after Ruth had been fired. They never met. Ruth Ross died of cancer a few years later, and sadly, would not witness the magazine she had named and helped launch become a media phenomenon.

I rarely came down to the ground-floor editorial offices, and when I did it was to usually say: "We have one law at *Essence*. We can't be late getting to the printer." This edict applied to the advertising side as well. In those days, ad agencies sent in layouts of advertising pages that shipped to the printer along with editorial page layouts. If either editorial or advertising layouts were late getting into the magazine, this meant the magazine was late shipping to the printer, and that meant we didn't make our newsstand distribution date.

The partnership had undergone a steep learning curve when it came to getting a handle on production during the first year of *Essence*'s operation. Costs associated with the mechanics of producing a publication are always the biggest line item in magazine publishing. Paper, printing, and distribution costs represented between 30 and 35 percent of our total costs, and we lost a lot of money on the first several issues of *Essence* because we didn't make our print schedule.

Meeting the schedule is critical in magazine production, since printing is basically an assembly-line operation with the large shops printing dozens, even hundreds of publications of all sorts within a month. Each magazine has its own schedule, and if you miss your print date, your publication is out of sequence, triggering a domino effect of lateness: The magazine will now be late getting to the wholesaler, which will make it late getting to the distributor, and this in turn makes it late getting onto the newsstand and magazine racks. A monthly magazine's shelf life on the newsstand is about four weeks, after which time newsstand operators get rid of the issue to make way for the new one.

Essence frequently missed its print schedule during the first year, and this cost us thousands of dollars in potential revenue and circulation because we were often on newsstands for only two or three weeks. We also discovered during our first year that we were being overcharged by our printer, Arcada, which in 1970 was the largest printer in the country. In trying to manage our printing costs, I started asking around to see what other magazines were being charged. Not as much as *Essence* was being charged, I learned.

Arcada was either blatantly taking advantage of the fact that we partners knew nothing about printing by overcharging us, or the company decided to charge us more for print runs whenever we were late. If this was the case, it was never disclosed. Whatever the reason, the practice was unacceptable as far I was concerned. Once our contract with Arcada was up, I secured bids from other printers for the *Essence* account. Unbelievably, Arcada had the nerve to try to get *Essence's* business back by making a bid when we went looking for a new printer.

Brown Printing eventually became our permanent printer and the vendor with which I developed the longest-running relationship. Brown's president, James Rifenbergh, and I became dear friends as well as business associates. It got to the point that Jim and I didn't even have to have a contract to do business. We just shook hands to seal any deal. He trusted me, and I trusted him. Few relationships operated like that in business, and in the case of *Essence* it proved to be very helpful whenever we were short on cash and had to pay late.

Besides problems with meeting our print schedule, *Essence* struggled through its first year caught in the middle of a dogfight between Triangle Corporation, one of the largest wholesale newsstand distributors in the country, and Hudson News, which at the time controlled the newsstands in all of the New York metropolitan area's travel portals—subways, bus terminals, and airports. It now controls newsstands throughout the country.

We didn't even know about the dispute, let alone its cause, but we soon enough felt the effects. I pretty quickly realized something was up because every time I passed a newsstand and didn't see *Essence,* I would ask the newsstand operator why. "Oh, we don't have that magazine dropped here," they would all say. Unbeknownst to us, Hudson News had taken *Essence* and dozens of other magazines off its newsstands for nearly a year in an effort to force concessions from Triangle. This meant that *Essence,* during its critical first year, was not on the newsstands in any subway station, at any magazine outlet in the Port Authority Bus Terminal, or at any of the three New York City metropolitan area airports. In other words, *Essence* was nowhere to be seen on any of the newsstands that millions of black people passed by every day in the biggest city and the biggest magazine market in the country.

Given how severely undercapitalized *Essence* was from the very beginning, having to face these distribution problems while trying to deal with an out-of-control partner and a new editor-in-chief who proved to have her own steep learning curve, forced The Hollingsworth Group to make changes in the hierarchy of the partnership. I had started talking to Russ Goings and Michael Victory, now on the *Essence* board, about the confusion Jonathan's wild-card behavior was starting to cause. They suggested that the partners meet to restructure the chain of command.

We held that fateful meeting on a steamy evening after work in August 1970. Clarence, Cecil, and I were in agreement that Jonathan had to go. Not as a partner, but as a problem. This meant we had to find a way to take away his power, but let him keep his pride and even his title of president. Jonathan was a founding partner and an *Essence* board director, so we couldn't exactly kick him out of the group. Instead, we added the titles of publisher and chief executive officer to the corporate officer titles, which were to be elected positions that would supersede his authority as president. The idea was to demote Jonathan by electing a partner to be over him who would now have the mandate to run the company. This would effectively end the one-equal-partner, one-equal-vote rule, because whoever became publisher and chief executive officer would have the authority to run the company as he saw fit.

Jonathan, not aware of our strategy to demote him, of course thought he should be elected to the new positions. But Clarence and I wanted the positions too.

At the meeting the three of us had the opportunity to present himself and say why he should be elected CEO and publisher of *Essence*. Jonathan reiterated that the idea for the magazine had always been his, and he should therefore continue to be the one speaking for the magazine in the exalted newly created positions.

Clarence explained he was the one out on the front lines dealing with Madison Avenue, selling the Essence Woman. He had the best knowledge of the advertising market and the black female audience, making him the best positioned to interpret both to the larger public.

I said I was the one bringing in the money, especially when we were in a pinch—getting that $13,000 early on from Freedom National Bank; that $50,000 emergency loan from Chase, and the big $250,000 investment from Playboy. While Clarence knew how to sell ads and Jonathan knew how to profile, I knew how to manage money and raise capital.

Cecil, the only one of the partners not making a bid to be in charge, was from the beginning the most entrepreneurial among us. He came to the *Essence* venture with both his own business and a wealth of business contacts that were very helpful in providing technical assistance when the partners were starting up. Yet Cecil always seemed to have a sideline going, even as a partner in the group that bore his name. He was a hustler in the best sense of the word—smart, creative, energetic, and open to pursuing new opportunities. As it turned out, all of his eggs were never in the *Essence* basket, and this would present its own problems further down the line.

Once Jonathan, Clarence, and I had made our election pitches, we put the decision to a vote. Only one vote was cast for Jonathan Blount—by Jonathan Blount. The three remaining votes, Clarence Smith's, Cecil Hollingsworth's, and mine, went to me, Edward Lewis. My victory, however, was only going to lead to a fight, because it didn't mean a thing to Jonathan. He continued to act as if being president meant he was in charge, still presenting himself in public as the one who spoke for the magazine.

At this point Jonathan had become close with Ida Lewis, who had been editor-in-chief for three months. Ida was also liked by Gordon Parks. Gordon and Ida had the European connection in common, both having been the chosen "first blacks" hired by *Life* magazine for groundbreaking European assignments in the late 1960s. Gordon's association with *Essence,* in fact, had been a reason Ida agreed to meet with the partners in the first place to talk about becoming editor-in-chief. And Jonathan, ever the status seeker, loved the idea of orbiting around these two former *Life* magazine stars who were now starring at *his* magazine.

At first I too was impressed with the international background Ida brought to the magazine. Given my own interest in international affairs, I think it's a plus when anyone has traveled or lived abroad. It broadens one's perspective. Ida was also smart and thoughtful, and seemed to have a real desire to be editor-in-chief. But it pretty quickly became apparent that she didn't have the editorial grounding or management skills of Ruth Ross. Though Ida could be sweet and cooperative and even seductive, she knew nothing about running a magazine, something Barbara Kerr, our astute executive editor, recognized from the beginning.

"I understand Ida worked as a freelancer in Europe for several years," Barbara said to me one morning as we were coming into the townhouse together shortly after Ida was hired. "What do you think that's going to mean in terms of what she brings to an *American* magazine?" she added pointedly.

Truthfully, I didn't really know, but I was about to find out. First, while Ida was smart enough to know she had to delegate and solicit help from her staff because she really didn't know how to run a magazine, she wasn't the best at organizing, multitasking, or handling pressure. And this led to the unforgivable: She couldn't get the magazine closed on time.

"Ida, I keep telling you," I said to her late one night in her office. "There is one law at *Essence*. You can't be late getting to the printer."

"I know, Ed," she said with a sigh. "I don't know what to do with these freelance writers. They never get their pieces in on time, then we have to scramble to edit them and sometimes even do a rewrite, and that makes us late."

I did not want to hear it. "Just get us to the printer on time," I snapped. Ida looked like she was about to cry. She would later accuse me of being mean and cold. I am sure those nights I laid down the law had something to do with that opinion. But warm and fuzzy has never been my style when poor management is costing the company money.

As *Essence* publisher and CEO I had the expanded authority to now become involved in all aspects of the magazine, including editorial. This brought me back to Marcia Gillespie, the young woman at Time-Life I had concluded should be a part of the *Essence* editorial team. Marcia evidently concluded the same thing, because she had already met with Gordon Parks, whom she knew from his days at Time-Life. Marcia also knew Gordon's oldest daughter Toni, then a photo researcher at Time-Life, who facilitated the meeting. Gordon recommended to Ida that she hire Marcia, which she did, bringing Marcia on board as managing editor in December 1970. Marcia was 26, and would eventually replace Barbara Kerr as second-in-command to the editor-in-chief.

Ida also brought in a couple of her own people, including a young associate editor from *Redbook* magazine named Sandra Satterwhite, and a young part-time beauty writer named Susan L. Taylor. At 25, Sandy Satterwhite was practically a veteran editor in the short history of black women working at white women's magazines. Having spent three years in *Redbook*'s articles department honing her skills as a writer and editor and developing media contacts, she brought a depth of experience to *Essence* unmatched by most of the other editors.

Susan L. Taylor was a 24-year-old wife and new mother trying to get a fledgling cosmetics business off the ground with her husband, a hair stylist. "I just like her," Ida said, explaining why she hired a young woman as a beauty writer who had little experience, but much energy, passion, and enthusiasm. Of all her editorial decisions, hiring Susan Taylor proved to be the best one Ida would make in her short reign as editor-in-chief.

Jonathan, meanwhile, wasn't exactly licking his wounds over being toppled as head of The Hollingsworth Group. He simply refused to recognize that a coup had even occurred. This head-in-the-sand, ass-in-the air posture would continue for the next thirty years as he perpetually fought to regain control, take over, and otherwise assert what he thought what was his rightful place as head of the multimillion-dollar company *Essence* would grow into during the coming years.

Like many adversaries who underestimate the strength their opponents, Jonathan never got over losing out to *me* as publisher and CEO. I was the quiet, unassuming partner in the group, more cerebral than charismatic, plainspoken, not glib, and more prone to listening, not just talking. Some people mistake these quieter qualities for weakness, rather than strength, or for being clueless instead of being shrewd and sometimes even cunning.

In the end, Jonathan, who was certainly a man of many talents, suffered the fatal flaw of hubris—the mistake of thinking he was the smartest man in the room whenever he was in the room with his partners. His partners had succeeded in taking him down a notch. Yet he seemed unwilling, or maybe was just unable, to accept that. This led to continuing confusion at *Essence,* which was unacceptable if the magazine was to survive. And this meant once the partners had taken Jonathan Blount down, we would have no other choice than to now take him out.

CHAPTER 12

R-E-S-P-E-C-T Find Out
What It Means to Me

Whenever any war story is being told, specific details of who shot whom, who got dragged from the battlefield mortally wounded, or who lived to fight another day tend to change with the years and with whoever is doing the telling. This has certainly been the case whenever the tale of that bloody fall-to-spring season of 1970–71 at *Essence* is recounted by those who were witness to the carnage. This was the game-changing season that would test the very survival of the magazine as personalities clashed, egos flared, and every line drawn in the sand upped the ante on respect.

A business is first and foremost an organization of people—good and bad, smart and less smart—and its success is always a function of how well those people work together on behalf of the enterprise. A black business is typically an organization of people working together who bring a particular and common racial history to the enterprise. And that history has inevitably been steeped in racial oppression that usually results in some element of psychological dysfunction—the consequence of any form of ongoing, debilitating oppression. The success of any black business, therefore, is invariably a function of how successfully dysfunction can be kept from throwing the business offtrack before it has a chance to get out of the starting gate.

What I was getting in my new role as *Essence* CEO and publisher were all the headaches that come with overseeing a struggling start-up trying to find its way amid conflicts and confusion. The Hollingsworth partners were certainly dealing with the conflicts and confusions caused by one Jonathan Blount, making our decision to neutralize him inevitable if the business was to continue and succeed. However, as publisher and CEO I would soon get dragged into personality and ego fights involving others at the magazine, not just the four Hollingsworth Group partners.

Which is how I came to look up one morning in late September of 1970 and see Annette Samuels, our fashion editor, standing in the doorway of my office, glaring at me. Annette, a petite, pretty woman in her early thirties, had a steely, outspoken toughness that could be a little jarring, given her small stature and stylish Halle Berry good looks. Taking a drag from the cigarette held in her trademark cigarette holder, Annette asked if she could speak with me. I told her to come in and have a seat.

"All right, Ed, I want you to know, I'm not putting up with this bullshit," she said, as she sat back, crossed her legs, and dramatically flicked a cigarette ash into the empty ashtray on my desk. She narrowed her eyes while blowing smoke into the air. "I know you heard about Ida taking her girlfriend—or whatever the hell she is—to the Paris shows. As you know, we only got *two* invitations to the shows, Ed, and as you also know, one of those invitations was for the fashion editor—*me*. I get to Paris, staying in the same hotel as Ida and her little girlfriend, but Ida had both invitations, so she and the girlfriend were the ones who went to all the shows, all the receptions, all the parties. Not me. I was locked out of *everything* because Ida never gave me my invitation." Annette took another long drag on her cigarette holder, then leaned forward to make her point. "*I'm* the fashion editor, Ed. Not Ida, and not her white bitch."

"Now, Annette," I said, not quite knowing what else to say besides the obvious. "I know you're upset . . ."

"Oh, no, Ed, I'm not upset. I'm way beyond upset. *I'm fucking furious! You hear me?*"

I do believe everybody on all six floors of the townhouse heard her.

"Why do you think *Essence* got invited to Paris in the first place, Ed? A new magazine that nobody can even *find* on the fucking newsstands? Because of my fashion pages, Ed. That's why. You think Ida and that little dyke girlfriend of hers give a shit about fashion? Please! Ida just wanted to go back to Paris to . . ."

I started to tune Annette out. Not because I didn't want to hear it, but because I had already heard most of it. By the time they returned from *Essence*'s first trip to the Paris prêt-à-porter shows in the fall of 1970, Annette's account of being royally "dissed" in Paris by Ida Lewis, *Essence*'s own editor-in-chief, was all over the office.

The twice-a-year fashion shows held in Paris, Milan, and New York during the spring and fall to debut the new ready-to-wear collections by the fashion industry's top designers are the A-list go-to shows for anybody who is anybody in fashion: editors, reporters, ready-to-wear buyers, designers, models, glittering celebrities, and accompanying paparazzi. Annette was right. Receiving an invitation to view the collections meant that *Essence*, a newcomer to the fashion scene, was already being noticed. Being at the shows was excellent publicity for the magazine, and would have certainly bestowed a certain cachet to its fashion editor. If she was not able to get in, I certainly understood why Annette was so angry.

Annette had worked in the fashion department of *Mademoiselle,* a major white-owned women's magazine, and as smart and talented as she may have been, she knew the odds of her or any other young black woman going to the Paris shows in 1970 as *Mademoiselle*'s fashion editor were zero to nil. To now be the fashion editor at a *black*-owned magazine and be shut out by a black boss at one of the most prestigious events in her industry would be an insult beyond imagining. If she couldn't get respect as a black professional at a black publication, where could she get it?

Annette left *Essence* shortly after meeting with me. It was never clear whether she left on her own or if Ida fired her.

I myself could not give two cuff links about fashion shows, but Ida and Annette had convinced me of the importance of *Essence* having a presence at the one in Paris. To think that the company may have wasted money on airfare and hotel costs because our editor-in-chief kept our fashion editor from doing her job—covering the shows in order to report in the magazine the latest fashion trends—was also beyond imagining. It was bad enough that Ida still couldn't get the magazine out on time. Now *this*? But to tell the truth, I wasn't sure how to handle *this*.

Ida's sexual orientation cetainly wasn't something I was comfortable getting into, though I knew it would have been just as inappropriate had Ida taken a *man* to Paris and given *him* Annette's invitation. The matter pretty much blew over when Annette left, though it did leave a bitter aftertaste.

Without Annette present, I could not confront Ida and try to get to the bottom of what had happened during their trip, nor could I really afford to fire Ida, even if Annette's account of the trip proved to be true. Ida was the third editor-in-chief at *Essence* in less than year, and had been at the magazine for fewer than six months. How many times could we keep firing our editor-in-chief and expect to keep getting the magazine out?

Caught between the proverbial rock and a hard place, I started kicking myself for even letting two strong-willed women talk me into sending them to Paris in the first place! This was one of the favors I had dispensed following the $250,000 investment by *Playboy* when *Essence* appeared flush and I was feeling generous. It did not take long for me to get over that.

At the heart of all of the bickering and infighting that would consume *Essence* during much of its thirty-five-year black-owned history was the very issue that had forced Annette to leave: respect. Ida did not respect Annette's role as fashion editor, nor even the magazine's position as a new business that could hardly afford to send one its editors out of the country and have nothing to show for it. Just as Jonathan did not respect my role as CEO and publisher, Ida was guilty of "dissing" one of her own staff—and the magazine—by preventing her from reporting on the fashion collections, the very reason she was sent to Paris.

Respect, or the lack thereof, is the racial dynamic that perhaps best sums up the entire history of black interactions in America, be they between other blacks or between whites. To a people whose fragile sense of worth is frequently based on the extent to which they feel they are being respected or valued, esteem issues become paramount in a black-owned business. The expectation among blacks working in a black workplace is that they will, at the very least, be respected for their humanity and their feelings, as well as for the talents and skills they are bringing to the business.

Yet in the peculiar "double consciousness" W.E.B. Du Bois talked about that results from internalized race oppression, I have found that blacks are the very ones more likely to act with disrespect when working for and with each other. The familiarity of working "with your own," a group that has historically been disrespected, does indeed breed contempt among some blacks, which leads to liberties taken that would never even be entertained in another workplace. Would Annette have flown into a rage with the publisher of Condé Nast because she felt slighted by *Mademoiselle*'s editor-in-chief? I doubt it. Would Ida have withheld an invitation from a *white* editor who was working for her at *Life* magazine, or wasted Time-Life's money by preventing the editor from doing her job? Absolutely not, no doubt about it.

Having to deal with double-standard thinking that leads black employees to behave one way in a black work setting and another way in a white one only adds to the collateral cost of running a black business. But there can also be specific advantages. Many of the black professionals I have worked with often brought a greater level of commitment to a black business, investing the kind of time and energy to ensure the success of the venture that they did not necessarily bring to another enterprise. *We are all in this together* was the unspoken feeling, thinking that as the success of the black business goes, so goes their own success.

This is why black-on-black disrespect in a black workplace can turn explosive. Being dissed as a black professional by other black professionals often feels more devastating than being dissed by whites, since white disrespect is never totally unexpected, given America's racial history. But disrespect from other blacks is never expected, especially in a professional setting, and tends to be less tolerated. In fact, professional blacks working in a black corporate workplace often expect *more* when it comes to the perks that connote value and success.

How large is the paycheck? How big is the office? How large the expense account? How big the bonus? How grand the professional title? These are the common indicators of reward and respect in any business, but for blacks working in a black business, such external perks frequently speak to their internal feelings of worth on a personal level as well as a professional one. Bottom line: The extent to which a black business makes its black employees feel respected, valued, and affirmed may be the first indicator of just how successful the business is going to be.

When the three of us partners voted to demote Jonathan, we respected him enough to let him keep his title as president. Yet he continued to disrespect us by acting as if our votes did not count. Left unchecked, such disrespect would jeopardize the very future of *Essence*.

Jonathan Blount may have been an ongoing pain to the partners, but he was continuing to become close with Ida Lewis, the editor-in-chief I was starting to have serious misgivings about. Ida seemed to have the loyalty of the rest of the editorial staff, however, as well as some of the staff in other departments. She could certainly be sweet and charming, as could Jonathan, which perhaps explained their affinity for one another.

I suspect, though, that Ida knew she was skating on thin ice with me, and joined forces with Jonathan to have both an ally and a buffer. Meanwhile, months after I had been elected publisher and CEO, Clarence, Cecil, and I were getting nowhere trying to rein in Jonathan. He remained the loose cannon, still speaking on behalf of the partnership, still soliciting potential advertisers on his own without consulting with Clarence, and still refusing to recognize me as the leader elected to run the company. The three of us partners decided to take the matter to a higher authority, our board of directors.

The *Essence* board of directors served in more of an advisory capacity, since they were rarely called upon to settle disputes among the partnership. Russ Goings and Michael Victory, our original business supporters and first board members outside the partnership, were continuing to advise us on financing strategies for the magazine and still helping to identify potential investors.

Though not a board director, Suzanne Warshavsky, a young associate at the law firm of Dewey, Ballantine, Bushby, Palmer & Wood, our legal counsel, attended all of our board meetings and took minutes. She was one of the two pro bono attorneys Dewey Ballantine assigned to handle the closing on the $130,000 *Essence* received in initial financing. Suzanne would eventually go on to head her own firm and take the *Essence* account with her, becoming our trusted counsel for more than thirty years.

Robert Gutwillig, the senior vice president at Playboy Enterprises, was our newest member to the board. As a condition of Playboy's $250,000 investment, one seat on the *Essence* board had to go a representative from Playboy. Bob was a shortish, slight, and wiry man, liberal in his politics and natty in his dress, given to wearing bow ties. He was the only board member who had a background in publishing, and consequently paid more attention to the editorial content of *Essence.* Bob originally came out of book publishing, and had also spent several years at Hachette, the French company that once published the women's magazines *Elle* and *Marie Claire.*

Initially Gutwillig appeared to be helpful, advising us on the kind of writing he would like to see in the magazine. The *Playboy* Interview was his standard, and he wanted all the feature writing in *Essence* to reflect the caliber of the incisive, well-crafted prose that came to be the signature of those interviews. Though Bob really had nothing to do with editorial beyond giving advice—it's not like he was stopping by Ida's office every day to read manuscripts—on some level he probably did think he could dictate and tell us what to do. But that was never going to happen. Not with all the strong personalities on both the editorial and business sides of the magazine.

Years later, recounting the story of Playboy's involvement in *Essence,* Ida Lewis would claim that Playboy Enterprises really wanted to take over the company and have her run it. Bob Gutwillig would regularly stop by her apartment, she said, offering to "give" her the magazine once it was acquired. I had never heard that one, but it would explain why a memo Gutwillig wrote on October 9, 1970, would take on incendiary proportions in the coming months.

Bob's job as a board member was basically to protect the investment of Playboy by keeping an eye on how money was being spent at *Essence,* how successfully money was being raised, and how the magazine was doing financially. He would regularly report back to his boss in Chicago, Robert Preuss, executive vice president, who in turn reported to Hugh Hefner.

Financially, *Essence* was still bleeding money. We were looking at ending the first year of operation with a deficit of more than a million dollars. By the end of 1971, our first full year of operation, circulation was less than 100,000–150,000 in subscriptions and 63,000 in newsstand sales—off by almost *half* from the 150,000 reader circulation originally projected for the first year. The fight between Triangle Circulation, our newsstand wholesaler, and Hudson News, our newsstand distributor, nearly killed us.

The fact that the magazine had been off the newsstand for almost a year in much of New York City, the largest magazine market in the country, meant we could not deliver our projected circulation to advertisers. And if we could not deliver the readers, we could not maintain our advertising page rates, which are based on circulation. The same was true if we did not meet the deadline with our printer, which is why Ida's continuing to be late in closing the magazine was unacceptable. If the magazine was late getting to those newsstands that *were* carrying it, or late getting to our subscribers, circulation was again compromised.

Cecil had scored a coup in getting Neodata, the largest fulfillment house in the country, to handle our subscriptions. At the time a subsidiary of A.C. Nielsen Company, the market research firm that measures television viewing, Neodata did all of our mailings, handled the subscription cards, and fulfilled subscription orders. Oddly enough, though Cecil Hollingsworth was named *Essence* vice president of circulation, he did not come to the company with a background in mass magazine circ- how many black men did in 1970?

But Cecil was one of those natural-born entrepreneurs who are quick studies—fast on his feet and nimble in his thinking. He always knew the right questions to ask, and the right people to ask the questions to. Circulation, like anything else, could be learned, and Cecil learned everything in pretty short order. Thanks to the invaluable contacts he acquired running his own business, Cecil was the partner who had also snagged Triangle Circulation as our wholesale distributor, which was considered a real coup at the time—until we got snagged by Triangle's fight with Hudson.

No doubt about it, we had enough start-up problems to deal with without continuing to be hampered by Jonathan and his out-of-control behavior. Taking him before the *Essence* board seemed to be the only way we could get him to understand that he no longer spoke on behalf of The Hollingsworth Group. I did.

––––––

Essence board meetings were usually held in the one of the conference rooms at City Bank's headquarters, located at 399 Park Avenue, not far from the *Essence* brownstone on 30th Street. All the board members were present the afternoon we met in the early spring of 1971 to specifically deal with Jonathan. Suzanne Warshavsky distributed the minutes from the previous meeting, which were quickly approved, and we then moved on to the matter for which we had convened.

"Jonathan, you know why we're here," Russ began, sitting at the head of the conference table, looking at Jonathan with paternal fondness. Russ always did like Jonathan. "The partners took a vote on how they want the group restructured, but it seems . . ."

Commotion could be heard in the hallway outside the closed double doors of the conference room. The doors suddenly opened and Ida marched in, accompanied by about ten other people—all of them from *Essence.*

"Excuse me!" Suzanne snapped with alarm. "This is a private meeting. I think you must be in the wrong room."

"No, we're not in the wrong room," Ida said calmly. "We are here at the invitation of Jonathan Blount, the president of *Essence.*" This caught Suzanne off guard. She turned to Jonathan, looking puzzled.

"That's right," Jonathan piped up. "I invited my staff to join us at this meeting today to support me. They have a stake in the company as much as the rest of us, and should know the truth about my partners. Our board meetings are not public, but perhaps they should be. The staff has a right to know how the company is being mismanaged."

"Cut the shit, Jonathan," Clarence said angrily. "You know the three of us voted you out as spokesman and voted Ed in as CEO and publisher. What *is* your problem?"

"I'll tell you what the problem is," Ida said, warmed up by Clarence's outburst. "None of the management staff at *Essence* had a say in who should be publisher and chief executive officer, because if we did, it would *never* be Ed Lewis." There was a murmur of agreement from the posse who had come in with Ida—the art director, the new fashion editor, two people I recognized from the production department, and a couple of copy editors. The rest I didn't recognize. All were standing, and had fanned out around the conference table, circling the wagons.

"As editor-in-chief I work more closely with Ed than probably anyone here, except maybe Clarence," Ida was saying, standing just behind Jonathan. "And frankly, I find Ed to be rather mean and cold. Jonathan is much nicer, much easier to get along with, and much more of a leader, as far as I'm concerned."

There were more murmurs of agreement from the posse. "Mr. Lewis doesn't even *speak* to me when I pass him on the stairs," somebody chimed in.

Who the hell was that?

I couldn't believe it. Jonathan's response to the partners taking him before the board was to try to do an end run with these stooges who had just barged in, trying to discredit me, no doubt hoping to be installed as publisher and CEO himself. I had heard enough.

"Listen, everybody," I finally said. "There is really no problem at all. You don't have to worry about me. I quit."

Stunned silence. Then Jonathan spoke up, his green eyes blazing. "What are you talking about, Ed? You can't do that!"

"It's done," I hissed. "I can't stand pettiness, and I don't have to put up with it. I'm out."

Russ sat speechless. Clarence and Cecil looked like they had just been sucker punched. Michael and Bob turned a whiter shade of pale. Even Ida looked shaken as I got up from my seat, grabbed my suit jacket, and headed for the door, turning around to look at everyone before exiting and saying, "I don't need this."

I went across the street to the little coffee shop where the partners would sometimes go after a board meeting. I needed a drink, but would settle for caffeine. Russ, Michael, and Suzanne came in about fifteen minutes later and found me sitting in a booth in the back, away from customer traffic. They squeezed in the booth with me.

"My God, Ed, if you leave there will be chaos," Michael said. "You know it will be the end of the company—you do know that, right?"

I said nothing.

"Come on, Ed," Russ pleaded. "We've come so far. The magazine has been your life, and you can't just walk away because you're mad. You'll get over being mad at Jonathan, but you'll never get over being mad at yourself if you walk out now."

I still said nothing. But Russ was right about one thing. *Essence* had taken over my life. Here I was, 30 years old, living in a little studio on East 70th Street, and working around the clock at a business that might or might not make it. I didn't even have a girlfriend. Maybe I needed to get a life beyond the magazine. All I seemed to be getting for all my work was a whole lot of disrespect from the very people I had lost respect for.

At two that morning I was still up, trying to cool out as I listened to Miles Davis's *Bitches Brew* album. *Very apropros*, I thought. The comment from the woman at the meeting who said I never spoke to her when we passed on the stairs was bothering me. I had heard that some people at work referred to me as "Stoneface Ed." With all I have on my mind, I can't believe there are people who are offended because I don't always speak when I walk by. *Black people take everything so personally.* These same people would sure take it a lot more personally if I couldn't meet payroll and give them a paycheck. No doubt about it. I've never been Mr. Personality, I know that—I'm shy. But *Stoneface Ed*?

The intercom bell rang. It was two in the morning! Cecil and Clarence were down in the lobby, asking to come up. I buzzed them in.

"Ed, what the hell are you doing?" Clarence said, pushing past me as soon as I opened the door. "I thought we all agreed. *You* are the one who's running the company now—forget about that asshole Jonathan." Clarence took a seat on my pullout sofa. Cecil sat at the dining table. I remained standing, leaning against the kitchen counter.

"Forget about him?" I said, looking at Clarence like he was crazy, though he was just a little drunk. Clearly he and Cecil had gone off after the meeting and had the drinks *I* needed. They must have closed out some bar before showing up at my door.

"Man, you know I can't work with that guy," I told Clarence. "I am not putting up with one more second of his disrespect."

"So what do you want to do?" Cecil asked.

"You know what I want to do. Get rid of Jonathan." Clarence and Cecil looked at each other, then looked at me.

"He's a partner," Clarence said finally. "He's got stock. His name is on all the company documents. He's on the board."

"I know that. Let him keep his damn stock—what's it worth? A penny a share?"

"Something like that," Cecil said with a smirk.

"This is the deal," I said. "You want me back, then Jonathan has got to go. I mean out completely. Out of the partnership, off the board, out of the damn townhouse. And I want to be the one to tell him—alone."

There was a moment of silence.

"Well, considering his behavior this afternoon, I don't imagine that Russ and Michael will have any objections to removing him from the board," Clarence said. "And Suzanne can take care of the legalities involved in getting him out of the partnership. Do you believe that idiot had half the magazine staff show up at the meeting? Jesus Christ. What a way to tear your ass."

I could hardly wait to tear that idiot a new one.

CHAPTER 13

Massacre on 30th Street

I will give him this: Jonathan Blount took his ass whipping like a man. The day following the staff's barging in at the board meeting, I was back at the brownstone, ready to deal with him. I had considered Clarence and Cecil's comments after their two a.m. visit to my apartment. They reminded me that we were all in this together. Much like a marriage, The Hollingsworth Group was a partnership, for better or for worse. Jonathan turned out to be the untrustworthy cheating partner we would have to divorce if *Essence* and the union among the three remaining partners was to survive and succeed. Cecil and Clarence had certainly invested as much in the business as I had, maybe more, considering they had wives and families to support. If they could take a chance on a venture that was still risky and continue to hang in when the going got rough, how could I do any less?

"We need to talk," I said to Jonathan, entering his office. He was on the phone, but hung up the minute I walked in.

"Sure, Ed," he said calmly, oozing charm as if nothing had happened the day before. "What can I do for you?"

"Let's take a walk. Get a cup of coffee."

Once we were seated at a table in the coffee shop across the street from the brownstone, I cut to the chase. "Jonathan, you know as well as I do, this is not working out. Clarence and Cecil came by my place practically at dawn this morning, asking me to come back. I told them the only way I'd do that is if you were gone. Out. I can't work with you, man. You're just too disruptive, too unpredictable. And you clearly can't work with me."

143

"So what are you telling me, Ed? That I'm being fired? That I'm no longer a partner?"

"That's exactly what I'm telling you. You're fired!"

Jonathan let that sink in for a second. I was surprised by how calm he seemed. So out of character for his usually unstable temperament. He did ask that I keep in mind the idea for the magazine had always been his mother's, and that in future references to how the magazine got started he hoped I would acknowledge that. Then he added a bit lamely, "About that meeting yesterday, Ed, you know, it was partly Ida's idea to bring the staff . . ."

"It's not about the meeting, Jonathan," I cut in. "It's about *you*. I'm the publisher and CEO and I can't work with *you*. The meeting yesterday just confirmed it."

Jonathan was silent.

"Look, man, no hard feelings," I said. "Clarence, Cecil, and I took a vote. You're out of the partnership, but you'll get to keep your 45,000 shares of stock. It's not worth much now. But maybe someday, who knows?"

The fight seemed to leave him. Jonathan agreed to pick up his last paycheck and clear out of the brownstone as soon as possible. He didn't ask for anything else—not that we had anything to give him. There was certainly nothing like a severance package to give out. Our attorney Suzanne Warshavsky would draft the resolution necessary to have Jonathan legally removed as a partner. He and I had nothing else to say as we left the coffee shop that warm spring April morning in 1971.

Now, you would think as a student of Russian history, I would have taken a page from the history of that country's revolution and recognized that if you are to effectively overthrow an existing order, it is not enough to take the czar out and shoot him. You must make sure you shoot him in the head—and his whole family too. But I wasn't up for firing anyone else after firing Jonathan. In his case the "whole family" would have meant getting rid of Ida Lewis and the ten or so *Essence* staff members who broke into the board meeting. Instead, I called a meeting of the entire staff on the afternoon of Jonathan's dismissal to say that in the best interests of the company Jonathan Blount had been asked to leave.

"I'm sure you've all heard about the board meeting yesterday in which

I resigned," I said to the group assembled on the ground-floor editorial offices and on the stairs. "Well, I have been asked by The Hollingsworth Group partners and the *Essence* board to return. We are here as a nucleus—as a family, so to speak—trying to do something meaningful as far as the magazine goes. The feeling is that Mr. Blount has become detrimental to our continuing to develop the magazine. That's why he is leaving. Going forward let's just let bygones be bygones and try to work together for the common good of the magazine I know we all believe in—*Essence.*"

That seemed to settle it. Everyone went back to work, but a message had been sent. It was a warning. Ida suddenly became ingratiating over the next few days. She even started acting as if she wanted to have more than a professional relationship with me. She would come into my office and try to sweet-talk me, saying things like, "Oh, Ed, you're so wonderful." I remember her once putting her arms around me from behind as I was sitting at my desk, and I felt the distinct sensation of a knife going through me.

Ida had really gotten on my bad side by firing Marcia Gillespie shortly before the board meeting, and only three or four months after hiring her. Marcia proved to be more capable than Ida in meeting deadlines and getting the magazine closer to closing on time. Barbara Kerr was still on board, but she had never intended to stay more than a year to help get an *Essence* editorial team in place. It was therefore critical that Ida and Marcia be able to work together.

Initially the two women did seem to work well together and even like each other. Ida could be sweet and charming, and Marcia, while no-nonsense and a hard charger, was a team player who did not come to the magazine in the beginning expecting to run it. Maybe if Ida had been a stronger editor, Marcia would not have perceived a weakness that she felt she could turn to her own advantage.

I will admit that I saw something very special in Marcia almost as soon as I met her. We would occasionally have drinks together after she was hired, and I liked the vision she outlined for the magazine. She talked in terms of *Essence* having "editorial spine" and becoming more relevant. Neither she nor Ida were into fashion and beauty, though Ida did understand the importance of both to the *Essence* readers, as well as their importance for selling advertising.

To be fair, Ida, while not the best manager, did bring her own editorial point of view to the content of the magazine. She had become close with Robert Gutwillig, the *Essence* board member representing Playboy's interest, and at his suggestion Ida launched the "*Essence* Interview," a monthly question-and-answer feature between the *Essence* editor-in-chief and a notable personality or public figure. Ida's first *Essence* Interview was with educator Shirley Du Bois, widow of W.E.B. Du Bois, the great African-American scholar and thinker. Subsequent interviews with people such as Aileen Hernandez, the president of the National Organization for Women; Gwendolyn Brooks, the Pulitzer Prize–winning poet; and the poet Nikki Giovanni, who in a clever turnaround interviewed Ida Lewis for *Essence,* gave the magazine both political and cultural heft, and an element of the unexpected.

There was fiction by Maya Angelou, and an excerpt from *Soledad Brother: The Prison Letters of George Jackson,* in which Jackson's poignant letter to his father was published. One fashion spread titled "Miles Davis's Boutique" photographed the enormous collection of shoes, belts, hats, shirts, jackets, and pants spilling out of jazz trumpeter Miles Davis's closet. Another fashion story called "A Dash of Ashe," featured the tennis star Arthur Ashe modeling African attire. At the dawning of the seventies, *Essence* covered the political and the cultural, showcased black men as well as black women, and gave larger esthetic meaning to the popular chant "Black is Beautiful!"

Within the first year of the publication's launch, *Essence* seemed to be finding its footing editorially as its editor-in-chief moved to establish a clear vision for the magazine. Ida's background as a writer and reporter covering international stories gave her a certain scope in creating a magazine that by definition would have to be many things to many black women. There was no other magazine directed to this new readership.

Notwithstanding Ida's international background, Marcia began to see her as incompetent. Marcia herself was well-read and outspoken, had a bachelor's degree in American history from Lake Forest College, and seemed more grounded than Ida in an understanding of the everyday concerns of black women. Marcia did not suffer fools gladly, and this meant she was soon making her feelings known to Ida. It didn't take long for Ida to feel threatened by Marcia, who was beginning to also make it known that she thought *she* should be editor-in-chief.

It wasn't surprising when Ida came to me to say she wanted to fire Marcia. I told her not to do that. She did so anyway. By this time the two women were having the kind of public fights in the office that had sunk to the level of personal mudslinging. I understand Ida once said to Marcia in a particularly vicious throw-down, "At least I'm not sleeping with the boss," and Marcia reportedly shot back, "Well, at least I'm sleeping with a *man*."

Like Jonathan's battles with his three partners, no one would give respect. I suspect, though, that the differences between Ida and Marcia had as much to do with differences in professional management style as with any differences in intellect or personal persuasions. Ida had a naturally engaging quality about her and easily gave the appearance of being nice, charming, and sweet. And to some extent she was. She encouraged staff input, liked to manage by cooperation, was quick to delegate, and had a coterie of people throughout the magazine who liked, respected, and were loyal to her. But Ida was the kind of manager who could also be passive-aggressive and duplicitous, which explained my wariness whenever she tried to hug me or otherwise "make nice."

Marcia, by contrast, was in-your-face assertive, hard charging, clear on what she wanted, and comfortable giving orders to make it happen. This kind of manager lacks the affirming bedside manner that can motivate a staff. She relishes the role of "boss lady," often making decisions that can feel tyrannical or dictatorial, and keeps her staff in line through fear and intimidation. But there is no confusion with an up-front boss. You know where you stand, you know what she wants, and if you meet her expectations, you will be fine. This kind of boss may not always be liked, but she is usually effective and respected.

I certainly respected Marcia, and was upset that Ida had fired her. Why tell me what you *want* to do, and when I tell you not to, you do it anyway? A classic passive-aggressive management move. Marcia was fired for insubordination, Ida said. Apparently, Ida had asked her to do something, and she refused. A classic in-your-face assertive yet defiant move.

By the end of 1970, after Marcia had just come on board and Jonathan was still acting like the de facto leader in charge, Ida tried to put a good face on the coming year with a memo she wrote to The Hollingsworth Group dated December 10, 1970. She summed up the uncertain climate at *Essence* this way:

When I joined ESSENCE magazine on April 15, 1970 as Editor-in-Chief, my first reaction was one of total awe. It was not only the greatest challenge of my life, but exceedingly gratifying to have the opportunity to participate in a venture I was certain would play an important role in elevating Black women to the level of excellence they so richly deserve.

I found Essence in deep trouble. Her infant heart, troubled by internal personal conflicts, could barely be heard. . . . Those summer months were the longest of my life . . . recognizing the task before me as Editor-in-Chief . . . I told myself Essence needs editorial 'spine,' which is not only in tune with current tastes and trends in the black community; but most of all, she needs to find her respectability in the Community. I strongly believe that goal has been accomplished. Internally, after some changes in personnel, we have found much peace.

Ida must have been talking about the kind of eerie peace that stills the waters just before a crashing tsunami rips through the surface, destroying everything in its path. Because in the next few months, as the magazine became convulsed by events both turbulent and embarrassing, I would sometimes think I should have taken Jonathan and Ida out when I first had the chance after that disrupted board meeting and then done what the Russians did to the czar and his whole family—shoot them in the head.

———

In the days immediately following the firing of Jonathan, Ida seemed to be holding more meetings than usual. Some with her staff. Others with people from other departments. I didn't pay much attention to this. Clarence had asked me to accompany him to Philadelphia to make a joint sales presentation to the Scott Paper Company, and I had started pulling some financial projections together for the pitch. With Jonathan gone, Clarence stepped up to become president of The Hollingsworth Group and national sales director.

Scott Paper was one of the giant manufacturers of durable goods and a natural advertiser, one would think, for the *Essence* market. Black women certainly used tissues, napkins, toilet paper, diapers, and every other paper product the company manufactured. Yet, like so many of the other "natural" manufacturers, Scott was not advertising in *Essence*. Much of Clarence and his sales staff's job in the early days of trying to sell to the black female market was to work on "breaking" resistant advertisers such as Scott Paper into the magazine.

The first issue of *Essence* had a scant 13 pages of advertising, but the second issue was even worse with a dismal 5 pages, and the next issue was up to only 9. It didn't help that we weren't making our print schedule and weren't on the newsstands in much of the key New York market because of distribution problems not of our making. But the majority of the advertising in the first issue of *Essence* were token ads taken out to placate the black social unrest still festering following the urban riots of the late 1960s. Advertisers were largely paying lip service to the idea of promoting black entrepreneurship by placing a few ads in *Essence,* but they didn't *really* recognize or respect the validity of the black female consumer market. They were either frightened by the prospect of angry boycotting blacks, or felt guilt-tripped into buying advertising in black media.

Even the advertisers who were a regular presence in *Essence*—the tobacco and liquor companies—represented a backhanded acknowledgment of the black American market. We couldn't sell advertisers on the idea of black women using toilet paper or napkins, but we didn't have any trouble selling them on the idea that black women drank and smoked.

Alcohol and tobacco use has always been disproportionately high in the black community, a reality reflected in the advertising of the first issue of *Essence*. The premium, most expensive advertising page positions in the magazine—the front inside cover and back cover—were both sold to cigarette advertisers, Kool and Virginia Slims respectively. In fact, these two advertisers bought a yearlong ad media schedule during our first year. It did help that *Essence* launched in 1970, the same year cigarette advertising was banned from television.

Because *Essence* was positioned as a black magazine, as well as a women's magazine, Clarence shrewdly also went after the one category of advertisers that typically never advertised in women's publications, the automotive industry. He knew that blacks have always been important to the new car market. So he was able to convince Detroit that while it might not consider the women's market to be important, the black consumer market was important, and the new car market among black families was dependent on black female *consent*. This meant if Detroit wanted to reach this important decision maker, the black woman, it had to advertise in media directed to her—*Essence*.

Still, the huge durable goods manufacturers such as Procter & Gamble, General Foods, Kellogg, and Scott Paper, along with the equally huge cosmetics industry, represented the lion's share of advertising dollars in women's magazines. If *Essence* was going to succeed in this marketplace, we had to get a share of *those* dollars.

While Clarence was pounding the pavement of Madison Avenue, working to sell ads to advertising agency media buyers, I became a fixture on the trade show circuit, working to meet the company decision makers who could tell the media buyers where to place their advertising. Since trade shows are the industry events where company presidents, vice presidents, and marketing directors socially convene to do business, I attended such shows looking to make business contact in a social setting with corporate top brass.

That is how I came to meet G. Willing Pepper, president and chief operating officer of Scott Paper Company. I don't remember the particular trade show, but I do remember "Wing" Pepper, as he was called. Personable and smart, he indeed possessed the "gift of sparkle," as a colleague said about him after his death in 2001 at age 92. When we met in early 1971, Wing seemed intrigued by the idea of a magazine for black women. He told me to have Clarence call his company, and he would see to it that we got a meeting with Scott's marketing people. Because I had facilitated the meeting, Clarence asked that I accompany him to the company's headquarters in Philadelphia. Also, in meetings like this, where Wing himself was likely to be on hand, my presence as his peer indicated just how important *Essence* considered the meeting to be. If the president and COO of Scott Paper was going be at the meeting, the publisher and CEO of *Essence* should be there as well.

Clarence and I took an early morning train to Philadelphia on a Friday, about two weeks after Jonathan had been let go. It was a two-hour trip, and I expected to be back in New York by early afternoon. I noticed that Ida seemed more preoccupied than usual—even somewhat distant.

But I was preoccupied myself, thinking about the trip to Philly. Getting Scott Paper to advertise in the magazine would be a real coup, the kind of break we could use as leverage to get P&G and General Foods into the magazine too.

Scott Paper Company's headquarters was actually closer to the Philadelphia airport than downtown Philly, which Clarence and I took a shuttle bus to get to. Located on a sprawling industrial campus in Delaware County's Tinicum Township, Scott Plaza, as the company site was called, comprised an impressive complex of corporate offices and warehouse facilities that occupied nearly 200,000 square feet of space and employed 1,200 people. Wing Pepper himself, along with two of his senior marketing people, greeted me and Clarence in the gleaming reception area of the headquarters building, then ushered us into a nearby conference room.

Clarence had just begun to outline the *Essence* market, giving figures on what percentage of our readers had children under the age of 5—a big demographic for tissues, paper towels, and disposable diapers—when the receptionist interrupted the meeting to say I had a phone call. "It's from your secretary in New York," she said apologetically, sticking her head in the door, "and it sounds important."

A bit annoyed, I excused myself. "Yes?" I said somewhat impatiently, taking the call from the phone on the receptionist's desk. "What is it?"

"I'm so sorry, Mr. Lewis," my secretary said in almost a whisper, "but I thought you should know. Miss Lewis just called a meeting of her editorial staff, and I heard her say something about forming a union. I'm not sure what's going on, but it doesn't sound good. People are talking about staging a walkout if anything happens to Miss Lewis."

What? I was stunned. I hadn't been gone from the office half a day, and Ida was talking about organizing some sort of workers' job action? *She's a dead woman,* I thought to myself. Returning to the conference room, I apologized to Wing and his people, saying an emergency back in New York required that I leave. I then said I needed to speak with my partner for a minute and asked Clarence to come out into the reception area with me.

"That call I just got from New York?" I said. "Seems like Ida is trying to organize a workers' union, and is calling for some sort of workers' strike. I've got to get back to the office and deal with her. You stay here and finish up the presentation."

"Yeah, yeah, sure," Clarence said, taken completely off guard by this piece of news. "I can handle the meeting. A workers' *union*? Jesus Christ. Go do what you got to do."

I knew I had to do what I should have done weeks ago. Fire Ida Lewis. I continued to be in touch with Marcia Gillespie after Ida fired her, probably because I knew firing Ida was inevitable. Just as I knew when that happened, I would bring Marcia back.

By the time I took the shuttle from Scott Plaza back to Philadelphia's 30th Street train station, then took the train back to New York's Pennsylvania Station and navigated Friday afternoon traffic across town by subway, I was doing a slow boil. When I got to the brownstone, I went straight to Ida's office and closed the door. "Just what do you think you're doing, Ida?" I said, standing over her as she sat at her desk, looking like the mouse that had just swallowed the canary. "You think I haven't heard you're planning a staff walkout if you don't get a workers' union? Now, I don't know what's going on in that cunning little head of yours, but you really leave me no choice. You're fired, Ida. I want you out of here. *Now*."

"Oh, Ed, I don't think you really want to do that," Ida said calmly. "If I go, my staff is prepared is to walk out with me. They're not going to sit here another minute and keep working for a mean man who fires people for no just cause."

"Oh, really?" I shot back. "Well, I'll show you how just mean I can be, because anybody who walks out with you is fired too."

Nonplussed, Ida stood up, opened her door, and went out into the editorial area. I couldn't hear what she was saying, but many on the staff started clearing off their desks while she was talking. These were some of the same people who had barged into the board meeting with her just a couple of weeks before. *The running lap dogs,* I thought. *Let them go.*

One of the editors, however, Sandra Satterwhite, had not been at the board meeting. Sandy was the most experienced of the editors in the department, having spent three years as an associate editor at *Redbook* magazine before coming to *Essence*. Although I knew she was close to Ida, I asked Sandy to stay, also knowing I would need a solid editor to keep the magazine going if too many on the editorial staff left with Ida.

Sandy declined to stay, but not without some soul-searching. "You know, working at *Essence* has never been just a job for me, Ed," she told me wistfully as I watched her pack up her desk. "It's been more like a mission on behalf of black women. And I've loved it. The intimacy of working in the brownstone with you and the other guys and all these other great black people. It's never felt like a job. I always felt like I was part of something really important. But Ida has been good to me, and I promised I would stand with her if she was forced to leave. And to tell you the truth, I also feel bad about Jonathan. The magazine *was* his idea, and now he's not even here. I feel bad for him."

One editor who did stay was Sharyn Skeeter, the fiction and poetry editor. So did Brenda Connor, Ida's secretary. Both women had held their own meeting with Ida to say they wanted no part of any plot by Ida to stage the coup of a job action. "We just wanted to do our jobs," Sharyn would say years later. And Sandy would say just as many years later that she continually asked herself over the decades if she did the right thing by choosing not to stay.

That Friday following the firing of Ida Lewis, half a dozen *Essence* staffers walked out with her: the art director, an associate editor, the fashion editor, the copywriter, the copy editor, and the production manager. The day came to be known in the history of *Essence* as the Friday Afternoon Massacre, because by Monday morning, when some of the dearly departed wanted their jobs back, I reiterated what I had said to Ida, "You're fired!"

Both Jonathan Blount and Ida Lewis were now gone—but not shot in the head. They would quickly rise again, taking a private fight public as their firings became fodder for a media circus that turned into a public relations horror show, starring Playboy's investment in *Essence* as the freakish villain.

CHAPTER 14

Getting Down

In the back of my mind I think I always knew Marcia Gillespie would be returning to *Essence*—I just didn't know when. Firing Ida Lewis answered that question. Within of a week of terminating Ida, I called Marcia to ask her to come back. Marcia was fired for insubordination, Ida said; Marcia said it was because she refused to make a last-minute change in the magazine ordered by Ida that would have caused us to be late getting on press.

"People hated me because I knew how to make the train run on time," Marcia said years later, talking about her ability to be a tough enforcer of deadlines—a quality I valued. No doubt about it, she was hard charging, straight shooting—and ambitious. Marcia had made it clear pretty early on that she thought *she* should be the editor-in-chief of *Essence,* and didn't try to hide her disdain for Ida. "I would have fired me, too, if I'd been in Ida's place," she admitted.

I don't recall when my professional relationship with Marcia turned personal—when business became romantic and attraction became sexual. I do remember it was Barbara Kerr, *Essence*'s executive editor, who first pulled my coat, saying, "You know, Marcia is attracted to you." I told Barbara I didn't believe her. "That's because you don't know women," she said.

That was very true. One thing I know about myself is that I can be a little bit naive when it comes to women. I may not be aware when women are attracted to me because my head is often just not there. I was so focused on running *Essence* that my primary concern regarding Marcia was that Ida had fired her. Now that Ida was gone, Marcia reiterated that the editor-in-chief's job should be hers. But selling that idea to the other two partners, Clarence and Cecil, was not going to be easy. They both had a say in who should be editor-in-chief, even if I did officially run the company.

First, Marcia was young—only 26. And she was brash, which she herself acknowledged. Her mouth had gotten her branded a troublemaker in her previous job as a researcher at Time-Life Books, where she had worked on an American history book series. Part of the series included a segment titled "The New Black Leaders," to which the venerable black historian John Hope Franklin served as adviser. Marcia was the only black person working on the research team, and part of her job was to do interviews in 1968 with black leaders as disparate as Jesse Jackson, Julian Bond, Harry Edwards, Ron Karenga, and Eldridge Cleaver. As she put it, "I got to meet all the boys."

The managing editor of *Life* exploded when he saw Cleaver's picture among the photos of the men deemed new black leaders. "What's that convicted felon doing here?" he said angrily, looking at the lineup during an editorial review.

Marcia fired back: "Regardless of what we may think about him, Eldridge Cleaver is a person considered to be a leader in the black community. He has an organization and a constituency. And do *you* get to say who our leaders are?" Marcia said later that she knew her chance of ever becoming "the black Brenda Starr" at Time-Life was pretty much over the minute she put that managing editor in check.

I happened to find Marcia's brashness somewhat appealing. She was clear and sure of herself, which I liked. I also found her physically attractive. She was a chestnut brown, curvy woman with nice legs, thighs, and posterior who got my attention. But Marcia's astounding intellect was the real turn-on for me. She grew up in Rockville Centre on Long Island, New York, and attended Lake Forest College, a rich little elite school outside Chicago, on a scholarship, graduating with a degree in American studies in 1966. Her ongoing interest in history was also appealing, since I've always thought of myself as something of a history buff. I found Marcia to be well-read, as well as a quick read who could get to the essence of a point very quickly. She was always thinking, always questioning: *What does it mean? What does it mean to be a woman? What does it mean to be a black woman?*

Personal feelings aside, though, my attraction to Marcia did not translate to my elevating her to the editor-in-chief position when she returned to *Essence* in the spring of 1971. Not only did the other partners feel she was too young to be editor-in-chief, Marcia had never even been an editor before coming to *Essence* just a few months before. She always said it was under the wonderful tutelage of Barbara Kerr that she learned her editing skills.

While Marcia kept pushing to be named editor-in-chief and I looked to find someone older and a little more experienced for the job, Jonathan Blount and Ida Lewis were still alive and kicking up what would turn out to be an embarrassing media firestorm over Playboy's $250,000 investment in *Essence*. On October 29, 1970, Bob Gutwillig, the Playboy vice president who served on *Essence's* board of directors, sent a memo to his boss Bob Preuss in Chicago, giving his assessment on the state of the magazine at that time. This is what he wrote:

I thought you'd be interested and pleased to know that yesterday John Hancock agreed to invest $265,000 in *Essence*.

I believe this will now be followed by substantial investments from General Motors, American Standard, the Franklin Corporation, other insurance companies, and possibly several more corporations.

As you know, all the original investors—except Playboy—have reinvested, and the Urban Coalition has also come back in a second time.

What this means is that the magazine will now have sufficient time and money to: 1) improve the basic product; 2) determine whether or not it is relevant to a substantial audience that is, in turn, meaningful to advertisers.

I am, of course, continuing to advise the *Essence* staff in the areas of my competence, and we continue to effectively dominate the Board of Directors with what now appears to be a solid coalition of five out of seven directors.

In short, it looks as if we'll get a damn good run for our money.

None of the partners, including Jonathan, who was still part of The Hollingsworth Group when Gutwillig wrote the memo, gave this document a second thought. Gutwillig's job was to keep the Playboy top brass apprised of what was happening at *Essence,* since $250,000 of their money was riding on the magazine. So the three remaining partners were completely blindsided when Jonathan and Ida called a press conference at the Overseas Press Club on May 5, 1971, to say they had been fired because they were trying to prevent Playboy from taking over *Essence!*

It was incomprehensible that the two of them would use a memo written seven months before to tell a monstrous lie. Yet there it was, a story appearing in the *New York Times* on May 6, 1971, written by veteran black journalist C. Gerald Fraser, which led with Jonathan accusing Playboy of trying to take over the magazine.

"The founder of *Essence,* a magazine published for black women, charged yesterday that *Playboy* was making a 'blatant' attempt to take over his magazine," the story began. It went on to say that when Jonathan asked the *Essence* board of directors to prevent the so-called takeover, he was dismissed. Clarence was quoted in the story calling Jonathan's allegations "a bunch of nonsense," which they were. But serious public relations damage was just starting to unfold.

Over the next few weeks Jonathan, who continued to refer to himself as the "founder" of *Essence,* not a cofounder, also continued to be quoted in both black and white media claiming that when he got hold of Gutwillig's memo, "Playboy ordered my removal." Jonathan passed out a copy of the memo at that first press conference, and the media picked up on the last two and most damaging-sounding sentences: "I [Gutwillig] am, of course, continuing to advise the *Essence* staff in the areas of my competence, and we [Playboy] continue effectively to dominate the board of directors with what now appears to be a solid coalition of five out of seven directors. In short, it looks as if we'll get a damn good run for our money."

Until that press conference the general public was not even aware of the $250,000 investment in *Essence* by Playboy. But once the story broke, hell followed suit. Could there be anything more loathsome than the idea of a white skin magazine trying to take over a black women's service magazine, and then firing the young brother, the *founder* of the magazine, for God's sake, when he tried to stop the assault? The historical and sexual implications were enormous. Talk of dominating the board of directors and "getting a good run for our money" smacked of two black American horrors: slavery and rape.

Everybody in black media circles and beyond, it seemed, had something to say about the Playboy attempt to "take over *Essence*." From cocktail parties to book parties, church sermons to sorority gatherings, black people were stunned and outraged, and given to endlessly discussing who *really* owned *Essence*. Never mind that Playboy's $250,000 represented an *investment*, not an *acquisition*, or that Hugh Hefner respected the black consumer market in ways that many of the white advertisers *Essence* was going after still did not. Never mind that the entire dismal episode was predicated on a blatant lie.

Unfortunately, *Essence* did not get in front of this incendiary issue with its own public relations spin to do effective damage control. We were caught with our drawers down, so to speak, exposed and thrown off guard by two disgruntled, fired executives who went out kicking, screaming, and fabricating. It would take years for the magazine to recover from this blowback, as many blacks continued to believe that *Essence* was really "owned" by Playboy at worst, or by some nonspecific white people at best.

Playboy sold its investment to Pioneer Capital, and Pioneer Capital in turn sold its interest in the magazine to Camille Cosby, who became a board director in 1986 and remained an *Essence* shareholder until the magazine was sold in 2005. After all was said and done, Playboy got a decent run for its money, though it did suffer some collateral public relations damage of its own in the wake of all the media flak over its *Essence* investment.

The Playboy episode was not the first time that *Essence*'s integrity as a black-owned business had been called into question by other blacks. This particular brand of scrutiny represents another "black tax" levied on black businesses and organizations by a black community demanding that its companies and institutions be all things to all black people. During the first year of the magazine's operation, Sonny Carson, then executive director of the Brooklyn branch of the Congress of Racial Equality, burst into the offices of *Essence* one night with his accomplice Lloyd Douglas, a Harlem activist. They said they wanted to make sure the magazine was going to be "relevant."

Carson was considered something of an outlaw type. A former gang member who had once stood trial for kidnapping and murder (he was acquitted), he opposed integration, despised black political moderates, and on the night he came to the office carried on as if he wanted to dictate *Essence*'s editorial. He told us the magazine needed to have more "militant articles." During the exchange, which got heated, Lloyd Douglas appeared as if he was going to make a move on Cecil, and I quickly stepped between them. "I'm from the Bronx just like you," I told Douglas, ready for a fight if he was. He backed off.

On another occasion a group of disgruntled black photographers literally stormed the office, angry that Gordon Parks was not giving them photo assignments. They said they were going to "liberate *Essence* from its bourgeois leaders." The partners were not in the office when the group barged in, but when we came back and saw they had trashed one of the offices and were still on the premises, a confrontation ensued. Jonathan walked up to one of the guys, slapped him across the face, then turned on his heel to walk away. Livid, the guy picked up a typewriter and was about to smash Jonathan over the head with it. I grabbed the guy from behind, putting him in an arm lock, which forced him to put the typewriter down. Perhaps if I'd been a little slower, my life would have been a lot easier, given the extent to which Jonathan would continue to be a problem in my life and the life of *Essence* for years to come.

———

Ida Lewis had backed the wrong horse in siding with Jonathan Blount. Her ouster followed his, which meant we were once again scrambling to find a new editor-in-chief for *Essence*. "Excuse me! I'd like to be considered," Marcia said repeatedly. I had already told her the partners thought she was too young and brash. She had made her views regarding all four of us pretty clear when she first came to the magazine. She thought Jonathan was full of himself and very egocentric. "I'm not impressed," she once said. She thought Cecil was "something of an enigma, but a very nice man—I just have no clue as to who he really is." Clarence, she said, "has the short man's syndrome. He doesn't like to be wrong, and I always feel like I'm being talked *at* when he talks to me." As for me, she said I was the one who was quiet, but also the easiest to communicate with. "Of the four partners, you at least listen," she said.

Marcia would prove to be prophetic in her assessments, though I wasn't listening to her demand to be promoted to editor-in-chief. That is, until she made two moves that caused me to me sit up, take notice, and finally give in. First, she put together an editorial mission statement outlining what she thought the breadth and scope of *Essence* should be. She wanted the magazine to speak to "strivers"—a term that Clarence Smith would take and run with in advertising pitches. *Essence* is for the "I *can* woman," the statement said. "Our core mission has to be inspiration, information and aspiration. Everything we do has to come back to one or all of those three things." This was the first time there had been a vision for the magazine articulated in writing, laying out a road map that would run true and sure.

The second move? Marcia simply packed up her desk one day and installed herself in the empty editor-in-chief's office. The editor-in-chief's workspace was one of the few real private offices, located in the back on the brownstone's ground-floor level. It had a door that could be closed and another door inside that led to a private outdoor garden area. While I was reaching out to women like Dorothy Gilliam, a writer at the *Washington Post*, to talk about becoming the next editor-in-chief, Marcia had commandeered the job by taking up a squatter's position at the editor's desk.

What could we partners say? Anybody as brash and bold as Marcia, and as on target as her editorial mission statement showed her to be, at least deserved a shot at the magazine's top editorial position. Besides, none of us guys was even trying to think about *removing* Marcia from "her" office by bringing in another editor to be over her. In the end, it's probably accurate to say that Marcia promoted herself to the editor-in-chief position at *Essence*.

My personal relationship with Marcia also gave her a degree of latitude that made such a move effective. Although I was dating Vicki Amos, a woman in Brooklyn (whom I learned years later had been the roommate of my second wife when they were students at Howard University), my most serious relationship at the time was with *Essence,* and Marcia was an integral part of that relationship. She herself was seeing a man she had dated in college who lived in another state.

I think Marcia basically viewed me as a good guy. I am not the type of man to dog women, so when our relationship turned personal, she knew she could trust me to be respectful and discreet. We were both single. We were both mature. And we both felt that having an intimate relationship would not prevent us from running the business, either in terms of her responsibility as editor-in-chief or my responsibility as publisher and CEO.

Our dates consisted of going to lovely dinner parties at her parents' home in Long Island. Sometimes we would take in a play produced by the Negro Ensemble Company, a popular live-theater company that launched the careers of actors such as Denzel Washington and Phylicia Rashad. We didn't publicly flaunt our relationship by going to places like the Cellar or Rust Brown's—two of the popular spots frequented by black professionals in the early 1970s.

Wherever we were, we endlessly talked—about the magazine business, about The Hollingsworth Group partners, about black women and men. It was a time of sweet passions and so many causes and agendas in the black community. I felt that working together actually enhanced the relationship. If I was going to be seeing someone at work, the editor-in-chief made the most sense, since it was more likely to be a relationship of equals based on us having so much in common around running the magazine.

Marcia once said she viewed our relationship as sort of a black counterpart to the romantic comedy *Woman of the Year*, the 1942 film starring Katharine Hepburn and Spencer Tracy, who portrayed a pair of reporters working at the same newspaper. In our case Marcia was the editor and I was the publisher at a black women's magazine, and Marcia thought "it could be really great to build an empire together."

The empire building did indeed begin under Marcia Gillespie's nine-year reign as *Essence* editor-in-chief. But within a year or so of our seeing each other we both concluded that in the long run continuing the relationship was not good for either of us. First, just from the standpoint of trying to manage a company, it could be problematic. I knew it created issues with respect to how other women felt. Second, I knew Clarence did not think it was a good idea for me to be seeing Marcia. He didn't especially like her—he had difficulties with women who were articulate. He had taken Marcia to lunch in the early days before the magazine launched, and when he told her the partners were thinking of calling the publication *Sapphire*, she told him in typically brash fashion, "I think you're out of your mind."

A few years after I had stopped seeing Marcia, I was having lunch at the Four Seasons restaurant with the venture capitalist Alan Patricof, founder and chairman of *New York* magazine. He first commented on the lack of beauty advertising in *Essence,* and when I told him, "It's because of racism," he steered the conversation to the black women working at *Essence,* many of whom were quite attractive. "My God, Ed, you must be fucking everything walking at *Essence,*" he said, "because Clay Felker sure is at *New York.*" Felker was a founder and at the time the editor of *New York* magazine. "You've got to be the Hugh Hefner of *Essence,*" Patricof concluded.

No, I wasn't. I did have one more personal relationship with a woman at work, but to me it never made sense to be involved with women inside the company when there were so many women outside the company to choose from. Besides, I still couldn't pull off the art of rapping or smooth talking women, even in my thirties. I was still shy, and never played on my position as publisher and CEO of *Essence* to attract women. I was more likely to not even mention it at all when I first met someone. I would just say I worked at the magazine because I wanted to have real interactions. I had already determined a woman would react to me differently if she knew I ran the magazine. I never wanted to use *that* as a playing card.

————

Marcia Gillespie's first issue as top editor of *Essence* was July 1971, though the partners didn't give her the editor-in-chief title until the August 1971 issue. She was listed as editor on the July masthead, positioned over the other editors and staff. Gordon Parks remained at the very top of the masthead right under the magazine's logo, as editorial director, though he had been long gone as a physical presence when Marcia took over. *Essence* still needed the cachet of Gordon's association with the magazine, even if it was literally in name only.

In short order, though, Marcia set an editorial course for *Essence* that took it from a magazine that had failed to meet its circulation projections at the end of its first year, to a publication that was touted as the "fastest growing women's magazine" in the industry by the end of the 1970s.

Like the *Essence* editors-in-chief before her, Marcia delivered the expected fashion and beauty features, service articles and celebrity interviews, home, and food and parenting information. There were also the unexpected features that made *Essence* distinct: a "Designer of the Month" spread that showcased a new black fashion designer in every issue; a dramatic black-and-white photo-essay of black women shot by distinguished black photographers such as Anthony Barboza, Roy DeCarava, Leroy Henderson, and Hugh Bell; a report on James Baldwin speaking with female inmates on Rikers Island that the magazine had arranged. Julianne Malveaux, the economist and former president of Bennett College, wrote her first mass magazine article for *Essence* as a young woman in her twenties. The bestselling author Terry McMillan became an *Essence* contributing editor long before she thought about waiting to exhale.

The *"Essence* Conversation," an editor-in-chief interview feature started by Ida Lewis and modeled on the *Playboy* Interview, continued under Marcia's editorship. Her first conversation in the July 1971 issue was with Jesse Jackson, who then headed the Southern Christian Leadership Conference's Operation Breadbasket program. The cover featured a striking black couple, nude from the breast up, regal with full Afros and full features. The cover line just beneath the photo read: "Rev. Jesse Jackson: 'Black men and women should have a oneness of respect.'" This cover and cover line in some ways was a harbinger of all the conversations about black male and female relationships that would rock black American culture into the new millennium. *Essence* was in the forefront of a new, sometimes combative dialogue between black men and women, and its editor-in-chief was leading the discussion.

Interestingly, the very things we partners thought would work against Marcia as editor-in-chief were actually assets: her youth and her passion. She in fact embodied the *Essence* Woman—young, educated, striving. And nowhere was Marcia's connection to the Essence Woman—the reader—more powerfully revealed than in her monthly editor-in-chief's column titled "Getting Down."

Unlike the typical editor-in-chief columns that characterized women's magazines in the 1970s when men were still running them and tended to use the editor's page only to talk about what was appearing in the magazine that month, "Getting Down" did exactly what it implied. It got personal and provocative on any number of subjects—sometimes painful, often helpful, and always illuminating. I would daresay that Marcia Gillespie was the first women's magazine editor who used her column as a platform from which to preach and protest.

In the tradition of the black abolitionist and journalist Frederick Douglass, whose mission was to agitate, agitate, agitate, or the black journalist and newspaper owner Ida B. Wells, who crusaded against lynching in the early twentieth century the way Harriett Tubman fought to liberate slaves in the 1800s, Marcia wrote on the cutting edge of a black perspective in order to educate and liberate. Her columns were often political, sometimes profound, and always intensely personal. The July 1975 "Getting Down" column began like this:

> When I was 16, I was in love with a guy who drove a pink Pontiac convertible. No, that's not quite correct—I was in love with a pink Pontiac convertible and the guy who drove it. In fact, I'm not really sure that I would have been nearly as infatuated as I was if he hadn't had that car. I can recall one my girlfriends describing why she dug a particular guy; her reasons were: "four wheels and a motor." Ok! We were 16, but those twisted values don't necessarily disappear as we get older.

The writing was good, honest, in your face—and readers loved it. In this same July 1975 issue, *Essence* launched a column called "Your Sexual Health," which featured readers' questions about sex and sexuality, answered by sex expert Joanne Tyson, Ph.D., coordinator of the Institute for Marriage Enrichment and Sexual Studies. Drs. William H. Masters and Virginia E. Johnson had aroused a generation with their landmark Masters and Johnson sex classics, *Human Sexual Response*, published in 1966, and *Human Sexual Inadequacy*, published in 1970. Both books were bestsellers, yet none of the more than 300 couples studied in the texts were black. Black sexuality was rarely discussed in the black community, let alone in larger American culture, so publishing a sexual health column in a black women's magazine was both daring and liberating.

There was some outcry from readers, but for the most part readers were pleased to see that *Essence* was taking on a subject that was still all but taboo. It was the first time a women's magazine talked openly and frankly about sex on a regular basis in a monthly column. As one reader in Los Angeles wrote in a "Letter to the Editor" after the first column appeared: "I, for one, did not realize how important sex really was to some

Black men until I met my fiancé. I think it is important for Black women to be able to have a source that could possibly help them in solving sexual problems."

One of our advertisers, however, did not agree. IBM was outraged that a column on sexuality was running in the magazine, and said it would not advertise as long as the column appeared. The partners took a stand and decided we were not going to roll over and let an advertiser dictate what the editorial content of *Essence* should be. Not that we could afford to lose a big advertiser like IBM—we couldn't. But neither could we afford to let an advertiser tell us what was right for our readers. The sexual health column remained. IBM walked. It would return as an advertiser a few years later when *Essence* was much too successful a magazine with a black female consumer market that was much too big to ignore.

Marcia's mix of beauty, fashion, service information, gutsy editorials, celebrity features, and hard-hitting political pieces caught on with black women whose growing numbers as readers began to prove the validity of the black female market our advertising department was trying to sell. By the end of *Essence*'s fiscal year, March 1974, *Essence*'s circulation was at 360,500, up from 200,000 the year before, and revenues were up by 52 percent. Advertising revenues increased by 41 percent, primarily because of a rate increase in March 1973. Subscriptions were up 44 percent, and subscription revenues increased by 66 percent.

New advertisers that Clarence Smith and his sales staff "broke" into the magazine in 1974 included Johnson & Johnson, Avon, Pillsbury, Posner's, Gillette, Rubbermaid, and United Airlines. Three years after its fourth editor-in-chief took over, *Essence* finally had the kind of smart, steady leadership and rich editorial mix that resulted in a growing circulation, making it possible to attract a growing number of new advertisers.

The magazine also had an editor-in-chief who would become a public personality wielding great personal power, much like Diana Vreeland, Helen Gurley Brown, and Lenore Hershey, the earlier doyennes of women's magazines whose names became synonymous with the publications they headed—*Vogue, Cosmopolitan,* and *Ladies' Home Journal* respectively. Marcia would not only help create *Essence* magazine, but in turn *be* created by *Essence* magazine. For better and for worse.

CHAPTER 15

Personal Power, Public Position

"Why don't you bitches *read*?" Marcia barked at her staff. She had just returned from a magazine luncheon and was now back in her office, chewing out the editors she had called in for some perceived shortcoming. Such outbursts were not uncommon. As an editor-in-chief Marcia Gillespie was often brilliant, but as a manager of people she could be arrogant and mean-spirited, even a bully at times. One associate editor at *Essence* in the early 1970s remembers Marcia saying something so nasty to her that a friend of Marcia's who had stopped by the office commented on it when she overheard the remark.

"Why are you talking to her like that?" the friend asked Marcia.

"Well, what's she going to do—where else is she going to go?" Marcia shot back.

This editor, who forty years later still sounds annoyed from the sting of that putdown, would in fact go on to become a senior editor at *Redbook* magazine, where she was quite successful, winning awards for the publication, despite being dismissed by Marcia a someone who had no career options beyond *Essence*.

For years *Essence* was the only national magazine directed at black women, and would inevitably be expected to be all things to all of them. This put enormous responsibility on its editor-in-chief. It also bestowed enormous power. The trouble with power, of course, is that it can corrupt. And the trouble with power in a top position is that there is sometimes confusion over what comes first: the position itself, which results in personal power; or personal power, which can lead to a top position.

Marcia Gillespie was a woman of great personal power, which led to her being named editor-in-chief of *Essence*. She was smart and articulate, could be witty and charming, and was always passionate, political, and demanding. I knew Marcia to be demanding because she viewed herself as smart—maybe smarter than most people—and could be quite disdainful of people she didn't think measured up intellectually.

This, coupled with Marcia's own brash personality, led to her tendency to be harsh and sometimes demeaning to her staff, the very women who resembled the *Essence* audience—the audience she affirmed, inspired, and celebrated every month in her role as editor-in-chief. Under Marcia's leadership *Essence* became the wise and sometimes tough-talking but loving big sister to a readership that started to identify with "their" magazine in a way white women reading *their* magazines seldom did.

Yet there was always a dichotomy between the public position of Marcia Gillespie as editor-in-chief to a publication loved by readers, and Marcia Gillespie the company boss who ruled with a heavy hand. This split between the "good face" a boss presents to the larger public and the tyrannical behavior he or she exhibits to a staff is not unusual in business. Hurt feelings at work are often collateral damage in running a business, as the award-winning actor Steve Carell deftly showed playing the insensitive, narcissistic boss on NBC's television hit comedy *The Office*.

But in a predominantly black office, a nasty remark, an unkind word, or a contemptuous attitude by a black boss reveals a double-edged sword that always cuts two ways.

Whether we admit it or not, most black entrepreneurs know our business enterprises are not always supported and even respected by blacks to the extent we would like. Many black consumers, given a choice between spending their dollars with a black-owned business or a white-owned business, choose to "buy white," believing that the white establishment is "better," and that a black business venture is somehow second best.

The inclination of blacks to buy white rather than support a black business offering similar services has been the bane of every black business owner trying to get a piece of the consumer pie in the American marketplace. It is another "black tax" that gets levied on black ventures. The truth is, white products, services, and institutions often *are* better than black ones. Superior monetary resources, greater brand recognition due to superior marketing capabilities, a larger consumer base—to say nothing of a 300-year head start in business by whites who were not enslaved in America for 300 years as blacks were—have all contributed to white businesses having the kind of market advantage that attracts black consumers to their goods and services in equal measure to white ones.

Given this, most black businesses are not started to *compete* with an existing white business. They are usually started to fill a void in the marketplace not being met by a white business. This is why the most successful black businesses tend to be ones geared to needs specific and germane to a black populace: black hair care and makeup products, for instance, or black media, with its emphasis on race-conscious information and affirming black images not found in mainstream media. Howard University is chosen over Harvard because of the supportive culture found in its black environment. Fashion Fair makeup is chosen over Revlon because it offers a greater choice of colors to complement the wide range of black skin tones.

Essence was started to affirm and inform black American women, who represented an untapped advertising market that none of the other women's service magazines recognized. Clarence Smith was great at selling this market to Madison Avenue, and Marcia Gillespie was just as terrific in building a fan base of loyal, devoted readers who would prove the existence of the very market Clarence was selling. These readers looked to *Essence* for not just the standard service information found in traditional women's magazines, but guidance, perspective—*an affirming way of being*—as black women coming into a new era of unprecedented opportunity.

Marcia's own way of managing as a black boss not only failed to affirm her staff, but at times even suggested the staff was perhaps "second best." She was notorious, for example, for not running a masthead in the magazine for months at a time. The masthead page lists the names and titles of the people who work for the magazine and matters to a magazine's staff the way a byline matters to a writer. Not running a masthead is equivalent to not giving any acting, directing, or production credits on a film. Marcia said the magazine saved money by not running a masthead page, but the result had the effect of devaluing the contributions of the staff by not granting the standard public recognition magazines give its employees. This failure to give recognition reflected the greater failure to give respect.

President Barack Obama and me at a 2013 Democratic
fund-raiser in the New York home of Harvey Weinstein.

Wedding to Carolyn Wright in 1991, with her daughters,
Nicole (*left*) and Haydn.

Photos are courtesy of Edward Lewis unless otherwise noted.

The four original *Essence* partners (*clockwise*) Jonathan Blount, Cecil Hollingsworth, Clarence Smith, and me.

My mother, Jewell Lewis Clarke; stepfather, George Clarke; and me at a disco to see Patti LaBelle perform.

My June 20, 1980, wedding to Michele Shay, with groomsmen Hughlyn Fierce and Erskine Perrone.

Me and my mother in the mid-eighties.

Me as an infant in 1940.

The launch party for *Latina* magazine in 1996 with (*left to right*) publisher Christy Haubegger; Clarence Smith; me; and Patricia Duarte, editor-in-chief.

Congresswoman Maxine Waters, the Rev. Jesse Jackson,
and me at the Essence Music Festival in 1997.

I received an award from Maxine Waters's women's political action group, which was presented by Camille Cosby in Los Angeles in the early nineties.

My graduation photo from DeWitt Clinton High School in 1958.

Clarence Smith, Earl Graves, Senator Carol Moseley Braun, and me at an
Essence reception to honor Braun in 1992. (photo courtesy of Gerald Peart)

I received an honorary doctorate
from Polytechnic University in
2003, given by David Chang,
the university's president.

I celebrated fifty years of friendship with my buddies from the
University of New Mexico in 2008. *Left to right:* Dr. Henry
Tobias, me, Steven Maurer, and Enrique Cortez.

Clarence Smith, Johnnie Cochran, and me
at the Essence Music Festival in 1997.

I met my future wife, Carolyn Wright, at the Men Who Cook fund-raiser in 1986.

Muhammad Ali received an award from TransAfrica in 2003. *Left to right:* Randall Robinson, executive director of TransAfrica, Ruby Dee, Angela Bassett, Danny Glover, Ali, and me. (photo courtesy of Solid Image Photographic Service, Ronald G. Baker)

Me, Suzanne de Passe, Ruby Dee, and Maya Angelou
at an awards program in 1985.

The Essence Music Festival circa 2005. *Left to right:*
Essence president, Michelle Ebanks, Rosie Perez, me, Lionel
Richie, George Wolfe, Macy Gray, and Terrence Howard.

Football coach Joseph "Doc" Weidman at DeWitt Clinton High School and me.

Me and my uncle Tracy Spencer. (photo courtesy of David Lee)

My daughter Nicole Wright and me with President Bill Clinton at Hillary Rodham Clinton's senatorial fundraiser on October 26, 1999 in New York City. (photo courtesy of Robert A. Cumins, Documentary Photographer)

Essence staff in the early seventies. Marcia Gillespie and Susan L. Taylor are in the front row on the right. Seated behind them are Clarence Smith, me, and Cecil Hollingsworth. Jim Forsythe is behind me and Cecil.

Me in the late sixties meeting with (*left to right*) Phil Smith of First National City Bank; Brady Keys, head of the All-Pro Chicken franchise; and Ed Glassmeyer, also of City Bank.

The Big Three in black publishing: John H. Johnson, publisher of *Ebony* and *Jet* magazines; Earl Graves, publisher of *Black Enterprise* magazine; and me.

The Hollingsworth Group partners reviewing the first issue of *Essence*.
From left: Cecil Hollingsworth, Clarence Smith, Ed Lewis, Cathy
Aldridge, promotion director, and Jonathan Blount, seated.

Now, this was not an attitude I ever fostered as the cofounder of a black business. If anything, I regretted not being in a position to compete when white magazines started hiring *Essence* employees with offers of better jobs and increased compensation—the surest indication that these employees were not considered second best by the competitors who were hiring them away.

Although I didn't agree with tactics that could demoralize *Essence* employees, neither did I interfere with my senior managers when it came to how they ran their departments. If I trusted you, that meant I trusted your judgment, and I'd let you be your own boss without trying to interject my own beliefs. The bottom line was this: I trusted Marcia's judgment because from a purely business standpoint she was a very successful editor-in-chief.

Essence became fully capitalized in 1974, three years after Marcia had assumed editorial leadership, helping to raise its circulation and ad rate base, attract investors, and give it status as one of the hottest publications in the women's service magazine field. Ironically, a large part of Marcia's success had to do with having talented editors working for her who bought into the mission of the magazine, choosing to stay with the company in spite of their boss's harsh management style because they, too, identified with the magazine and the audience. As one editor said, "What better place is there for a black female journalist to be than *Essence* magazine?"

Marcia clearly helped build *Essence*'s success, but the magazine in turn just as surely contributed to her own personal power and public success. She achieved high media visibility—becoming a black star in the predominantly white magazine publishing world and a leader in the African-American community—precisely because of her affiliation with *Essence,* the magazine that gave her the platform and the resources to build a national constituency. *Essence* bestowed similar status and power to every editor-in-chief that followed. Just as it did to all of us partners in The Hollingsworth Group.

However, the question of what comes first—the public position that leads to personal power, or the personal power that can elevate one to a public position—would test the very mettle of The Hollingsworth Group. How much is corporate status, celebrity, and opportunity a function of a position held, and how much a result of personal power? The answer was about to force the ouster of a second partner, leaving only two partners still standing.

———

We partners recognized from the very beginning that the success of *Essence* would give us all a certain cachet, putting us in a position to benefit personally because of our association with the magazine. That's why we also agreed from the beginning that if any of us ever had what we called "a corporate opportunity" to make money privately because of our *Essence* positions, a percentage of whatever he made would be shared with the company.

It was no secret that Cecil Hollingsworth, the most entrepreneurial of the partners, always had a side venture going. But when it came to my attention in 1974 that he was working on the sort of deal that would have had a great financial benefit, I approached him about it. He didn't confirm or deny anything, but he did make it clear that whatever profits he made with any separate venture on his own would be his alone.

"What I do outside of *Essence* has nothing to do with *Essence*," he said.

"That's not true," I said, reminding him of our agreement when the partnership was formed. "Why do you think you're approached in the first place with business offers? Because you're one of the *Essence* partners, that's why."

Cecil was convinced that it was his own personal power—his talent and savvy as a businessman—that led to others seeking him out to do deals, and he therefore didn't owe the company anything. I was just as convinced that without the public platform and visibility that his *Essence* partnership position gave him, there would be no business offers, thus a share of the profits was due.

I honestly don't remember the particular deal that Cecil was working on. Some say he and Don Cornelius, then host and producer of the hit television dance show *Soul Train*, were working to produce the program internationally. Don Cornelius had been quite helpful to *Essence* in our early days by bartering advertising: His *Soul Train* program would be advertised in *Essence*, while *Essence*, in exchange, would be advertised on *Soul Train*.

It was also rumored that Cecil was working on a television special in

Australia with Lorne Greene, star of the popular TV western *Bonanza*. Whatever the deal or deals, Cecil made it clear that *Essence* would not be getting a share of any financial gains from any of his ventures.

This to me was a serious breach. If Cecil had taken this hard-line position during our first year of operation, that would have been one thing. But by 1974, capital investment in *Essence* had reached the $2 million mark. From an investment standpoint, the magazine was now successful, though not yet turning a profit. We were known in the industry and in the African-American community. Popular media in any community is powerful. Surely Don Cornelius recognized the value of an *Essence* partner facilitating his television expansion. What black business wouldn't want an *Essence* principal affiliated with its enterprise? A principal who had access to hundreds of thousands of black women every month?

I've sometimes wondered whether *Essence* could have succeeded *without* the partnership of The Hollingsworth Group. Could any one of the four us have started the magazine on his own, independent of the other three, and made *Essence* the success it became? Good question. Hard to answer. I do know that the individual strengths Clarence Smith, Jonathan Blount, Cecil Hollingsworth, and I brought to the enterprise got us through the toughest of those early days. Clarence, Jonathan, and Cecil were all superior salesmen—whether selling ad pages, talking a star like Gordon Parks into joining our ranks, or stoking business contacts for everything from free technical advice to expanded office space. I was the banker who could raise money and manage the bottom line. The fact that we started a business as partners made us rare and unique as black entrepreneurs and no doubt accounted for much of our success. The fact that the magazine also survived and thrived long after the original partnership died spoke to the strength of the initial partnership foundation.

However, at some point individual partner goals may start to diverge from group partnership goals. One partner wants to sell, the others do not. One wants to go in the direction of A, while the others want to take route B. Individual egos can also start to clash, with one wanting to be the "star" of the enterprise or another wanting to break the rules. None of the four of us in The Hollingsworth Group were friends when we established the partnership—didn't even know each other, and at times didn't much like each other. It was actually pretty remarkable that we four young black businessmen managed to subsume our egos for as long as we did. Even Jonathan lasted two years before his ego got him ousted.

Now here was the ego of Cecil Hollingsworth refusing to share profits made as a result of his position at *Essence*. This was unacceptable, since acquiescing would have meant that any of the rules agreed upon by the partners could be broken at will. Jonathan had already tried that by refusing to recognize his demotion when I became publisher and CEO of the magazine. I felt that Cecil, like Jonathan, would have to leave *Essence* and the partnership if he didn't honor the corporate opportunity agreement.

However, Cecil was not going to leave voluntarily, and I did feel he deserved an opportunity to present his case to the *Essence* board. If the board agreed that he could keep any financial gain he made as a consequence of his affiliation with the magazine, then so be it. I would not try to go against that decision.

In the end, the board, which now included Marcia Gillespie, sided with me, voting unanimously to remove Cecil from the company and the partnership if he continued to refuse to show profits from his outside ventures. It wasn't as if Clarence and I expected to *personally* benefit, nor did we expect Cecil to share the majority of his profits. One-third seemed reasonable, and it would go to the company in which he was a partner. We felt it was unreasonable that he refused to share anything, especially since we had all agreed at the outset on the concept of sharing a corporate opportunity.

Like Jonathan, Cecil left the partnership with his 45,000 shares of *Essence* stock. He also took his name, effectively dissolving The Hollingsworth Group as the name of the partnership. The new corporate entity that emerged from the split was Essence Communications Inc. (ECI), and it would soon have a new corporate headquarters at 300 East 42nd Street before moving to its permanent headquarters, 1500 Broadway, in 1975.

Though Cecil Hollingsworth and Marcia Gillespie would both go on to have more personal and business success after leaving *Essence,* neither achieved the level of success their public positions at *Essence* afforded them.

James Mtume, a Grammy Award–winning jazz and R&B artist, once told a group of *Essence* senior editors that the reason the Rolling Stones continued to be a successful rock group long into their sixties was that nobody ever left the band. "Mick Jagger might have done a solo album every now and then," Mtume said, "but he never left his band." For more than forty years, Jagger and his three partners, Keith Richards, Charlie Watts, and Ron Wood, had managed to subsume egos, work out personal differences, and stay with the band, which is why they are still standing as legends of rock and roll.

The partnership among the band of four young black men who started a magazine for black women was not as resilient. In two years, the partnership of four was down to three; in less than five years it was down to two. Clarence Smith and I would continue the partnership for the next twenty-eight years. For the majority of that time Clarence and I recognized that whatever personal power we brought to ECI was enhanced in our public positions as partners. Together we were mightier than we were apart.

This was the conclusion Jonathan Blount, Cecil Hollingsworth, and Gordon Parks apparently also reached. Because three years after Cecil left, they would all come roaring back, united, ready to fight to take control of what they thought was rightfully theirs—*Essence.*

CHAPTER 16

Crunching Numbers
and Taking Stock

Of the three partners, Cecil Hollingsworth is the one I'd say I got along with best. He was smart and personable, the kind of man who was easy to hang with, whether having a drink or a conversation. He was also equal if not superior to Clarence Smith in sales ability.

Cecil Hollingsworth and Jonathan Blount, on the other hand, couldn't stand each other, which made their alliance a few years after they'd left the magazine a curious, questionable partnership that would turn into one of those backfiring deals made with the devil. Yet I'm sure in their mind *I* was the devil who had done the dirty deal of forcing them out of the partnership and the company. In their mind *I* was the partner who was mismanaging the company—never mind that *Essence* became fully capitalized in 1974 and would turn a profit in 1977.

Jonathan no doubt thought the company was being badly managed because he was no longer affiliated with it. Cecil felt betrayed by my hard-line stance insisting that he had to turn over a portion of the profits from his outside business ventures to The Hollingsworth Group. Both men considered themselves to be smarter, shrewder, and savvier than I—the calm, quiet one.

Now, I am never going to be the guy sitting at the bar bragging about his latest business deals, trying to impress any and every one. Nor am I likely to get rattled when the going gets tough or the tough try to get up in my face. I know there is strength in silence and circumspection.

Remaining calm allows one to focus and to think. Like many opponents who mistake these quieter virtues for weakness, Jonathan and Cecil would continue to underestimate my ability to prevail.

Though my friendship as well as my partnership with Cecil ended when he left *Essence,* the magazine will be forever indebted to him for hiring James Forsythe, the white circulation manager who came on board as his assistant. As circulation director, Cecil was never really interested in the details involved with crunching demographic numbers. His strength was working the newsstand wholesalers around the country, getting them to give *Essence* good positioning on the newsstands and on in-store magazine racks. He was the point man, the first one we sent out on the road to do the sales pitch on why a start-up magazine for black women should get prominent display space.

Positioning is important in newsstand sales because rack sales represent largely "impulse buys." A magazine, with its cover and cover lines, has to grab a reader's attention instantly. And where it's displayed on a magazine rack can mean the difference between the publication being seen immediately or being lost in a sea of other magazines. The closer a magazine is to eye level, to the front of the rack, or to where store traffic is heaviest is likely to have a positive impact on newsstand sales.

Jim Forsythe, who would replace Cecil as vice president of circulation, came to *Essence* from *Look* magazine, the giant pictorial publication where he had worked in circulation analysis. He would bring the same talent to analyzing *Essence* numbers and demographics that Cecil brought to positioning *Essence* on magazine stands. Jim joined *Essence* in 1972 at age 27, coming from Des Moines, Iowa, where *Look* was based. He lost his job when the magazine folded that year.

Big, tall, and sandy-haired, Jim had an easy, affable manner and spoke in the flat-note twang of the Midwest. He was offered a job as an auditor with the Singer sewing machine company around the same time he received the *Essence* job offer. Initially he thought taking the *Essence* position over Singer would be "ridiculous," he said, because he didn't expect *Essence* to be around another six months when he came on board. *Essence* was in New York, however, and "that was too attractive for a guy like me coming from Des Moines to turn down," he would recall forty years later.

Essence's circulation at the end of its first fiscal year was less than

100,000—63,000 from newsstand sales and 15,000 from subscriptions. By 1972, when Jim joined the magazine, total circulation had reached 125,000, up only 25,000 from the very first issue of the magazine, which had sold 100,000 copies. The drop in sales between the first issue of the magazine and its sales at the end of the 1971 fiscal year reflected the fight between our newsstand wholesaler and our newsstand distributor, which kept *Essence* off newsstands in the New York metropolitan area for much of 1970.

In looking at the demographics for the readers *Essence* wanted to reach, Jim learned this unexpected truth: The majority of black women do not buy magazines from freestanding newsstands, because outside of major urban areas such stands don't really exist. Most magazines are bought off the magazine racks in stores—in major supermarket chains like Safeway, convenience stores like 7-Eleven, or the superstore retailers like Walmart. The key to reaching black women would be finding the stores with a heavy concentration of black traffic and pushing for the magazine to be carried in those outlets.

Circulation runs on the twin engines of newsstand sales and subscriptions. To be successful with its circulation, a magazine must find the winning balance between the two: the number of people who buy the magazine on a newsstand rack, versus the number of readers who pay for an ongoing subscription to the magazine. Subscribers are usually considered the more desirable readers. They have paid up front for the magazine, which suggests a loyalty to the publication and a buy-in of the brand. They are also easier to identify and measure, giving a clearer picture of the specific demographic your market represents.

Yet newsstand sales also yield vital information about a market: Where is it concentrated? What kind of magazine subjects and covers grab the attention of readers passing by a newsstand or a store magazine rack? Is there a season of the year that magazine sales do better than at other times of the year? These can all be measured by newsstand sales.

Cecil and Jim built *Essence*'s circulation by first coming up with a formula to assess where it made sense to push the magazine on stands, and the rule of thumb was this: If a store outlet or newsstand did not get traffic that was at least 10 to 20 percent black, *Essence* would not be placed in that outlet. They considered it a waste of time and money, since the magazine was less likely to sell in outlets that had little black traffic.

Outside of large urban areas such as New York, Chicago, and Los Angeles, the largest overall concentration of blacks was the South, making it the most important regional market for *Essence,* and this led to what became known as our "southern strategy" in newsstand marketing. Cecil, who was the salesman on the road pitching *Essence* to white wholesalers in the South, had to first persuade this reluctant group to distribute a little magazine for black women to their retail customers, then persuade the retail customers—the store owners—to give the magazine prominent positioning on their display racks.

This was no easy task among southern wholesalers and retailers who had even less interest in a "black female market" than the advertisers did on Madison Avenue. By now, though, thanks to Marcia Gillespie's leadership on the editorial side, *Essence* had a growing readership that Cecil knew would translate into heavy sales in the South. He practically guaranteed the wholesalers and retailers that if a store's black traffic was 25 percent or more, *Essence* would outsell *any* other magazine on the racks. This was the southern strategy, and it worked. Time and time again *Essence* outsold other magazines in stores throughout the South where black customer traffic exceeded 25 percent. It would be economically unwise for distributors *not* to carry *Essence.*

As the analyst crunching the numbers, Jim Forsythe soon realized that *Essence* was never going to be a major newsstand publication because no market had a high enough concentration of black women. To reach critical mass in circulation the magazine would have to be subscriber driven. "This is the rough truth," Jim would say. The readers that *Essence* was going after—the well-educated, well-employed black female strivers with money to spend and aspirations to achieve—were just as likely to be in Seattle or Cincinnati or Houston or Denver as in urban big cities. And the key to building circulation among this group would be through subscriptions.

Direct mail subscription drives became the engine fueling most of *Essence*'s circulation growth in the early 1970s, with the biggest direct mail campaign undertaken in 1973 when *Essence* did a mail blitz to 1.3 million potential subscribers. Subscription cards placed in black magazines and other outlets such as black hair care packages were used to target desired readers. The campaign yielded a 4 percent response rate, which is *huge* in the magazine industry, where most direct mail promotions average about a 1.5 percent return. A 4 percent response rate on a mailing of 1.3 million translated into 52,000 potential new subscriber readers.

Jim was terrific at analyzing exactly who these readers were. Using census tract information, zip code overlays, and block group markers, he could identify how many black households were on one side of a street; what the occupants did for a living, their income, education level, number of children, and seemingly endless other data critical to targeting the kind of audience *Essence* wanted as subscribers.

The winning circulation balance for *Essence* turned out to be a 75/25 ratio of subscriptions to newsstand sales, meaning that three-fourths of its circulation needed to come from subscriptions and the remaining quarter from newsstand and retail store sales for the magazine to maximize its circulation numbers. This was a complete reversal of the 63,000 newsstand sales to 15,000 subscriptions ratio existing at the end of *Essence*'s first year of operation. By the end of its first decade, *Essence* was not only the fastest-growing women's publication in the magazine industry, it also had the highest market penetration of any women's magazine geared to a niche audience. And by the time the magazine was sold in 2005, circulation had been holding steady at over one million for more than a decade.

Yet for all of Jim Forsythe's skill in building circulation, and all of Clarence Smith's talent in selling advertising, and all of Marcia Gillespie's vision in creating a product that Jim and Clarence could sell, in the spring of 1977 *Essence* took on a stock fight in which all of this would be at stake—and in danger of tumbling down.

It never occurred to us when The Hollingsworth Group was formed that the 45,000 shares of stock issued to the four of us partners would one day be at the center of bitter fights for control of the magazine. At the time the 180,000 shares were issued, *Essence* stock had a floor value of one cent a share, making the partner holdings worth all of $450 apiece. Over the years, however, the value of the stock would increase as the magazine grew in circulation, advertising, and equity investments.

As a privately held company, *Essence* stock valuations were not based on public trading, but on the assessments of independent accounting firms that measured the magazine's present earnings, growth, and future earnings potential. In 1974 when *Essence* became fully capitalized, the magazine had raised $2 million in total equity investments—including that first $25,000 we borrowed from the four Shearson partners and Freedom National Bank; the $130,000 we raised to launch the magazine, another $167,000 we had borrowed from First National City Bank in the first three months of the magazine's operation, and the $250,000 Playboy investment that came later in 1970.

By 1974, new investors such as John Hancock had come into the magazine, and previous ones such as Chase and Pioneer Capital had reinvested. Chase, for example, after almost reneging on the $50,000 it had pledged to help launch the magazine, would continue to invest, raising its total equity stake to $450,000. Pioneer Capital also returned to the investor table, buying out Playboy's stake. Playboy was the only early investor that did not reinvest, spooked by the public relations scandal that erupted when Jonathan Blount and Ida Lewis charged that Hugh Hefner was trying to take control of *Essence*.

Once *Essence* became fully capitalized, we were now self-sustaining from the revenues generated by advertising and circulation sales and equity investors. Even before the magazine became fully capitalized, the partners created an opportunity for our employees to share in the company's growth with a stock compensation plan. Set up in 1973, the plan offered employees 500 to 1,800 shares of Essence Class A voting stock, entitling them to vote for two-thirds of the *Essence* board of directors. An employee had to have been with the company at least two years before being eligible for stock, and Essence Communications Inc. had the right of first refusal if any employee wanted to sell his or her stock shares.

Essence investors were also shareholders, but they were issued Class B stock, which entitled them to vote for one-third of the *Essence* board. Class A stock gave shareholders the control position, and this would take on great significance in the coming years, since virtually every fight that ensued at *Essence* during the thirty-five years leading up to its sale would be about the power—and the right—to control the magazine.

I must say, that first stock fight for control took me completely by surprise. The notice came on Friday, April 15, 1977, a day for me that still lives on in its own infamy. Jim Forsythe and I were in my office going over the newsstand figures for the February issue. Circulation was continuing to grow, ad sales were up, and if we stayed the course I was projecting we might turn an actual profit by the end of the 1977 fiscal year. We did. *Essence* earned $177,000 in net income that year. For a magazine whose middle name could easily have been "struggle," that first profit was very sweet indeed.

Almost from the beginning, a number of our investors had been pushing me to "just sell the magazine." New magazines typically run a five-year course before they show anything resembling a profit, but some of our investors were impatient. They felt *Essence* was taking too long to make money, and just wanted to get out with whatever gain there was to be had. Fortunately, they couldn't win in a vote on this, and I wasn't about to budge on this. I didn't sign on to run a magazine only to be forced off the track before it had a chance to show what it could do once it got up to full speed.

The day Jim and I were in my office going over the newsstand numbers, my secretary walked in with a package for me to sign for that had just been given to her by a messenger. It was from the law firm of Debevoise & Plimpton, one of the most prestigious international law firms in the city, if not the country. "Wonder what this is," I muttered to Jim, puzzled, as I opened the package. Inside was a letter signed by one of the firm's partners, along with thick pages of legal documents. The letter stated Debevoise & Plimpton represented Jonathan Blount, Cecil Hollingsworth, Gordon Parks, and Oscar Tang, whose aggregate shares of *Essence* stock now gave them control of the company.

What the hell . . . ? I quickly showed the letter to Jim, before hurrying down the hall to Clarence's office. "Mr. Smith is not in," his secretary said. "He's out with Gordon Parks, playing tennis, but I expect him to call in shortly for any messages."

"Tell him he needs to call me right away," I said, not really hearing what she had just told me. I then added, "On second thought, tell Mr. Smith he needs to get back to the office *right now*." I went back to my office and called Suzanne Warshavsky, the young lawyer who had started out as an associate for the law firm that once represented The Hollingsworth Group. Suzanne now headed her own firm, Warshavsky, Hoffman & Cohen, and was Essence Communications Inc.'s legal counsel.

"Suzanne, I don't know what's going on, but I just got a hand-delivered package from Debevoise & Plimpton, saying they represent Jonathan and Cecil and Gordon and Oscar Tang, who have enough shares to take over *Essence*."

"What about Clarence?" Suzanne asked. "Did he get a similar letter?"

"I don't know. I doubt it. He's not in. In fact, I was told he's out playing tennis with Gordon!"

"All right," Suzanne said calmly. "I know the partners allowed Gordon to acquire 3,750 shares of *Essence* stock as part of his compensation when he was editorial director—"

"So what do you think this about? I interrupted.

"Without seeing the documents, I can't say exactly," Suzanne answered. "My guess is, Jonathan and Cecil are planning to mount a proxy fight, and with Gordon's shares, they feel they have enough shares to control the company. But I don't know how *Oscar Tang* fits in."

That name threw us both. Gordon was once married to Genevieve (Gene) Young, his third wife, who was the sister of Oscar Tang's wife, Frances Young. Gordon and Gene divorced, but Gordon and Tang remained close long after they were no longer brothers-in-law. Now it looked as if Gordon had persuaded Tang to join him, along with Jonathan and Cecil, in a fight for control of *Essence*. Oh, my. I knew Oscar Tang could be a formidable adversary.

Tang came from money as old as China's dynasties. Having fled his home country in 1949 with his parents when the Communist Party came to power and overthrew China's moneyed ruling class, Tang arrived in New York at age 11. He attended elite Phillips Academy, graduated Yale undergraduate school and the Harvard Business School, then amassed *billions* as an investment banker heading his own firm.

We soon enough discovered how Tang fit into a looming fight for control: He had bought 15,000 shares of *Essence* stock from one of our investors, John Hancock Life Insurance, following a dispute I'd had with one of Hancock's officers. I couldn't believe it! Jonathan Blount was *back*—this time with his revered Gordon Parks in tow, who brought along his deep-pockets favorite ex-brother-in-law. The group would be going after control of the company by either buying stock or getting proxies of employees and investors.

Suzanne suggested we meet at my apartment later that afternoon. She also advised me to invite three of our outside board members to the meeting: Michael Victory, our original board member and still supportive champion; Fred Brown, a lawyer who had been with the Goldman Sachs investment firm; and Harriet Michel, who was then executive director of the New York Foundation, and the first black woman to head a major foundation. Since we didn't know what *Essence* employees or investors might have already been approached by Jonathan Blount et al. to turn over their proxies or sell their stock, we thought it best to meet outside the office, away from prying eyes and ears.

For the life of me, I could never figure out why Cecil would join forces with Jonathan to try to take over *Essence*. I knew Jonathan pretty much despised me; but I also knew Cecil pretty much felt the same way about Jonathan. I can only surmise that both men never got over being booted from the partnership. Jonathan always claimed the idea for the magazine was his, and felt it had actually been stolen from him when he was fired and voted out of the company. Cecil was not used to losing out on his business deals, and *Essence* represented the biggest of the deals he had lost out on.

I learned years later that *Essence* meant more to Gordon Parks than any other undertaking in his long and illustrious career, which he may not have even realized until he was no longer with the magazine. He probably wanted back in more out of sentiment than ego, though I'm sure Jonathan's stroking of Gordon's ego didn't hurt in persuading him to fight to come back as an owner of the magazine. As for Oscar Tang, whose pockets were as deep as the Yangtze River, *Essence* was most likely just an interesting investment that his beloved brother-in-law was down with, so he would be down with it too, even if it meant paying hefty costs to mount a protracted legal battle. That was beside the point, since he could afford it.

I myself was so pissed that these guys were trying to take over the company after all these years that I broke out in hives the afternoon I received the notice from Debevoise & Plimpton—just as I sometimes did when I got stressed playing football back in college. Clarence was also stressing me out that afternoon. *Where is he?* I kept wondering. We didn't have cell phones in those days. He hadn't called in; he hadn't returned to the office, and by the time I left my office at 3:00 to meet with Suzanne, there was still no word from him.

He showed up at my apartment later that evening, flushed and agitated. "What the hell is going on?" he wanted to know. Clarence said Gordon had called him earlier that morning, inviting him out for a game of tennis. Gordon took him to lunch after the game and then invited him back to his apartment in the luxury United Nations Plaza building, where Jonathan and Cecil were waiting. They were later joined by Oscar Tang. It soon enough became clear that they were gathered to coax Clarence into throwing his stock in with theirs.

"Whoa, let's hold on a minute," Clarence told them, looking at the documents that had been drawn up and placed before him for his signature. "I need to speak with my partner about this. Let me talk to Ed."

That was the game changer. I don't know what Jonathan and the others said to Clarence; what they promised him or what they told him about me. I only know if he had thrown his stock in with theirs it would have given them control of *Essence,* and I would have been out. Clarence held the winning hand with his 45,000 shares, and he chose to play it with me, his partner. For that I will be forever grateful.

Even so, Essence Communications Inc. would spend the next two years fighting Jonathan, Cecil, Gordon, and Oscar Tang in court and out of court, filing motions and countermotions; both sides rounding up proxies from employees. The Sunday after receiving that Friday notice from Debevoise & Plimpton, I was on a plane to Chicago to secure the proxy of Tom Rivers, head of our Midwest sales office, who held about 1,200 shares of employee stock.

Jim Forsythe was later approached by Cecil to pledge his stock to him and Jonathan, but Jim refused the minute he heard Jonathan was involved. Even after I had fired him, Jonathan would periodically show up at the office, pretending to still be with the company. On one such occasion he stormed into Jim's office and told him he was fired because he wasn't showing Jonathan proper respect.

I once held a private one-on-one meeting with Oscar Tang during the escalating and costly court battle to see if we could resolve the matter without further financial bloodletting. He looked at me and said, "You do not know the Chinese. We dig in, and we are patient. You have met your match."

"You do not know *me,*" I calmly told him. "You have met *your* match."

We fought on. Somewhere along the way Tang and the gang changed law firms, bringing in the bigger guns, Mudge Rose Guthrie Alexander & Ferdon, Richard Nixon's old law firm. I was urged by Clarence to do the same—to bring in a big white-shoe legal firm to replace Suzanne Warshavsky—which I refused to do. Clarence and others in the company could be sexist. But like me, Suzanne was often underestimated. People didn't realize she was a gunfighter, a street-smart, tough little Jewish pistol who had gone to Barnard College as an undergraduate, and New York University's law school, graduating in the same class as Rudolph Giuliani, another New York City gunfighter.

Suzanne could outwork and outthink the best of them, and that's exactly what she did in terms of crafting a response to every motion that was thrown at her by the other side. It turned out that a number of the shares Tang purchased from employees were not legal because Essence Communications Inc. had not been granted its right of first refusal.

Finally, in 1979 the court ruled that the plaintiffs did not have enough shares to take control of *Essence*. I still had the support and proxies of key shareholders in the company, including Clarence Smith, Marcia Gillespie, and Jim Forsythe. Oscar Tang, Gordon, and Cecil eventually sold their shares to Bancap and MECCO, two minority enterprise investment companies.

But the fight took a financial and emotional toll. Legal costs ran about $250,000, and *Essence* didn't turn another profit until 1979, two years after the first one in 1977. Plus, I occasionally had my own meltdowns. I remember being out with my former banking buddies, Hughlyn Fierce and Frank Savage, the day after I'd received the letter from Debevoise & Plimpton. Hugh was now CEO of Freedom National Bank and Frank was a vice president at the Equitable Insurance Company. We were standing at the curb of Lexington Avenue and 41st Street when a taxi brushed by us. In a flash of fury I punched the taxi's trunk—that's how angry I was with Jonathan and Gordon and Cecil.

At that moment I knew exactly how it felt to be Ratso Rizzo, the crippled loser character played by Dustin Hoffman in *Midnight Cowboy*, who pounded a taxi's hood while crossing in front of it, yelling, "Hey, I'm walkin' here!" Jim Forsythe would tell me later that the first weekend of the takeover fight was my finest leadership hour as I quickly moved to secure proxies and mount a counterattack, while appearing to be cool. Truthfully, I was identifying more with Ratso Rizzo than John Shaft.

Still, once again I prevailed over Jonathan Blount. His partners Cecil Hollingsworth and Gordon Parks had retreated, leaving him alone on the battlefield. As *Essence* moved into the next two and a half decades, marked by a long, uninterrupted era of great expansion and enlightened editorial leadership, there would be a new stock fight and battle for control of *Essence* by a new, unexpected outside force.

And like a run of bad luck, there would still be Jonathan Blount, who continued to spring from the bushes, in attack mode, refusing to concede defeat, or give up the ghost.

PART IV

Getting Over

(1980–2005)

CHAPTER 17

Moving On

Marcia Gillespie resigned as editor-in-chief of *Essence* in 1980 at age 35, leaving the magazine at the top of her game. She needed to move on, she said; she was burned out and wanted to pursue other interests. During her nearly ten-year run she had become something of a celebrity in her own right—a popular speaker on the lecture circuit and a respected leader in the magazine industry. In 1976, under Marcia's editorship, *Essence* won a prestigious National Magazine Award, presented by the American Society of Magazine Editors.

The award is the equivalent of an Oscar in the industry, and *Essence* won in the fiction category for the short story "Isom," an epic 10,000-word family saga written by Hortense Spillers, a professor of black studies at the University of Nebraska. A few years after leaving *Essence*, Marcia would receive the prestigious Matrix Award from the powerful New York Women in Communications organization for outstanding leadership in magazine media, and *Time* magazine would name her One of Fifty Faces for America's Future.

Essence's circulation had reached 600,000 by the time Marcia left—up more than half a million from the less than 100,000 in circ at the end of *Essence*'s first year of operation. This rate of growth made *Essence* the fastest-growing women's service magazine during the 1970s, an achievement that would not be duplicated by any other *Essence* editor-in-chief who followed, since no magazine sustains this kind of growth indefinitely. By the dawn of the '80s *Essence* had clearly found its niche, becoming successful financially, and respected and popular among both the black women it served and the industry of which it was a part.

I knew Marcia felt she could find a larger career platform once she left *Essence,* maybe run a major white women's magazine. She did, in fact, become editor-in-chief of the feminist magazine *Ms.* in 1993, a position she held until 2001. And this did make her the first black woman to run a white women's magazine. Yet *Ms.* never achieved the large circulation numbers, financial success, or award-winning stature of *Essence.* It was never as "major" in the magazine industry as *Essence* had become. Another decade would have to pass before black women started being named to top editorial positions at large, white mainstream publications.

Although I was sorry to see Marcia go, I'd have to now say in retrospect it was probably a good thing, because it paved the way for Susan L. Taylor, the woman whose editorial leadership would bring *Essence* stunning popular success for the next nineteen years. Marcia told me to keep an eye on Susan as a possible editor-in-chief even before she had decided to make her own exit. But Marcia didn't recommend Susan for the job when she left. Her recommendation was Daryl Royster Alexander, *Essence'*s editor, the number two position.

Daryl, originally from Minneapolis, had done two stints at *Essence.* The first was when she came to *Essence* from *Mademoiselle* magazine in 1974 as an associate editor. She had worked as an assistant in the art department at *Mademoiselle* after graduating from the University of Minnesota in 1969 with a degree in journalism. When a copywriting position at *Mademoiselle* opened up, she took the writing test required for the job, but didn't get the job, despite learning that she had performed better on the test than any of the other applicants. She was told she didn't have the experience to be a copywriter.

Recognizing that her chances for career advancement as a young black woman were probably limited at imperial Condé Nast, the parent company of *Mademoiselle*, Daryl decided it was time to look for another job. She wasn't really familiar with *Essence,* she admitted years later, making her perhaps one of the few black women in the early 1970s with a degree in journalism who weren't tuned in to a magazine for black women. It was Daryl's husband, Rodney Alexander, who suggested she consider *Essence* as an employment possibility. I had met Rodney when he interviewed me for a project he was doing while working for the Council on Economic Priorities. Daryl heard about a position at *Essence,* applied for it, and then heard from Marcia, who hired her.

Daryl left *Essence* for the first time in 1976 when Rodney took a position in Atlanta to help establish Morehouse College's medical school. He and Daryl lived in Atlanta a year and a half, during which time Daryl remained in touch with Marcia and accepted some freelance assignments. The couple returned to New York in 1978, and Daryl rejoined the magazine as managing editor. When Sheila Younge, *Essence*'s much loved and highly respected executive editor, died after many years of battling cancer, Daryl was promoted to her position, and then became the magazine's editor, the newly created number two spot.

I pretty much kept out of the decision making for Marcia Gillespie's replacement, leaving the selection up to her. Though I would have final approval on any editor-in-chief, I trusted Marcia's judgment regarding who she thought would be best to follow her. Daryl made sense as the successor for several reasons. First, she was smart and attractive, had worked her way up the *Essence* ladder, understood the mission of the magazine, and proved to be skilled at general organizing and managing copy flow.

Daryl was also the first editor-in-chief who was married and a young mother, having given birth to her son in 1979. She reflected our ideal demographic. Once *Essence* was up and running in the black, I made it a point to ensure that new mothers like Daryl had *paid* maternity leave for up to four months. "It was extraordinary to have that kind of support as a young mother," Daryl would recall thirty-three years later. "I was quite grateful."

Though Daryl seemed more than capable of leading *Essence* as its editor-in-chief, it wasn't long before there were signs that the magazine was headed for trouble. Circulation director Jim Forsythe was the one who sounded the alarm. Newsstand sales were down, he told me a few months into Daryl's tenure. So were renewals from subscribers. Subscription renewals are critical to keeping circulation up. If you have a satisfied subscriber, getting her to renew a second or third time is just easier. This is the reader you no longer have to entice with discounted subscription rates; she will pay the full subscription price for the magazine, which is key to making circulation profitable.

I remember *The New Yorker* magazine being the envy of the entire magazine industry during the 1970s because its renewal rates reached as high as 80 percent. A perennial National Magazine Award winner, *The New Yorker* never had huge newsstand circulation, but its subscriber base was loyal and devoted, and constituted an intellectually curious, well-educated, and high-income demographic that is the dream of every editor and publisher. High renewals means the magazine is delivering exactly what the reader wants.

A drop in renewals indicates just the opposite. More disturbing than a drop in renewals is what's known in circulation as "request cancel." Subscribers are desirable readers because they take the time to fill out a subscription card, send it in, and then follow up by sending payment. If a subscriber is particularly unhappy with the magazine, she may take even more time to call or write to ask that her subscription be canceled before it expires. A few request cancels is not uncommon or particularly alarming in magazine circulation, but when they start to increase, as they did under Daryl, it is cause for concern.

Essence in many ways during Daryl's tenure was more literary than it had ever been. Fiction continued to be stellar. Profiles of women as varied as Harlem Renaissance writer Zora Neale Hurston and Chicago U.S. congresswoman Cardiss Collins, a labor story on domestic workers, and a personal essay about the black expatriate experience were the kind of articles that gave *Essence* an intellectual heft that had always set it apart from other women's magazines. Daryl's first issue as editor-in-chief, June 1980, ran a lengthy book excerpt titled "Family Heroes" from basketball player Bill Russell's 1979 memoir, *Second Wind: The Memoirs of an Opinionated Man.*

The July magazine was a special issue on Africa, featuring the Somalian model Iman on the cover, who showcased Africa-inspired attire on the inside in an eight-page fashion spread. The location was Jamaica, though, not Africa. In retrospect, this wasn't the best idea, but the thinking then was justified by Jamaica being touted as the Caribbean region most like the regions of Africa most familiar to black Americans. Food, beauty, and home décor features in that issue all had an African theme. Rounding out the issue was a critical piece on the Ugandan dictator Idi Amin, reprinted from a story written by Les Payne, a black Pulitzer Prize–winning journalist, editor, and columnist at the Long Island newspaper *Newsday.*

Diana Ross was the surprise December 1980 cover, marking the first time the Supremes star had appeared in the magazine. Like Iman, she was the featured model on the inside pages in a ten-page fashion spread titled "In the Spirit." Though landing Ross as a cover and fashion feature was something of a coup, by December it was clear that *Essence* was not resonating with readers as it had with Marcia. While *Essence* never lost circulation during its thirty-five years as a black-owned publication, the rate of request cancellations started to spike under Daryl, along with the number of nonpayers—people who simply don't pay for the magazine after taking out a subscription. If either of these trends continued, declining circulation was sure to follow. I would have to take action before that happened.

Fair or not, the buck stops with the editor-in-chief when it comes to gauging the success of a magazine. As request cancellations neared the 10 percent mark, it became increasingly clear that something was wrong with *Essence*'s editorial approach—perhaps not so much with the magazine features themselves, but maybe with their timing, emphasis, and packaging.

An entire issue devoted to Africa, for instance, may have been ahead of its time in 1980 despite the huge popularity of the TV miniseries *Roots* in 1977, and the special fashion issue the magazine had done in Senegal in 1974. And Jamaica as a stand-in for Africa was surely a stretch. Running stories on Zora Neale Hurston, Cardiss Collins, a labor union for household workers, and the experiences of a black woman living in Sweden all in the same November 1980 issue may have been just too ponderous a mix. And a cover of Diana Ross without an inside cover *story* to accompany her fashion spread was no doubt something of a letdown to readers.

Daryl could be shy and even remote, which didn't always result in a forceful editorial vision. Yet perhaps most significantly, her editor-in-chief's editorial column, "Common Ground," was less effective as a platform to connect with readers than the editor-in-chief's column had been under Marcia. For starters, the "Common Ground" column ran without a photograph of Daryl for all of 1980, making it impossible for readers to even visualize who was speaking to them every month, let alone have an emotional connection. And though the writing and diverse subjects of the columns were fine, the tone lacked the fire-in-the-belly, take-no-prisoners spirit of the previous editor-in-chief, who became famous for "getting down" every month.

In her first column Daryl told readers: "Our lives overlap and we share a common ground as Black women. Our bonds weather winds of change, endure and grow. They hearten us, giving us hope in a world that is increasingly haphazard and disposable."

The column ended with readers being urged to share their stories of "How you cope. How you learn from yourself and your mistakes, your hurts and your joys. . . . Tell me about the sisters too busy, too shy, too humble to talk about their works for the church, the community and the world. Write to me. Let us share our common ground."

For readers used to an editor-in-chief whose editorials inspired, affirmed, and led the charge to think outside the box and act with courage and conviction, being told by a new editor that all black women share common ground "giving us hope in a world increasingly haphazard and disposable" didn't exactly ignite reader passions. *Essence* had achieved astounding growth during its first ten years by having an editor-in-chief who was a thinker as well as a charismatic personality, which in turn made her popular, and the magazine a popular success. Daryl was no less a thinker than Marcia, but she was less charismatic—and that made the magazine less successful. This would force me to do something I hadn't done in ten years: fire an *Essence* editor-in-chief.

I probably should have warned Daryl that slipping circulation was putting her job as editor-in-chief in jeopardy, and maybe give her a chance to try to turn the numbers around. But in my mind I had already moved on to Susan L. Taylor, the woman who would become *Essence*'s sixth editor-in-chief in less than a dozen years.

Susan started as a part-time beauty writer for the magazine in 1970, hired by then editor-in-chief Ida Lewis. The title of fashion editor was added to her responsibilities when Marcia took over as EIC in 1971. Coming to *Essence* as a 24-year-old wife and mother, Susan grew up in Harlem and Queens, and had briefly been a model and an actress, working with the Negro Ensemble Company. She did commercial work and landed a small part in the Roman Polanski film *Rosemary's Baby* in the late 1960s. At the time she joined *Essence,* Susan was planning to launch a line of beauty products with her husband, Billy Bowles, a hair stylist, but the marriage turned abusive and she left her husband soon after arriving at the magazine. A part-time writing job would now become a full-time fashion and beauty editor position.

As fashion and beauty editor Susan had already shown the organizational, leadership, and style qualities that would contribute to her a success as an editor-in-chief. Tall, model thin, strikingly attractive, and always fashionably turned out, she epitomized the very "essence" of the Essence Woman. Charles Watson, who had been a senior media planner at Young & Rubicam before coming to *Essence* as an advertising salesman in the early 1970s, remembers coming up with an idea for a fashion advertorial that he pitched the Monsanto Company to underwrite. His thinking was to do a fashion insert in the magazine featuring the clothes of such top black designers as Willi Smith and Stephen Burrows.

"I asked Susan to accompany me on the sales pitches," Watson said, "because she represented the *Essence* reader in terms of look and presentation. She was stylish, attractive, and well-spoken in making the case for the magazine." Monsanto didn't buy the idea, and fashion would remain a hard sell in *Essence* for many years to come, but Susan would become experienced at interacting with advertisers, an invaluable background when she became editor-in-chief.

The *Essence* fashion and beauty team also had its own status under Susan Taylor's leadership. "I used to see Susan and her team—Mikki Garth, Ionia Dunn-Lee, and Sandra Martin—at the fashion shows," recalled Monique Greenwood, who was an up-and-coming editor at Fairchild Publications at the time and would replace Susan as *Essence*'s seventh editor-in-chief in 2000. "They were all so striking. They would all come in together, turning heads, stay for just a little while, then leave for another show. It was very impressive. I felt so proud seeing these regal black women at the shows who worked at a magazine for black women, but also looked like they could have been in the magazine themselves as models."

Sandra, the associate fashion and beauty editor, was single, but Mikki, the beauty and accessories editor, and Ionia, the associate fashion editor, were both married young mothers. And it was Susan who affirmed her team in motherhood as much as she affirmed the women professionally. "I was supported in every way," Mikki said. "For example, when my last two children were born in 1984 and 1985, I had a crib in my office, and when I came back to work as a nursing mother, they came with me."

During the trip to Jamaica to do the special issue on Africa, Susan, who was still the fashion and beauty editor, supervised the fashion shoot and allowed the model Iman to bring along her 2-year-old daughter, Zuleka, who became a part of the shoot. Susan's own daughter Shana often accompanied Susan on out-of-town fashion shoots as well when she was a youngster.

Susan's capacity to recognize the real-life needs of the women she worked with were based on those needs being in common with her own. This resulted in an enlightened management style that probably had as much to do with the success of *Essence* as any of the magazine's editorial content. This was the quality I recognized in Susan with respect to how she connected with women—she had empathy and understanding. Plus, I thought Susan *looked* like an editor-in-chief. But most important, she quickly stepped up to lobby for the job when it became clear Daryl would have to go.

Like Marcia, Susan put forth a mission statement and an editorial vision statement outlining the kind of magazine she thought *Essence* should be. She wrote an issue plan for the magazine, giving feature ideas as well as ideas for the magazine's shorter department stories. She contacted editors at other magazines she wanted to hire to help with the enormous new task she was lobbying to take on.

Because Susan was coming from a fashion and beauty background, rather than a journalism or liberal arts background typical of most EICs, she knew this would be perceived as a liability if she didn't have a strong editorial staff. Rosemary Bray, a senior editor and Yale graduate, who was a gifted writer as well as a sharp editor, was already in place. So was Stephanie Stokes Oliver, a Howard University graduate who ran the magazine's "Contemporary Living" department and would later be the magazine's second-in-command as editor. Stephanie had modeled for the magazine during her junior year in college when *Essence* did its annual college issue and featured coeds from Howard University.

Susan would bring back Cheryll Greene, who had been at the magazine in the 1970s, to be a senior editor and later executive editor. Cheryll conceived and assigned many of the international stories that set *Essence* apart from other women's magazines. Valerie Wilson Wesley, an editor at *Scholastic* magazine, joined the magazine as a senior editor, later becoming executive editor, and launched *Essence's* first short-story fiction contest, discovering the then unknown Haitian writer Edwidge Danticat, who won the first contest and went on to become a critically acclaimed, award-winning novelist. Valerie herself would become a bestselling mystery and romance writer after leaving the magazine.

Essence's arts and entertainment editor Benilde Little also became an award-winning novelist after she left the magazine, while her successor, Gordon Chambers, who had been an *Essence* editorial assistant, went on to became a Grammy Award–winning songwriter. Joy Duckett Cain, a former *Sports Illustrated* writer and the married mother of three, ran the magazine's "Parenting" department, and along with Pamela Johnson, a Stanford University graduate and arts and entertainment editor, wrote excellent general magazine features. Susan McHenry, a Radcliffe graduate and former editor at *Ms.*, was the *Essence* editor known for her encyclopedic memory. Linda Villarosa was the magazine's first openly lesbian editor. Careers editor Lena Sherrod, an economist by training, launched the popular "Work and Wealth" department.

Susan brought in magazine writer and editor Audrey Edwards, a former associate editor at *Redbook* and *Black Enterprise* and a senior editor at *Family Circle*, to be her first executive editor and then editor. And all of the editors contributed to bringing in such exceptional freelance writers such as Bebe Moore Campbell, Pearl Cleage, Jill Nelson, Betty Baye, Laura Randolph, and Betty DeRamus.

While I was fairly certain Susan should be the EIC to follow Daryl, my partner Clarence Smith was not. First, he had never been happy with Susan's fashion pages. He thought the clothes were dated, not attuned to what was going on in the fashion industry, and he thought the price points were too high for the magazine's audience. The truth is, fashion has always been a hard sell for *Essence* because the magazine is not perceived as a fashion publication. It's not a *Vogue* or a *Harper's Bazaar*. Never has been, and that fact made it a tough sell to advertisers. But in my conversations with Susan I realized she was sensitive to what black women wanted, and I saw how these women reacted to her. I knew her connection to black women would be pivotal in turning around *Essence's* request cancels.

Surprisingly, Susan Taylor and Marcia Gillespie got on as the best of friends. I say "surprisingly" because the two women couldn't have been more different when it came to management style, temperament, and attitude. Marcia's management could be harsh and demeaning; Susan's was gentle and affirming. If Marcia was known to be moody and temperamental, Susan was equally known for her great kindness, generosity, and fairness. Susan was never less than impeccably styled and groomed. Marcia not so much.

What the women did have in common and no doubt bonded over was passion for their work and audience, enthusiasm, standards of excellence, and a sharp political consciousness. Under Marcia these qualities made *Essence* a fast-growing financial and popular success; under Susan these qualities made the magazine *hugely* popular and financially successful. It also elevated the position of editor-in-chief to that of a celebrity. This was something that John H. Johnson, the founder and publisher of *Ebony* and *Jet* magazines, had once warned me about. "Ed, be careful about how much power you let your editor-in-chief have," he quietly told me. I was to learn many years later exactly what he meant by that.

CHAPTER 18

Spirit Rising

"I will tolerate ineptness a moment longer than I will tolerate rudeness," Susan Taylor was saying to her editorial team during one of her weekly Tuesday morning meetings. "Say thank you to Francine when she buzzes you in! Can you imagine having a job where what you do all day is go *bzzzz* to let people in? Say thank you."

These Tuesday morning meetings were part editorial production review, part pump-up pep talks, and always lessons in living respectfully. Susan paid as much attention to how staff members treated one another as she did to the quality of their work. A receptionist buzzing employees in at the front desk was no less worthy of respect and appreciation than I was as publisher and CEO, she would tell her staff. It was a rule she herself lived by, and expected others to as well.

Under Susan Taylor's leadership there proved to be a direct and positive correlation between how people were affirmed and how well they performed their jobs. By creating a climate in which staff members were praised and supported, encouraged and valued, they were motivated to do their best work, and this resulted in the best editorial product.

As it had been with Marcia, it was Susan's monthly editorial column, titled "In the Spirit," that would elevate her personally, making her an editor-in-chief who not only struck an emotional connection with readers, but a spiritual one as well. This spiritual connection was to be the defining feature of her reign as editor-in-chief. It marked the beginning of a nearly twenty-year period of enlightenment that would for the first time introduce spirituality as a component of women's magazines and influence everyone from Oprah Winfrey to Iyanla Vanzant and Maya Angelou.

In her first editorial, titled "Choosing to Win," appearing in the June 1981 issue, Susan set the tone and the direction that would guide black women for a generation. Here is how she introduced herself to her audience as its new editor-in-chief, at age 35, the first to recognize the value in making such an introduction to readers. It was the first act of connecting.

> After nearly a decade as *Essence*'s fashion and beauty editor, I move to this place with high spirits. High spirits buoyed by a universal truth: we are the rising tide of Black women, the first in many centuries who have the ability to choose. We can choose to win!
>
> For me choosing to win means focusing—making conscious, well thought-out decisions. It took years of scattered direction for me to realize I could chart my own course, guide my own life. Through positive self-direction, I'm breaking those old habits that kept me going around in circles. Life is like a boomerang—what you give her she gives you back.
>
> Every day, moment to moment, we must *choose* to win. *Choose* to think positive thoughts and to distance ourselves from negativity.

Like Marcia Gillespie's, Susan Taylor's editorials could be highly personal. They were also empowering. Borrowing from the teachings of the Bible, the legacy of African-American history, the prescriptions of self-help gurus and tenets of the Black Church, Susan's messages were always ones of hope, optimism, and the abiding belief that black women had the God-like power to transform their own lives. "God is within you" became the mantra-like homily repeated monthly in various ways through her editorials.

Such thinking might have been considered almost blasphemous in the writings of an editor less connected to her readers. But in the editorials of Susan, a woman whose queenly cornrows, regal bearing, and aristocratic good looks gave her the imprimatur of a goddess, her own tales of struggle as a single black mother struck an empathetic note that readers would come to respect and love her for. Like her readers, Susan admitted to being sometimes fearful, impatient, not loving enough of self, too harsh with her child, too compliant or too harsh with men. Whatever the struggles of her readers, she had been through them too, and wasn't afraid to say so through her editorials.

The act of public, personal confessing became its own source of power and inspiration. Oprah Winfrey made it the hallmark of her hugely successful television show, which debuted nationally in 1986, five years after Susan took over as editor-in-chief of *Essence*. Oprah would often say that she read Susan's "In the Spirit" columns faithfully.

The power to inspire, transform, and educate through disclosures in a personal essay was not confined to Susan's "In the Spirit" editorials. Her first issue as editor-in-chief, June 1981, featured a reprint of a story that had appeared in the *Atlanta Journal and Constitution*, written by Roger Witherspoon, a health and science writer for the newspaper. Running in *Essence* under the title "Father's Day," the story was Witherspoon's harrowing personal account on how his joy at being present in the delivery room to witness the birth of his first child quickly turned into the nightmare of watching his wife miscarry. It was gripping and heartbreaking, and delivered in equal measure an education on the science of miscarriage and a riveting look at its emotional devastation as seen through the eyes of a black father and skilled writer who articulated both with powerful storytelling.

I don't know how the Witherspoon story came to Susan's attention, but her decision to buy and publish it as soon as she became editor-in-chief characterized the good instincts and good taste she used in selecting everything from stories to publish to models to put on the cover. Not every idea or cover choice was always successful, but Susan's great strength was that she listened, encouraged input, learned from her mistakes, and surrounded herself with a smart staff she could trust and rely on.

Susan's first request when she became editor-in-chief was that I give her a budget to do focus groups with black women to gauge what articles they wanted to see in the magazine. I told her the money would be better spent if she traveled the country herself, getting to know readers firsthand in the vastly different geographical regions that make up America. I had learned long ago just how big this country is. I crisscrossed it many times by car when I'd go home to the Bronx during my years as a student at the University of New Mexico, driving through the mountains and the desert, the major cities and the small towns. Everywhere there were black people, black women, who shared much in common, but also experienced differences based on the distinct cultures of their varied locales. I knew the best way to get to know these women and get a sense of what they wanted in a magazine directed to them would be to go out and meet them personally.

By now *Essence* was in better shape financially and could afford to send Susan on the road to meet readers when she was invited to do speaking engagements. I have to say, I believe these "road shows" are where Susan's reputation and popularity as a charismatic leader and speaker became cemented. She was a natural at working the crowd: gracious and inspiring, taking the time to listen to the concerns and desires of the readers. She was never too busy or too grand to talk to anyone, be it a sorority president who invited her to speak at an event, or the chauffeur driving her from the airport.

Susan was no less inspiring back at the office. Though her workload would increase significantly over the years as she became more in demand as a public speaker, went back to school for a college degree, and entered into a second marriage, the magazine was always her first priority. She approved every idea, read every manuscript, conducted every meeting from layouts to production to cover lines, wrote all of her own "In the Spirit" columns, and brought more story ideas to the table than any of her other staff editors—often based on ideas she'd received from *Essence* readers she met during her travels.

The "Father's Day" story was an emotionally searing piece of reporting that set the stage for future magazine articles, as did the front-of-the-book fashion story on fitting bras for full-figured women, which also appeared in Susan's June 1981 debut issue. As fashion and beauty editor for ten years, Susan knew that the average black woman was not a size 6 or 8, the ideal body size portrayed in white women's magazines. Black women's body types were larger, fuller, with size 12 or 14 being more the standard. The June fashion story on fitting bras for full-figured women recognized this reality with good service information on how to purchase a bra for bigger breast sizes.

Essence, under Susan, in fact, would be the first women's magazine to regularly showcase fuller-figured women (called "voluptuous" in *Essence*) in its center-of-the-book fashion spreads. Recognition of the value, beauty, and growing market potential of plus-sized women no doubt contributed to the launch of *Mode* magazine in 1997, a fashion publication specifically geared to this group that published for four years.

If the seventies was the era in which black women came into their own on the two fronts of civil rights and women's rights, the eighties was the decade in which their romantic dealings with men erupted in what was called "a crisis in black relationships." The crisis was spurred in part by the idea that black women had started to outpace black men in employment gains and other areas because of their newfound social opportunities. But shifts in the American economy—the loss of manufacturing jobs to countries overseas and the advent of technology—were the real forces that put a particular strain on the economic prospects of black men, leading to strained relationships with their women.

Turning the crisis into a full-fledged skirmish between the black sexes was the huge popularity of two books written by black women in the 1980s, *The Color Purple,* by Alice Walker, and *The Women of Brewster Place,* by Gloria Naylor. Both were published in 1982. Both won National Book Awards and both were made into films—*The Color Purple* was a major motion picture, produced and directed by Steven Spielberg in 1985; *The Women of Brewster Place* was the first made-for-television movie miniseries produced by Oprah Winfrey and Harpo Productions in 1989.

The two books, coming a few years after two other works by black women in the seventies, *Black Macho and the Myth of the Superwoman,* by Michele Wallace, and the incendiary play *For Colored Girls Who Have Considered Suicide When the Rainbow Is Enuf,* by Ntozake Shange, led to charges that black female writers were making their fortunes and their literary mark by writing works that demonized black men.

While the works of these writers did indeed cast black men in a less than favorable light, the real issue was that black men were under siege by a number of other alarming forces that had nothing to do with black female writers. Black men were disproportionately less likely to be college educated than black women, and more likely to be incarcerated, unemployed, unable to take care of their families, and victims of early death through gun violence. The picture was so grim the media started calling this at-risk generation of black men "an endangered species."

This media-fed "crisis" became the lightning rod that sparked what would prove to be Susan Taylor's best idea as editor-in-chief of *Essence:* a special November issue of the magazine devoted to black men. Her thinking was brilliant for two reasons. First, November is traditionally a slow month for women's magazine newsstand sales because the approaching holidays typically leave women with less time and thus less interest in buying magazines. Second, women, whatever their ongoing preoccupations, are *always* interested in what men are thinking, and may be more likely to buy a magazine if it's about men. A slow November sales month was the perfect time to try out the new concept of a "men's issue" to see if women would in fact depart from tradition and pick up such an issue of the magazine.

The first men's issue of *Essence,* November 1981, had just one line splashed across the cover, and it read: "In Their Own Words . . . The Truth About Black Men in America Today!" The cover photo was a tight shot on the faces of a black male and female model, lightly pressed together cheek-to-cheek in a portrait of uncertainty. The four major feature stories inside included an essay titled "What Do I Tell My Sons Who Are Black?" by writer and editor Phil Petrie, a father of three sons, who wrote about the challenges of raising black boys to be both safe and responsible as men. Writer Martin Simmons took a hard-eyed look at the meaning of friendship among black men in his essay "My Main Man."

Editor and writer Elliot Lee wrote an open letter to his father who had been absent from his life. *Newsday* reporter Sid Cassese did a provocative Q&A interview titled "Black Men and the Law" with Judge Bruce Wright, the controversial New York City civil court judge who routinely released black men on their own recognizance who were brought before his bench, earning him the moniker "Turn 'Em Loose Bruce." The fashion story that month, titled "Behind Every Dynamite Woman Is a Designing Man," featured glamorous models posed with the black male designer who had designed the outfit she was wearing.

Like Roger Witherspoon's miscarriage story, all of the feature stories in the first men's issue were powerful, beautifully written first-person accounts by black male writers that exposed raw emotions, told terrible truths, and illuminated the landscape of black male thinking in a way that had never been shown before in *Essence*—or any other media. The issue flew off the newsstands. And November would become a perennial bestselling newsstand month for *Essence* because of its special men's issue published annually for the next twenty-five years. Over the years other women's magazines would take note of *Essence*'s November issue and begin publishing their own special issues devoted to men.

Essence under Susan Taylor became the forum that not only began a healing dialogue between black women and men in the pages of the magazine, but became increasingly popular to a black male audience. Within a few years of Susan's editorship, nearly 25 percent of *Essence*'s readers were men, and some of the best writing in the magazine was done by men. James Baldwin, James McBride, Kevin Powell, Touré, John Wideman, Ishmael Reed, and Alex Haley are just a few of the great black male writers whose work has appeared in *Essence* as either personal essays or assigned features. The magazine became the honest and respected place where black men could tell black women exactly what was on their minds, and this made *Essence* popular among a dual audience. Also, many of the brothers who started reading *Essence* admitted they just liked looking at all of the beautiful women featured in the magazine.

————

By 1980, I was having something of a crisis in my own relationships. I turned 40 that year, and I still wasn't married. I had certainly dated any number of beautiful women during the first ten years of the magazine's run, but my most committed relationship for much of that decade was with *Essence* itself. Despite all the opportunities I had as the publisher and CEO of a successful black women's magazine to date and squire about town any woman I wanted, that was never my style. My judgment always told me it was never a good idea to use my position to attract women. To me that was courting potential problems with respect to running the business. I needed to concentrate on watching the bottom line—on making sure the magazine had enough cash, and that I was allocating resources in a way to keep us alive and surviving.

But when I hit 40 the magazine had become enough of an established success that I could think about doing something else—like getting married. This wasn't an abstract idea, since I was living with Michele Shay at the time. She was a wonderful actress I met at a reception in 1978. Ironically, it was Marcia Gillespie who introduced us. I remember being struck by Michele's sheer loveliness and loving spirit when we met. She was a member of the Negro Ensemble Company, the highly respected black theater company founded and run by Douglas Turner Ward. She was also a regular cast member on *Another World,* making her one of the first blacks to star in a soap opera in the late seventies.

A Louisiana native and graduate of Carnegie Mellon University, Michele is a full-figured, voluptuous woman whose light-skinned exotic looks give her the chameleon-like ability to look Hispanic or Asian or biracial or just homespun light-skinned, depending on the role she is playing. I loved that about her. I also loved that our values were compatible. She came from a strong, loving black family like I did; was articulate and quick to think outside the box, and had traveled extensively, something I've always felt was important because it gives one a larger perspective.

Like a lot of blacks whose spiritual quests in the late seventies led to paths that diverged from traditional Christian teachings, Michele was into Eastern religion, having become a follower of Siddha Yoga. This would turn out to be a value we didn't share, though I tried to become involved by learning to meditate, but was never converted into a true believer. Nevertheless, in 1979 Michele and I decided to live together.

For me it was important to determine if the relationship had legs to stand long term before entering into a marriage. I knew I wanted children. So did Michele. We both had busy careers, and I was the one in a position to help hers. This meant as publisher and CEO of *Essence* I did something I had never done before: told the editor-in-chief whom to put on the cover. As I recall, Daryl Alexander, then the new EIC at *Essence,* didn't object to putting Michele Shay on the June 1980 cover of *Essence,* though she could have certainly and rightly accused me of nepotism of the most blatant sort.

While I was never one to use my position to attract women, I did think it was appropriate to use my position to help someone I loved. A magazine cover for any actress is certainly wonderful publicity, but I didn't think of Michele Shay as just *any* actress. She was a serious actress who had been formally trained, worked regularly, won awards, and had the great respect of her peers in the business.

She was also the woman I came to love and would marry. As an *Essence* editor said when another editor complained that I had put my light-skinned wife on the cover of the magazine: "Hey, he married a *black* woman—I don't care what her skin shade is—and he *owns* a magazine with a cover to put her on. I have no problem with that. He's *supposed* to put her on the cover if it will help her career."

The June 1980 issue with Michele on the cover sold very well, I must say. Readers evidently liked the fresh, pretty round face of the woman being featured. And I loved the same woman walking down the aisle in Columbia University's St. Paul's Chapel to become my wife that warm day on June 20, 1980. Maybe other black couples were in crisis, but I had found the woman who was to be my soul mate, as well as my wife.

Over 500 of our closest friends attended the wedding. On the show business side were guests like actors Phylicia Rashad, Adolph Caesar, and Janet League. On my side was the *Essence* team, of course: Clarence Smith and Susan Taylor, Jim Forsythe, and Marcia Gillespie. Personal and political friends included my buddies Earl Graves and U.S. congresspersons Maxine Waters and Charles Rangel. Former New York City mayor David Dinkins, my bank buddies Hughlyn Fierce and Frank Savage, and my good friend Tom Burrell, head of Burrell Advertising in Chicago, were also there. The noted activists and theologians, Rev. Dr. Eugene Callender and Bishop Joseph Francis, officiated the ceremony.

It had taken decades for me to make a legal and spiritual commitment to marriage. But it would not take nearly as long for the spirit rising in me filled with hope and optimism in a new marriage to turn into emotional heartache. And this heartache, in both my professional and personal dealings, would result in a physical challenge that was nothing less than life-threatening.

CHAPTER 19

A Brand Is Born

"Jonathan Blount has escaped from the mental institution and is heading this way!" Susan Taylor announced theatrically, addressing her staff during one of the weekly Tuesday morning editorial meetings in the fall of 1985. "We understand he was hospitalized at a facility somewhere in New Jersey and just walked off the grounds. He said he intends to kill Ed Lewis, Earl Graves, and Roger Wilkins."

That certainly jolted everyone to attention in a way their morning cups of coffee never did, as ripples of nervous laughter and worried looks shot around the room. Susan always had a flair for the dramatic, but in this instance she was not overemphasizing the seriousness of the matter. Jonathan Blount was back—not in person yet, but as a menacing threat, running loose and unpredictable, who might show up at our offices at any minute to do who knows what.

I had heard that Jonathan was being hospitalized for "emotional exhaustion," and I knew he still harbored a deep a hatred for me over having "taken" *Essence*, "his" magazine, away from him. I didn't even try to figure out why Earl Graves, founder and publisher of *Black Enterprise* magazine, or longtime civil rights activist, journalist, and university professor Roger Wilkins were also on his hit list. I just knew I needed to move quickly to secure the safety of *Essence*'s staff and property.

A security firm was hired to provide us with a guard who was stationed outside the bank of elevators that opened onto the *Essence* floor. I had hired my stepfather, George Clarke, a few years before to be a security presence near the mailroom. But this was one of those soft jobs that allowed me to show my love and respect for him by giving him comfortable employment after his years spent working in the garment district. I knew that as an older man of gentle spirit, Mr. Clarke would be about as effective a security presence in a confrontation with Jonathan as a Yorkshire terrier taking on a pit bull.

Jonathan might have been crazy, but he was never crazy enough to give up his *Essence* stock, even after he was booted from the company. As a shareholder he was entitled to see the company's annual financial statements that showed Essence Communication Inc.'s mounting profits. Though ECI was still not paying out dividends, the magazine was rapidly growing in editorial popularity, which translated to increased ad sales and rising circulation. It must have galled Jonathan no end to see the success his magazine idea was becoming as we moved into the decade of the eighties.

His threats against me and others in addition to Earl Graves and Roger Wilkins never amounted to anything deadly, but they did have an unsettling effect. Michael Victory, for one, the former Shearson, Hamill executive vice president who was an original *Essence* board member, an early supporter of the magazine, and now a good friend, was greatly spooked when Jonathan threatened to kill him and his family. Jonathan had made such threats against my family as well. This led to my not only retaining the services of a security firm, but arming myself for personal safety by carrying a gun. I also made sure the security firm included private investigators I retained to keep track of Jonathan's every move, even years after his threats subsided.

Essence was not just growing in profitability during the 1980s, but was quickly gaining stature and public visibility as its editorial content intersected with news events occurring in larger American culture. In September 1983, a 20-year-old Syracuse University coed named Vanessa Williams made history by becoming the first black woman to be named Miss America. It was a collective triumph for black women that *Essence* documented by putting Vanessa on the cover of its January 1984 issue. A feature story on Vanessa ran in the magazine's "Contemporary Living" department, written by the department's editor, Stephanie Stokes Oliver.

The story's lead paragraph referenced the sniping that occurred almost immediately among some in the black community who felt Williams won the Miss America title "only because she has light skin and straight hair." Vanessa fired back in the article, saying, "The only reason I won was because I was qualified. It's too bad people couldn't feel proud." She called such negativity "pretty unfortunate."

Essence was often a public media forum in which volatile racial issues surrounding things like skin color, hair, or political attitudes got addressed through articles, essays, and editorials that were often celebrity and even reader driven. A personal essay page titled "Say, Brother" was launched in 1982, written by our male readers, who then represented about a quarter of *Essence*'s total readership. "Speak" was the reader editorial page written by women and men alike that ran on the last page of the magazine. Both pages were highly popular outlets for reader opinions and ideas that helped to cement our readers' buy-in of the *Essence* brand.

If *Essence*'s readers were vocal in their written opinions, their buying decisions resonated loudest on the magazine's bottom line. Newsstand sales for January are typically down for magazines across the industry, the result of post-holiday slumps. Yet the January 1984 issue of *Essence* with Vanessa Williams on the cover sold very well—her hair and skin color notwithstanding. The majority of *Essence* newsstand readers apparently wanted to know more about "their" Miss America.

While monthly women's magazines rarely run a cover of the same celebrity twice in the same year, Susan and her editors believed that running another cover of Vanessa Williams in 1984 could be a newsstand bestseller too. September 1984 would mark the end of Vanessa's one-year reign as Miss America. It was also the month of *Essence*'s annual fashion issue. The decision was made to put Vanessa on the September cover and spotlight her inside modeling clothes in one of the fashion layouts for that month. There would also be an accompanying feature story about her year spent as Miss America.

Then the *Penthouse* bombshell hit. A few weeks before a new Miss America was to be named, *Penthouse* magazine announced it would be publishing exclusive nude and pornographic photographs of Vanessa Williams *in its September issue!* The photos were taken when Vanessa was a 19-year-old college student and aspiring model, and promised to be graphic and scandalous, warned *Penthouse* publisher and editor Bob Guccione.

Rather than mount a counterattack so close to the end of her reign, Vanessa decided to resign as Miss America before the damaging photos came out. She would get to keep her pageant scholarship money and could move on with her life. Vanessa made the announcement during a press conference held on July 20, 1984, at New York City's Sheraton Centre Hotel. *Essence*'s senior editorial staff was in attendance. It was less than a month before the magazine was due to hit the newsstand with Vanessa Williams on the cover.

"What are we going to do?" Susan whispered to her executive editor during the press conference, sounding a little panicked. Actually, there was nothing we could do. The magazine was already on press. Pulling it at this stage of production was out of the question. We would just have to ride out the storm of controversy that was sure to be coming our way.

Savvy marketing thinkers like Clarence Smith, however, thought the September issue would be a newsstand hit. "*Essence* is showing Vanessa Williams with her clothes on the same month *Penthouse* is showing her with her clothes off," he said jokingly. Susan, on the other hand, knew readers had no idea of the lead time involved in producing a magazine, and would surely think *Essence* had deliberately made a decision to feature Vanessa during the same month *Penthouse* was running its lewd photos of her. Susan believed this could be disastrous for circulation.

In this instance, both Susan and Clarence proved to be right.

The September 1984 issue of *Essence* had the highest newsstand sales in the history of the magazine at that time, with a 71 percent sell-through—meaning that 71 percent of the September issues placed on newsstands sold out that month. This kind of newsstand sell-through was unheard of for most publications. *Essence* usually had a newsstand sell-through in those days of about 50 to 55 percent, still very respectable for a magazine whose circulation was driven by subscriptions, not newsstand sales.

The curiosity factor turned out to be enormous among readers who had evidently grown tired of all the hype surrounding Vanessa's upcoming nude *Penthouse* photos, and welcomed a change-of-pace magazine cover and story that indeed showed her with her clothes on. Vanessa was modeling sophisticated fall career suits in a six-page fashion spread. The timing made *Essence* look like something of a marketing genius in getting ahead of the *Penthouse* steamroller, as regular readers and first-time buyers alike snapped up the September issue.

Subscribers, by contrast, were outraged that *Essence* appeared to be celebrating a woman who had not only posed nude, but in compromising positions with another woman, as the *Penthouse* photos revealed. Our subscriptions dropped to an all-time low, and it would take nearly a year for us to get back the readers who canceled or failed to renew their subscriptions because of the Vanessa Williams September 1984 cover.

Like much in business, both the success and the failure of that issue were due to the accident of timing and circumstance. *Essence* editors made a decision to profile Vanessa Williams at the same time Guccione made a decision to also profile her—in very different ways. *Essence* benefited newsstand-wise by this accident, but paid a severe cost on the subscription side. These are the kind of unexpected occurrences that even the most astute editors and advertising salespeople can never anticipate in planning and selling a magazine.

Nor did *Essence* anticipate what would then be its worst-selling issue ever: the July 1984 magazine with Jesse Jackson on the cover. In 1984 the Reverend Jesse L. Jackson made a historic run for president of the United States, which led to his being on the cover of *Essence*'s July 1984 issue just before the Democratic National Convention in San Francisco. The inside story was an editorial-like essay written by executive editor Audrey Edwards that amounted to a rousing cheer of Jackson's candidacy. I also wrote a "Publisher's Page" that month discussing the historic significance of the Jackson campaign and the importance of blacks getting out to vote.

The close-up cover photo of Jackson showed him in profile, looking serious, if not downright somber, which was a striking departure from other *Essence* covers depicting vibrant-looking models and celebrities. A small banner across the magazine's upper-right hand-corner touted July as a Special Issue, and the large lead cover banner read, "Winning Spirit." Beneath it the lead cover line read, "Jesse Victorious!" The overall cover effect, however, was heavy, dark, and moody. The issue bombed on the newsstand, selling less than 30 percent.

Because *Essence* is not a political magazine, readers weren't buying a "special issue" that suggested editorial content that month dominated by politics. The cover was out of sync with what readers expected. Yet when it comes to historic race moments, as the Jesse Jackson presidential candidacy certainly was, I believe we in black media have an obligation to document the moments, even if they are at the expense of newsstand sales or go against reader expectations for a particular month.

In the case of both the Vanessa Williams and Jesse Jackson covers, history has shown that *Essence* did the right thing in recognizing the importance of their respective moments. Vanessa Williams would go on to have the most successful career of any Miss America in the pageant's history as an award-winning recording artist, Broadway star, movie and television actress, and author. She would also grace the cover of *Essence* again. The candidacy of Jesse Jackson paved the way for Barack Obama, the first black U.S. president, elected twenty-four years after Jackson's bid for the presidency. Obama and his wife and family would be bestselling *Essence* cover subjects several times in the years that followed.

As for Jonathan Blount, his murderous threats never went beyond the selling-wolf-tickets stage, though I did take out an order of protection on him in 1985 when his threats momentarily escalated. In 1990 Essence Communications Inc. bought out 44,500 shares of his stock for $1 million—not a bad return on a stock that was valued at a penny a share when he was booted from the company twenty years before. Jonathan took the money, and eventually took his leave, moving to Florida. Of course, we had not heard the last of him. He still had 500 shares of stock.

———

At the time of Jonathan Blount's buyout, *Essence* was entering a flush period that would be marked by large cash reserves and high visibility leading to a number of business expansions that firmly established "the *Essence* brand." The first branding was *Essence: The Television Program*, a joint venture with the New York local station WPIX that launched in 1984. The show was the brainchild of Kathy Sheperd, a black executive producer at WPIX who was looking to broaden the station's reach into the African-American market, and approached *Essence* about doing a weekly television show together. At the time, only a handful of consumer magazines were attempting to bring their editorial content to a television format, and *Essence* became the first black magazine to do so.

Essence: The Television Program, was originally produced by the *Essence* editors and starred Susan Taylor as host and executive producer, who introduced segments, interviewed celebrities, did a live version of her "In the Spirit" column, and effectively cemented her status as a celebrity editor. The show eventually left WPIX and went into national syndication, running for five years. The most popular stories appearing in the magazine were often featured as subjects to discuss on the television show. One such segment assembled a panel of men to talk about why men cheat in their relationships, and remained a subject of conversation long after the show aired. A reader told one of the *Essence* editors that she had overheard two women on a bus having a heated conversation about the segment a few weeks later. Having a television platform from which to promote the magazine clearly enhanced the magazine's success.

Unfortunately, the syndication markets were limited and the time slots for airing the show even more so. In New York and California, for instance, the country's two largest television markets, the show aired at six o'clock on Saturday mornings. Even so, by the time the show's run ended, ECI had established a television division headed by Gene Davis, an African-American syndicator who had worked at CBS.

ECI also developed a mail-order catalog business in 1984, and began a licensing business that put the *Essence* name on eyewear as well as a hosiery and undergarment line. This branding of the magazine became an important asset in continuing to move ECI to business ventures beyond publishing. The brand also became the target of a black competitor who would try a hostile takeover of the company not unlike that mounted by Jonathan Blount, Cecil Hollingsworth, and Gordon Parks back in 1977. In fact, much of Essence's time and money in the mid-eighties was spent on fighting this takeover attempt and also fighting to protect the Essence name, which by 1984 was worth a fortune at least symbolically, if not yet financially.

Our 1984 operating year was the only one in the eighties in which Essence was not profitable. First, there were the hefty costs of expanding into television and the mail-order business. But there were also the enormous legal costs of fighting the various business entities that wanted to cash in on the Essence name. General Motors, for one, wanted to name a new Buick line Essence. The Philip Morris tobacco company wanted to name a new cigarette Essence. There were jewelry lines named Essence, and fragrances with the Essence name. In every instance these manufacturers were going after the black female market, and it would cost Essence Communications Inc. more than a quarter of a million dollars in legal fees to keep them from using the Essence name to do so. ECI could have made a ton of money allowing some of these ventures, but we were not car manufacturers and didn't think a car named Essence was appropriate. Nor would we ever endorse a cigarette called Essence.

By 1985 the company had successfully fought back every attempt at encroachment on the Essence brand. That year also marked the fifteenth anniversary of the magazine, an event celebrated with a dazzling May special issue featuring Lena Horne on the cover. At 68, Lena stood triumphantly on the cover, the perfect embodiment of black womanhood, looking fierce and fabulous in a floor-length gray matte jersey gown designed by Giorgio Sant'Angelo. Former executive editor Audreen Ballard, writing under the name Audreen Buffalo, wrote the cover story documenting Lena's fifty years in show business. She also wrote a profile of the longtime married political activists Amiri and Amina Baraka.

The issue published essays, poetry, and prose by women who comprised a veritable who's who among contemporary black female writers of the day: Alice Walker, Ntozake Shange, Bebe Moore Campbell, Gloria Naylor, Marita Golden, June Jordan, Nikki Giovanni, Paule Marshall, Vertamae Smart-Grosvenor, Marcia Ann Gillespie, Jean Carey Bond, and Jean Wiley.

The peerless Toni Morrison penned the magazine's last-page "Speak" column that month, writing a luminous tribute to the greatness of black women titled "A Knowing So Deep." Here's a sample of what she had to say about the legacy of African-American women: "What doesn't love you has trivialized itself and must answer for that. And anybody who does not know your history doesn't know their own and must answer for that too. You did all right, girl. Then, at the first naming, and now at the renaming. You did all right."

Lee Iacocca, the iconic chairman and CEO of the Chrysler Corporation, spoke during a luncheon held for a few top editors of women's magazines at Chrysler's Detroit headquarters shortly after *Essence*'s May anniversary issue came out. He gave passing mention to some of the magazines headed by the editors present. But when he got to *Essence*, he made specific reference to the May issue and gushed unscripted, "I have *always* loved Lena Horne!"

Our advertisers also loved Lena Horne and the fifteenth anniversary issue. The magazine had a record 230 pages that month, with a record number of advertising pages. It was the first time the magazine's pages exceeded 200. *Essence*'s ad pages traditionally spiked for May anniversary issues, as Clarence and his sales team sold against what advertisers knew was a perennial newsstand bestseller.

More significantly, other special themed issues of the magazine had become so branded in the minds of *Essence* readers that advertising pages could be sold in greater numbers against these issues as well. The February "love issue," the September "fashion issue," and the November "men's issue," were all months that typically had greater ad sales due to the reader popularity of these annual special issues. I don't know of any other women's magazine that had such reader buy-in of its brand and special themed issues, except for perhaps *Vogue*'s annual September fashion issue.

––––––

If familiarity breeds contempt, the success of *Essence* bred a second take-over attempt in 1985. The would-be corporate raider was none other than John H. Johnson, venerable founder, publisher, and editor of *Ebony* and *Jet*. Johnson is the godfather of black magazines, and his rags-to-riches story has become the stuff of legends.

Arriving in Chicago in 1933 following a flood in Arkansas that left him and his mother homeless and on the move, he worked for a while in the insurance business, then launched his first magazine, *Negro Digest*, in 1942 at age 24. He financed the venture with $500 in capital he had borrowed from a white-owned Chicago bank using his mother's furniture as collateral. *Negro Digest* would be folded into a new magazine called *Ebony* in 1945. *Jet*, a pocket-sized weekly digest of black news, was launched in 1951.

John understood perhaps better than anyone the virulence of racism, and the powerful need for black media that could present news from a black perspective and also affirm and celebrate the accomplishments of African-American men and women, something white media rarely did. There were a handful of black magazines being published during the late

1940s and into the '50s. *Sepia*, a *Life* magazine–sized publication premiering in 1947, was black-owned and based in Fort Worth, Texas. It featured articles on the achievements of African Americans, but also wrote about obstacles facing blacks—from lynching to the Ku Klux Klan. Ownership of the magazine eventually became white, and by 1983 circulation was only 160,000. Other magazines such as the now-defunct *Bronze Thrills*, *Black Confessions*, *Black Romance*, and *Jive* were published by Sterling/MacFadden, publishers of the mainstream romance titles *True Confessions*, *True Story*, and *True Romance*. The black-oriented publications in Sterling/MacFadden's stable were the forerunners to what we now call "urban street lit" in book publishing, but these magazines never reached the large circulation numbers of Johnson's *Ebony* and *Jet. Tan* magazine, a digest-sized publication that dispensed "Dear Abby"–style relationship advice, was also published by Johnson Publishing, and was incorporated a few years after its launch.

Although *Ebony* and *Jet* were general interest publications not in direct competition with the black female market that *Essence* was reaching, all three magazines were targeting a black consumer market. And Madison Avenue did not always make such fine distinctions between a black dual audience and a black female one. This meant Chicago-based Johnson Publishing and Manhattan-based Essence Communications Inc. were frequently going after the same advertising dollars. *Black Enterprise* had its own separate struggle trying to sell advertising in the smaller business community.

Johnson and I had developed a friendly relationship over the years, though I would never think of him as a business friend the way I did Earl Graves of *Black Enterprise*. John and Earl and I occasionally joined forces to make presentations at agencies on Madison Avenue to talk about the viability of the black consumer market in newspapers, radio, and magazines. During these times we were not trying to pitch our respective publications per se, but to make an overall case for the importance of advertisers buying into *all* black media if they wanted to reach black consumers. Such joint presentations were rare, however.

John had been the first and only black magazine game on Madison Avenue for so long that he never really got used to the idea of four young upstarts launching a magazine for black women two and a half decades after he'd pretty much single-handedly laid the groundwork. And that ground had been hard indeed. I remember my mother telling me that when *Ebony* first came out in 1945, blacks would hide it from whites for fear of reprisals if they were caught reading a *Life*-sized glossy magazine that celebrated Negroes, published by a Negro company. And there was always the ever-persistent challenges of selling advertising in a Negro magazine.

Although I knew the value of partnering, John did not, due to his early experience as the lone pioneer in publishing. This is why I could never get him to consider joining forces with *Essence* to do things like joint di-rect-mail campaigns or buy printing paper together. These were the kind of shared activities that would have saved money for both companies and enhanced our overall efficiency. "Ed, I just can't do that," John would tell me. Then he would say, "Madison Avenue will not allow *Ebony* and *E* into *Jet* to come together."

John felt racism was so powerful that advertisers would never support two black magazines joining forces to share certain expenses. I never believed that. There is always *more* power in partnering, as the growing success of *Essence,* a magazine started with four partners, clearly showed by the early 1980s. In fewer than twenty years, the magazine's circulation was rapidly gaining ground on Johnson's magazines, the largest circulated black publications in the country. This fact was not lost on John, and probably explains why a few of our disgruntled investors successfully ap-proached him about buying their shares of *Essence* stock.

Early investors had been after me almost from the beginning to sell *Essence* so they could get their money out, since ECI was still not paying any dividends. I always refused. I shouldn't have been surprised that some of them would eventually try to unload their *Essence* stock by selling it to a likely suitor. And who was more likely than John H. Johnson, a friendly enough competitor and colleague, but also a tough businessman who would love nothing more than to have an opportunity to demolish the competition? Strangely enough, John admitted he never really trusted white people, never felt at ease doing business with them. Yet he relished being the only black game in town—the only black at the party or in the boardroom or in the publishing arena—with entrée to white wealth and white privilege.

For many years Johnson was considered the wealthiest and most successful black man in America, with his company, Johnson Publishing, landing number one year after year on *Black Enterprise*'s annual list of Top 100 Black Companies. Johnson would eventually be toppled from the top spot by black billionaires such as the late leveraged buyout specialist Reginald Lewis and media mogul Oprah Winfrey. The fact that *Ebony* magazine never covered the astounding success stories of either Lewis or Winfrey (who is based in Chicago like Johnson Publishing) said everything about how Johnson viewed blacks whose achievements were greater than his own: He simply ignored them.

Essence and the Essence brand were too threatening to ignore, however. I always believed Johnson's decision to buy up shares of *Essence* stock was fueled by his thinking about his own mortality. I think he wanted to insure *Ebony* and *Jet*'s longevity by aligning those publications with another important black magazine—*Essence*. What this boiled down to, though, is that Johnson would try to get control of ECI.

John initially bought the stock of a couple of our impatient investors who were looking to sell and just get out. But I soon realized Johnson was looking to do a more hostile takeover of *Essence* when he started going after the shares of some *Essence* employees. This prompted me to make my own move to buy more stock.

On the advice of ECI's legal counsel Suzanne Warshavsky, I quietly started acquiring *Essence* stock from employees who were willing to sell. I also enlisted the aid of two *Essence* board members, Congresswoman Maxine Waters and businessman J. Bruce Llewellyn, who together with me formed a consortium to buy back *Essence* stock. I was able to secure the shares of Marcia Gillespie during this time, which I bought for a premium price, though for much less than they would be worth when the company was sold twenty years later.

Clarence could not step up as strongly as I did in purchasing more stock. He acquired some new shares, but not enough to be a part of the consortium. I was now in the position of owning more stock than my partner, which would have serious consequences in the years ahead.

John Johnson, for his part, was never able to acquire a controlling stock position in Essence Communications Inc., a defeat he took with grace. "Ed, you won fair and square," he told me by phone from his Chicago office when it became clear he could not win against me and the consortium. "I'm not going to come to your board meetings or your shareholder meetings," he said. "All I ask is that you send me financial statements, and every once in a while, you pay dividends. That's what I expect."

True to his word, John never tried to interfere with the running of *Essence* or attempt another takeover. He remained the quiet shareholder who had paid $10 a share for the initial stock he bought from the unhappy investors. Unlike other stockholders who over the years would sell to various parties for various prices, John held on to to his shares of *Essence* stock until ECI was sold to Time Warner in 2005. By then the stock was worth more than $400 a share, and he received the largest payout from the deal—$38 million! No doubt about it, John H. Johnson was nothing if not a consummate and shrewd businessman.

CHAPTER 20

Serious as a Heart Attack

It was probably just jet lag. I had taken my first trip to Zimbabwe in the summer of 1988 to attend an annual conference sponsored by the American Travel Association. *Essence* was trying to get a piece of the African market for travel advertising. We had already been successful with the Caribbean in advertising the islands as a destination spot for black American travelers. Africa represented the next natural destination, especially in newly independent countries like Zimbabwe, the former British colony known as Rhodesia, now headed by Robert Mugabe, the country's first African president.

Essence was present for Zimbabwe's anniversary celebration in 1981 marking Mugabe's first year in office. Susan Taylor assigned writer Alexis De Veaux to cover the occasion, just one of the many international stories *Essence* would commission and publish during the decades of the 1980s and '90s, as it sent writers to do political coverage in countries such as Haiti, South Africa, Nicaragua, Grenada, and Burkina Faso. In another first, *Essence* was the only women's service magazine during this time that included assigned international political stories as a regular part of its editorial mix.

Zimbabwe was certainly a long way from home, and despite a layover in London, I was feeling the effects of the twenty-two-hour trip by the time I arrived back in New York in late July. The first morning back home I went for my usual jog through Central Park. Suddenly, I had to slow down, then I came to a dead stop. *Jet lag.* I ran another four or five hundred yards, and had to stop again. Still thought nothing of it. I even played tennis that afternoon.

A week later as I came up out of the subway at 43rd Street and Eighth Avenue and started walking along 43rd Street on my way to the *Essence* offices at 1500 Broadway, I stopped dead in my tracks. I was standing in front of the *New York Times* building and couldn't take another step. *My God! Something is wrong!* I couldn't move and was sweating profusely. The sweating slowly subsided, and I just as slowly made my way another half block down 43rd Street and crossed Broadway to my office. It was about eleven or twelve o'clock.

I called my doctor, Adrian Edwards, as soon as I got to my desk. He told me to come in that afternoon. I took a cab to Adrian's office on East 71st Street at about three o'clock, forgoing my usual subway mode of transportation. Adrian examined me, then did an EKG and a stress test, both of which were inconclusive, though his medical assessment sounded ominous. "There's something going on with your heart," he said, "but I don't quite know what it is. I'm going to schedule you for more tests tomorrow morning."

The next morning, lying on the base of a huge X-ray scanner at New York Hospital, I watched as the lab technician slowly injected contrast dye into one of my arteries. "Just relax, Mr. Lewis," he said, while monitoring the dye's flow. "I know your doctor told you we'd be performing an angiogram. Basically, what we're going to be doing is taking a picture of your heart and surrounding blood vessels to see exactly what's going on."

The angiogram showed that a left coronary artery was 99 percent closed! *Oh my.* The doctors told me the only reason I was still alive is that I was in excellent physical shape. But they also told me I wouldn't be around much longer without an angioplasty procedure to open up my closed artery.

A few days after the angiogram, I checked into New York Hospital for the recommended angioplasty. It wasn't open-heart surgery, thank God. In this type of procedure, a catheter is inserted into the groin and threaded through the main artery or aorta up to the coronary vascular bed in order to access my closed vessel. A stent, which is a short, narrow tube made of mesh, is attached to the catheter on top of a balloon and inserted into the artery to keep it open.

Although I came through the angioplasty quite well, thanks to my overall physically fit condition, I would have to be on a low-cholesterol and low-sodium diet for the rest of my life. No beef or pork, and few dairy products. I made a basic decision to forgo all those foods. Not because I thought I would live a day longer by doing so. I know when my time comes, it'll come, but I'm not going to help it come any sooner by engaging in behavior that can be injurious to my health. I have control over that. I can control my diet and my exercising. I also felt that I had a responsibility as publisher and CEO of *Essence* to stay in the best shape possible. My doctors and I worked out a rehabilitation program combining diet and exercise, and I slowly got on track to restoring my health.

What I learned I couldn't control was a genetic predisposition for heart trouble. My mother told me that my father may have suffered from heart disease. His death at age 54 was probably the result of an undiagnosed heart condition made worse and perhaps ultimately fatal by years of drinking. Uncle Freddy, my father's brother, had also died of heart disease. Now here I was at age 48, not a heavy drinker, never a smoker, and in good physical shape, but maybe headed down the same path as my father and uncle if I wasn't careful.

About six weeks after the first angioplasty, I experienced the same symptoms that had sent me rushing to Adrian's office in July. The stent had prematurely closed, and this would require a repeat angioplasty. For a number of reasons stents can close after an angioplasty, though advanced stent procedures now greatly reduce the likelihood of such an occurrence.

Even though I had to have a repeat angioplasty, I never thought my heart condition would present any serious problems. I was planning to attend the annual Congressional Black Caucus weekend in Washington, DC, in September, a huge political event hosted by the African-American members of Congress. The caucus gathering draws literally thousands of blacks in politics, business, entertainment, education, civic, and religious groups from all across the country. It's a great time to attend workshops and symposiums on issues pertinent to the black community, to do business, entertain, catch up with old friends, and make new contacts.

I was out walking in Central Park a few days before the caucus weekend when I felt the same heart symptoms I'd experienced less than three months before—and I'd just had a *repeat* angioplasty. A little troubled by this, but determined to keep to my schedule, I headed to Penn Station the Friday afternoon of the Black Caucus weekend to take the Metroliner train to Washington. I stopped off at the private club bar in the station for a quick drink.

"Sir!" the bartender blurted out, looking at me strangely. "Are you all right? You look like your world is coming apart." And that's exactly how I felt. I was short of breath and disoriented, and could barely move. I knew I had to get to the hospital right away. There was no way I could make the caucus weekend that year.

Back at New York Hospital, I was told I would need *another* angioplasty. Now I was furious. What was the point of watching my diet and exercising faithfully if I was going to continue to have heart problems? How many times would I have to be subjected to the poking and prodding of a stent procedure? Why wasn't it *working*?

Adrian wondered the same thing, and concluded that I needed the skills of an exceptional specialist in the field of angioplasty to perform the procedure a third time. The specialist, whose name I no longer remember, was world-renowned in performing angioplasties and bypass surgery. Unfortunately, he was not available. His office informed Adrian that the doctor was out of town attending a weeklong medical conference in New Orleans where he was presenting a paper. "That's okay," Adrian told me in my hospital room. "We'll just wait."

My heart, however, would not.

On Friday, September 23, 1988, while lying in my hospital bed, my heart started beating so rapidly I thought it was going to jump out of my chest. I was having trouble breathing. *Really* having trouble breathing. *What's going on?* Doctors and nurses came rushing into my room. Adrian was there. "We can't wait, Ed," he told me, sounding and looking alarmed. "We're going to have to operate immediately—first thing tomorrow morning. I've found another doctor who is very good. He's an expert in heart bypass surgery, which is what we have to do."

Bypass surgery? Now *this* would be open-heart surgery. Adrian said my condition had deteriorated to such an extent that a single bypass heart operation was necessary for long-term success. The left internal mammary artery would be used to bypass the blockage in order to keep my heart functioning properly. I was stunned—and terrified.

The next morning, just before going under the anesthesia, I stared at the large, circular flat-paneled fluorescent light fixture hanging above me in the operating room and wondered if my life was about to flash before me. It didn't. But every stress and strain that had eaten at me over the last few years certainly did: *The end of my marriage to Michele. Clarence's bull-headed explosions. Susan's diva popularity. Susan and Clarence's constant butting of heads. My shutdowns. Quiet rages. Therapy sessions.*

Oh, yes, I was fully aware of all the demons that got me wheeled into the operating room on the morning of September 24, 1988. They were as serious as a heart attack.

———

I doubt if it's entirely coincidental that my heart troubles surfaced in 1988, nearly six months after my divorce from Michele Shay became final. After living together for a year, we married in 1980 and separated in 1986, discovering, as many couples do, that we were not compatible. We loved each other in the beginning. Traveled together a great deal, especially to the Far East. Singapore and Hong Kong and Bali. Bali is still my favorite place to visit. I just fell in love with it. The first time I went to the Far East was with Michele.

Michele and I both had busy careers, and I always supported hers. Financially backing theater projects she was involved with, putting her on the cover of *Essence*, maintaining the household whenever acting jobs took her out of town for long stretches—these were some of the ways I showed my support. I will admit I could never quite get with her Siddha Yoga religion. I was raised Baptist in the Bronx. But I know that faith is a private matter, and I respected Michele's right to practice whatever faith she chose.

If we had been honest with each other, though, I think we would have realized in our first year that we were having some difficulties and perhaps should not have stayed together. I ended up going into therapy in an attempt to understand myself and see if there was something I was doing that contributed to our problems.

My therapist was a tall, Germanic woman named Barbara Munk, whom I met in 1983 during the banquet at a conference sponsored by the Puerto Rican Legal Defense and Education Fund. We were seated at the same table and started having a discussion about behavior. I was struck by the idea that maybe there was something wrong with my own behavior—

with my reactions or my inability to communicate—and maybe Dr. Munk could help me. She gave me her card, which I kept, and about a year later gave her a call.

That was in 1984, the year of Michele's miscarriage. We had always wanted children, and were devastated by the loss of our baby. But I don't know how well I communicated my feelings to Michele during that awful time. Opening up was not something I'd ever been comfortable doing. And I realized that sharing my own feelings of loss with her might have helped us both cope a little better.

I wasn't always coping effectively in the *Essence* workplace either with the outsized personalities of the company's two principal department heads, Susan Taylor and Clarence Smith. They were both larger than life, especially when compared to my own low-key persona. Susan, a naturally gifted speaker, spoke in a soft and breathy voice as distinctive as her sleek cornrows, a hair style, by the way, that was copied by thousands of black women in the 1980s. Clarence had been a glib-talking smoothie for as long as I'd known him. Though he would pursue many other business interests over the years, his sheer talent for *sales* would remain his greatest gift. Both he and Susan were persuasive and charismatic.

As strong personalities will do, they often butted heads. Clarence, the company president and national director of sales, routinely tried to get Susan to do editorial features that could help sell advertising. Running a career story on the twenty best companies for black women to work in, for instance, were the kind of features Clarence would push for so the *Essence* sales team could then go after those companies listed to pitch for advertising. Susan usually refused such obvious selling, though I have to say on some levels she was ahead of her time when it came to cooperating with the advertising department.

Back in those days there was an absolute separation of church and state between editorial and advertising powers in magazine publishing. No self-respecting editor ever wanted to be accused of exploiting editorial content in order to help sell advertising. *Essence*, however, was forced to march to a different beat. Because selling ads was always difficult, we had to use all of the resources at our disposal to attract advertisers, and that increasingly meant getting the editorial department to run stories in support of advertising.

One such story published early in Susan's tenure as chief editor was a perfume survey asking readers to rate the perfumes they liked best. Getting perfume advertisers—the high-end ones in particular—to buy advertising in *Essence* had always been an uphill battle. The Chanel No. 5s and Estée Lauders and Ralph Laurens preferred to reach the readers of *Vogue* and *Harper's Bazaar* and *Women's Wear Daily*. The idea in doing a perfume survey was to show these advertisers the extent to which black women used their products. Clarence did such marketing surveys all the time, and used them in his sales pitches, but he believed a perfume feature story in the editorial well of the magazine would be more effective in making the sell to perfume advertisers. It was another way to go after ads.

Clashes between Susan and Clarence were usually over editorial content. He exploded, for instance, any time the magazine made a negative reference to cigarette smoking—the tobacco industry was a big *Essence* advertiser. Susan, as editor-in-chief, considered herself a guardian of the well-being of her readers, whether that meant running health stories that told readers to stop smoking or her complaining about "those awful wig ads that run at the back of the magazine," which, like tobacco, were regular advertisers in *Essence*.

I always thought that Clarence was driven by the *need* to be right, while Susan was driven by the *certainty* that she was right. This made for all sorts of head butting. Clarence could be loud and bombastic. He was once in Susan's office and yelled at her so ferociously that after she had calmed down, she marched into his office and told him in her breathless voice that could cut like a knife when angered, "Don't you *ever* speak to me like that again—*ever!*"

Sometimes I felt more like a reluctant ombudsman than a corporate CEO, meditating conflicts between these two. I was the quiet one. A good listener. I understood that my ability to listen to what Susan had to say about Clarence or what Clarence had to say about Susan was part of my strength as a manager. They were talkers and needed someone to bounce ideas off of, someone to give them feedback and support.

Yet as time went on, Clarence and Susan's big personalities started to overwhelm and even overshadow my own calmer temperament. They got most of the attention in public, simply because it was impossible *not* to pay attention to them. Susan especially. The *Essence* logo that ran on the contents page in the magazine pictured a woman in profile with flying braids, evoking the image of Susan's illustrated picture on her "In the Spirit" editorial page.

Her popularity grew so enormous that readers started to believe *she* owned *Essence*—that she had started the magazine, built it, ran it, and even had a magazine logo that looked like her to prove it. This didn't make me happy, though I never spoke on it. I didn't speak on a number of things, partly because I am quiet, but largely because I have never felt the need to be out front. I have always been more comfortable in the background. Plus, *Essence* is a magazine for black women, so it made sense that a black woman would be in the public forefront as editor-in-chief.

This would present its own problems. My quietness was unnerving to some people who either thought I had nothing to say or was clueless, or worse yet, that I might just not be that bright. I remember giving a speech in 1980 after receiving an award from the Interracial Council for Business Opportunity, an organization created to help blacks get into business. Afterward, a very well-known black advertising executive came up to me and said, "Ed Lewis, I'm stunned. I have never really heard you talk. I didn't even think you could talk."

Now, you can't head a magazine for thirty-five years and be clueless or dumb—or not know how to talk. Being quiet in my case, though, had left me emotionally shut down and often unable to express what I was feeling precisely when I most needed to express my feelings. My tendency to keep things locked in, to be "Stoneface Ed," sometimes resulted in smoldering rage that was not healthy for me either physically or emotionally. By my late forties I would be forced to undergo open-heart surgery. Before that I voluntarily went into therapy.

To tell the truth, I never saw myself as someone who would ever seek the help of a psychiatrist. Therapy was not something black men did. That was for white people. I know that's nonsense now, but at the time that is what was in my head. Initially, I started seeing Dr. Munk because my marriage was in trouble. I persuaded Michele to attend a therapy session with me, but she came only once. I think she believed that Dr. Munk and I had already established a history of relating, and that perhaps her needs wouldn't be heard. I later thought she probably regretted not coming back.

Dr. Munk was helpful in getting me to open up, but not helpful enough to keep me and Michele together. We separated in 1986 and then went through a long and very stressful divorce that took two years. I thought because we didn't have children, a divorce would be fairly easy. But there were assets to divide and emotions to sift through. It was a wrenching time. In the end, I believe Michele and I got most of what we wanted.

After seven or eight months of therapy, I had a clearer perspective on my own behavior, learning to appreciate its strengths as well as deal with some of its weaknesses. On the plus side, my quiet, low-key demeanor gave me an ability not only to listen, but to ask the right questions and choose the right people on whom to rely. I understood that power in a multifaceted business such as *Essence* was one of *shared* dependency.

I had to depend on my partner Clarence Smith to bring in 60 percent of the company's revenues through advertising. I depended on Susan Taylor, my editor-in-chief, to deliver an editorial product that brought in the other 40 percent. I depended on my circulation manager, Jim Forsythe, to keep the balance between newsstand sales and subscriptions. I depended on Harry Dedyo, my chief financial officer, to give me daily reports as they pertained to *Essence*'s cash flow. I depended on my production manager, Bill Knight, to hold the line on publishing costs and get us to the printer on time. These were the top five executives at *Essence*—the five fingers on a corporate hand that wielded shared power in making *Essence* run smoothly and profitably.

As head of the corporate body, I knew my five top managers, my department heads, depended on me for judgment and leadership. I always let my managers do what they needed to do to accomplish goals, and rarely interfered. I allowed for mistakes to be made, but I also expected my managers to own up to their mistakes. I am very critical of people who don't take responsibility. I have always taken responsibility in my own life.

Being honest with myself, however, was something I needed to work on. What was really going on with me? How could I communicate better? What could I do to be more articulate in expressing my feelings? These were some of the challenges Dr. Munk helped me work through. I took the initiative after Michele's miscarriage to see if there was something medically wrong with me. The miscarriage was caused by an ectopic pregnancy, and I wondered if that was because of something I had done. Was there something wrong with my sperm? The answer was no, but just going through the exercise of trying to find out helped me to get in better touch with my real feelings.

Two years before I experienced my heart problems I met the woman who would become the true love of my life—and my second wife. My feelings were on full display the day we met. I was not only in touch with my real feelings, but ready to act on them with purpose and passion. And that, no doubt about it, is what saved my life.

CHAPTER 21

Oh My!

My God, what an incredible-looking woman, I remember thinking when I saw her come into the great hall. There were about 100 of us black men lining the perimeter walls of the room, standing behind our respective tables serving food. We were at International House, a residence for graduate foreign students near Columbia University in upper Manhattan. The house had large public meeting spaces often used for big fund-raising events.

Oh my. I continued to stare at the woman who had just entered. So striking. She was tall and slender, and had an air about her that combined good looks with terrific personal style. She quickly passed by my table, stopping to chat with two other women who were at another table, sampling a dish. I recognized one of them: Joy Moore, who worked on the *Essence* television show. But I couldn't keep my eyes off the woman who was now talking to her. *Who is that?*

It was Sunday, February 9, 1986, the day of the popular Men Who Cook fund-raiser hosted by Lana Turner, a Harlem impresario known for originating innovative events to support the arts. Men Who Cook was her yearly benefit held to raise money for the Children's Art Carnival, a Harlem arts program for school-age children. The event featured a smorgasbord of great food prepared by some of New York City's most prominent black men—lawyers and journalists, doctors, politicians, photographers, advertising executives, and magazine publishers—who volunteered to cook and serve their favorite recipes as their donation to the benefit. Paying guests always had a wonderful time sampling the culinary delights of men they typically didn't associate with boiling an egg, much less concocting a mean gumbo.

This was the first year I had participated, and I made my special roasted chicken and potato salad. The beautiful woman I was staring at didn't even stop by my table for a taste!

————

I did notice this gentleman at the far side of the room wearing an ascot and a bit more hair than he needed. I saw him looking at me. But he looked so serious and distant that I just assumed he was arrogant, so I passed by his table without stopping. I was in New York at the suggestion of my friend Matt Robinson, a writer on The Cosby Show, *who had put me in touch with Lana Turner. Lana suggested I come to the Men Who Cook event to see if it was the kind of fund-raiser that could be replicated back in Los Angeles where I lived and worked as a lecturer and consultant for the King-Drew Medical Center. King-Drew, located in L.A.'s South Central district, was a medical school on the West Coast that trained students to work with minorities in urban and rural areas.*

In addition to my job at King-Drew, I advised the dean of the school on ways to raise money for the center, as well as how to publicize the work it was doing. The dean knew I had been married to a physician—the chief of obstetrical anesthesiology at Cedars-Sinai Medical Center—who had a number of celebrity patients and friends. The dean hoped I would use some of those contacts to help raise money. He had also asked me to consult with a group of doctors' wives who did their own fundraising.

I was meeting my sister Linda at the Men Who Cook event, too. She lived in Washington, DC, but was a friend of Joy Moore, a writer for Essence TV *show. Linda had come up to New York to attend the fund-raiser with me. I spotted them at a table across the room. Joy had suggested that I try to meet Ed Lewis while I was in town. He was going to be one of the men cooking at the event that year and could be helpful in getting a story placed in* Essence *about the King-Drew Center. I knew who he was, but had no idea what he looked like.*

————

My wife still tells the story of thinking I was a bit stuck-up when she first caught me staring at her at Men Who Cook. I had not stopped staring when she and Joy and another woman walked up to my table. Joy introduced me to the first woman, Linda Shaw, a friend of hers from Washington, DC, and then to Linda's sister, Carolyn Wright from Los Angeles. I broke out in the biggest grin, listening as the lovely lady from L.A. told me how she had come to Men Who Cook hoping to meet me. I gave her my card; she gave me hers. Our eyes met. I called her office in Los Angeles first thing the next morning. She wasn't in. I left a message telling her assistant to have her call me as soon as possible. *You need to get to know this woman,* I was thinking to myself. *Find out what she's about.* I felt there might be something happening here, and my instincts were telling me to go for it.

I didn't hear back from her for two weeks.

———

"Did you get a chance to meet Ed Lewis?" Joy asked, when I joined her and Linda at a table where one of the men was serving a delicious shrimp dish he'd cooked. She pointed to the gentleman across the room wearing the ascot. Oh, dear, there goes the story for the school, I thought, if he realizes I deliberately walked by his table because I thought he was arrogant. We quickly walked back to his table. His face lit up with the most beautiful smile as we approached, giving me such a different feeling about him. He had a warmth and openness that was so unlike the arrogance I thought I had first seen in him.

The next day I flew to Atlanta to meet with the CEO at the Coca-Cola Foundation to talk about the King-Drew school. I was also starting a two-week vacation, and planned to spend some of the time with my oldest daughter, Nicole, who was a student at Spelman College. The school's annual mother-daughter weekend was the following weekend, so I would stay for that. I planned to take a real vacation this year, and deliberately did not call my office for any messages while I was away. The office knew how to reach me if there was an emergency.

I was a bit surprised when I got back to Los Angeles to see that the first message on the Monday following the Men Who Cook event was from Edward Lewis. I called him back. I could tell from his tone that he was not accustomed to people taking as long as I had to return his phone call.

———

I admit I was a bit put off by the fact that I didn't hear from Carolyn Wright for two weeks after I'd first called her. But I was so delighted once I did hear back that I got over any annoyance, especially when she told me she had been on vacation spending time with one of her daughters. I was planning to be in Los Angeles for a business meeting in the next couple of weeks, and I told Carolyn I'd like to meet with her over drinks while I was in L.A. to talk about the King-Drew Center. We met for drinks, which led to dinner, and that would lead to the beginning of a long-distance, whirlwind romance—with 3,000 miles separating us—that has gone on for twenty-seven years through dating, living together, and marriage.

Carolyn and I started seeing each other every two or three weeks. Like me, she had her own life, her own career, and her own power. As a speech pathologist, she had spent twenty-two years in private practice, in addition to consulting and serving on boards dealing with a variety of educational, social, and political issues. She was divorced, a professional working woman, and a mother to two almost grown-up daughters who were 19 and 21 when we met. Like their mother, Haydn, 19, and Nicole, 21, were beautiful. Nicole (we call her Nikki) took to me much faster than Haydn did. Haydn was the more guarded and questioning of Carolyn's two girls, no doubt a bit suspicious of the quiet man from New York who was spending so much time with her mother.

I like to say that Carolyn was already an heiress when I met her. She had pedigree. I am the one who married *up*. Originally from Darlington, South Carolina, where her people were quite well known, Carolyn's great-grandparents on her father's side were respected educators. A school is even named after her great-grandfather. Carolyn and her two siblings were all class valedictorians in high school, continuing the legacy of importance of education in the family.

Carolyn's father, Allard A. Allston, finished college at 17 and went on to become a millionaire as a supplier of office and school equipment and graduation paraphernalia for the majority of black businesses and schools in segregated South Carolina during the 1950s and '60s. He had a virtual monopoly in most of the state, and also developed an early interest in the stock market, parlaying the proceeds from his business into lucrative investments. After her divorce, Carolyn requested that her father guide her investments as well. The success of his efforts assured her financial independence.

Mr. Allston and I had much to share in our conversations, and I was fascinated listening to his experiences as a black businessman in the Deep South. We had an abiding respect for each other right from the start. Carolyn is the oldest of three children. Her brother, Allard Allston III, is an attorney in Columbia, South Carolina, and her younger sister, Linda, is a photographer, formerly employed by the ABC-TV affiliate in Washington, DC. She is married to Bernard Shaw, the retired CNN national anchor.

In addition to having her own life and career, Carolyn had her own money. She also had an ex-husband and two daughters. I realized a relationship with her would be a package deal. Her children and ex, her parents and siblings, even her former in-laws, were all part of a new family mix I found very satisfying. I was an only child. I had also always wanted children, and though Carolyn's daughters were nearly grown when we met, I would nevertheless come to view them as my daughters, and they would later refer to me as their "other father"—not stepfather. I loved how Carolyn interacted with them, and I thought it was very appealing to see the way these incredible-looking women bonded. Carolyn's ex-mother-in-law, Mrs. Ruth Wright, adored her, and once told me that letting Carolyn go was the worst mistake her son had ever made. I did not intend to make the same mistake.

———

Ed is the only man I've met who never leads with who he is, what he does, or why you should be impressed with him. Which is exactly why he impressed me. All of the accomplished men I had known, and that included my father, could hardly wait to tell you what they do or who they are. I was also impressed with Ed's integrity. For example, as a CEO, Ed always believed company bonuses should be tied to job performance, not job entitlement. It always galled him to see how top executives at companies that were losing money would nevertheless compensate themselves with large year-end bonuses. To him that represented the worst kind of management.

On our first date Ed told me about his divorce proceedings. He and Michele had recently separated. I had been divorced since 1985, but separated for eight years before then. It was very important to me that I be clear about what I wanted in a relationship at this stage of my life. Ed and I were both in our forties. Neither of us was rushing into marriage. I loved that Ed always encouraged and supported me in my professional work, and wasn't looking for a trophy or corporate wife. Ed had expressed a desire to have children. Realizing this, I told him I couldn't have any more children. I elected to have a partial hysterectomy while married to my first husband because I had planned for two children. As Ed and I talked about what we wanted in life, I was delighted to see that he was a man who valued my input and my concerns, and wasn't rigid in his thinking. We also shared similar values regarding family and community.

We had been dating for about two years when Ed had his heart episode. I knew he was going to need care in recovering from his bypass surgery, and realized I wanted to be the one to care for him. This would mean moving to New York and staying with Ed for as long as it took to nurse him back to health.

"Ed will need care when he comes home," I told my daughters, "and I'm thinking of moving to New York for a while." Neither of the girls lived at home at this point, but still, their mother was thinking of going across country to live with a man. By then I had a part-time practice as a speech pathologist and my consultancy jobs, both of which gave me the flexibility to take time off.

Ed and I lived together for about eight weeks in New York. Our relationship deepened. On February 9, 1990, the anniversary day of our meeting, we became engaged. On February 9, 1991, five years to the date of our meeting, we married. Our marriage has been a bicoastal one since then. By the time we were married, I had lived in Los Angeles for twenty-seven years, raised my children here, built my practice here, and was not fond of New York winters. Maintaining a home in Los Angeles, even after I married, seemed perfectly reasonable to us.

It was just as reasonable that Ed continue to live in New York. He is a native New Yorker. As the CEO and publisher of Essence, *with its corporate headquarters in New York, Ed would spend a portion of the year with me in Los Angeles, and I would spend a portion in New York. I know this kind of relationship can work only on a strong foundation of trust.*

Ed and I have an element of the loner in us, a quality also conducive to a long-distance marriage. We are both comfortable with our private, independent time. The occasional time apart from each other makes the coming together that much more romantic.

———

My world got better the minute Carolyn came into it. I don't know if I would have made it through my heart surgery without her by my side, taking care of me, loving me. She dispensed my medications, consulted with the doctors, researched my medical options, and kept me focused on diet and exercise as I worked on getting better. She was there for me during the most frightening health challenge of my life, and that made all the difference in my recovery. Even my mother recognized this when she came to see me in the hospital. "I knew you were in good hands," she said about Carolyn.

Carolyn is also a true helpmate in every sense of the word. I consider her one of my most trusted advisers. Whether discussing with her my interactions with Susan and Clarence, or my negotiations with Time Inc. during our merger talks, her feedback and advice have always been spot-on. She even helps me write my speeches. And when I started spending more time on the West Coast during our initial courtship, she was pivotal in introducing me to her vast network of friends and contacts, who would became important to me personally and to *Essence* professionally.

I continue to be in good hands with Carolyn as a wife and a friend, a lover, and a kindred spirit. She challenges me and also comforts me. I love her incredible intellect; her impeccable style permeates everything she does, from the artful way she dresses to her exquisite taste in decorating our homes in New York and Los Angeles, creating a loving and calming sanctuary in both. I am always astounded by her ability to think outside the box, to embrace complexity and unconventional ideas—like a long-distance marriage, which we have made work for more than two decades.

One of the blessings I took from my marriage to Michele Shay and her practice of Siddha Yoga was learning to meditate—learning to get still, centered, and focused. That skill would be of great benefit during my ongoing fractious dealings at *Essence.* But my favorite talisman is the one I have carried in my wallet for nearly thirty years. It's a candid photo that Linda Shaw, Carolyn's photojournalist sister, took of us back in 1986 on the day we met at Men Who Cook. Carolyn had come back to my table. In the photograph we are in profile facing each other—Carolyn earnestly talking to me, and me looking at her, grinning like a loon, my Afro standing on end. I love that shot. It is a picture of me falling in love.

CHAPTER 22

Cash Is King, Queen, Jack . . . and Ace

"How's your cash, Ed? How's your cash?" my buddy J. Bruce Llewellyn would always ask me about *Essence*. He was a member of the magazine's board of directors, so he had a right to ask. But Bruce was also a multimillionaire businessman who in 1969 had bought out the chain of ten Fedco food stores in Harlem and the Bronx, making him the only black owner of a supermarket chain in New York City. In 1985 he would become a co-owner in the Philadelphia Coca-Cola Bottling Company with a group of partners that included Julius Erving and Bill Cosby. Consequently, Bruce knew firsthand the importance of running a business from a strong cash position.

Magazines, it turns out, have the potential to generate large amounts of cash once you have stabilized your business costs, expanded advertising, and built circulation. *Essence* had done all of this by the end of the 1980s. At the start of the '90s, the magazine was making such a great return on its bottom line that it was now in the enviable position of having large cash reserves that would allow it to expand to multimedia platforms. The five skilled fingers on the corporate hand were turning the wheel of a virtual cash machine.

On the editorial side, the magazine reached the height of its popularity during the 1980s and '90s, as circulation grew from 600,000 under Marcia Gillespie to more than 1 million under Susan Taylor. As a result, subscription costs stabilized because of high renewals. A magazine may have to pay direct-mailing costs to get a new subscriber, but once you have that reader and she continues to renew, it doesn't cost anything to keep her, and now subscription fees represent pure profit. The same with advertising. As *Essence* continued to break new categories of advertisers who committed to twelve-times-a-year advertising schedules or bought more than one page of ads in an issue, the profits generated from advertising increased.

Essence's longtime black production manager, Bill Knight, was superb in negotiating paper costs, holding down mailing expenses, and keeping us to an efficient print schedule, which resulted in stabilized production costs. And Harry Dedyo, who joined *Essence* in 1988 as our crackerjack chief financial officer, was the one I called every day from wherever I may have been in the world to ask, as Bruce always asked me, "How's our cash, Harry? How's our cash?"

Large cash reserves would allow *Essence* to expand its print base to other media and business platforms such as television, a mail-order catalog, a licensing division, and part ownership in Amistad Press, a black-owned publishing company. We were also able to create an awards program and a music festival and offer our employees the opportunity share in *Essence*'s wealth through an employee stock plan. For me the purpose of a black-owned business is not to just make money, but to employ blacks and use the black wealth generated from the business to enhance the lives of both our employees and those in the larger black community. "What are you running here, Ed, a business or a social service organization?" some of our board members would ask me as the magazine started to take public positions and make financial contributions to both political and social causes.

To me personally, cash allows you to provide for the basics you need in life and facilitate the lifestyle you want. I know I am a wealthy man, but I have never been the kind of man who needs to spend his money on fine cars or lavish second homes to display his wealth. I don't even own a car in New York, since you don't really need one, and I'm perfectly comfortable getting around by subway, a private car service, or walking. Nor do I have a summer place in New York's Hamptons resort community or any other high-end, second-home enclave. I can afford one, but it doesn't bring me any kind of psychic comfort to say to the world, "I've made it."

I have lived in my two-bedroom, two-bathroom rent-stabilized apartment a block from Central Park since 1975. The rent has gone from $615 to $4,000 a month during that time, but a comparable non-rent-stabilized apartment in the same area rents for about $12,000 a month. I do own two condominium apartments in Los Angeles, which my wife Carolyn and I share, along with the New York apartment. The bigger L.A. apartment is a 4,000-square-foot, four-bedroom, five-bath residence that Carolyn has made exquisitely beautiful with soothing neutral colors and African and Asian art. The smaller 1,000-square-foot, apartment is used for visiting guests. I did buy my wife a Porsche in Los Angeles, since a car is mandatory in Southern California.

My spending weakness is on clothes. How I present myself matters very much to me, a trait I acquired from my mother, who thought dressing well was important. "I want you to buy good quality, Sonny," she would tell me, "because it will last you a long time." She set the example. Good-quality clothes, not overly flashy or in-the-moment trendy, are the investments I make in myself. I also like good service and I like to be treated well, which to a great extent is certainly brought about by money. But I've never been into using money to show off.

As a businessman, however, I know money talks many languages and can help solve a myriad of social and economic problems. If a business is run right and does well financially, it is then in a position to do good. I have always tried to use the wealth generated by *Essence* to do good works, which many times can be good business too. Money can also be used as a weapon to leverage concessions or take political positions. *Essence* has used its cash to do both. Over the years I would learn that cash is not just king or queen, jack or ace. It is the whole game.

―――――

I had dreamed of seeing *Essence*'s name splashed across the marquee of Radio City Music Hall, home of the Rockettes and the fabled *Nutcracker* children's show. Now here we were in May 1990, hosting the twentieth-anniversary celebration of *Essence* at this majestic theater anchoring Rockefeller Center. I couldn't imagine a more fitting venue. As limousine after limousine delivered the entertainers, politicians, and business-people who would help *Essence* celebrate its rise into a third decade, I was humbled by how far we had come and how much we had proved to the world. Hosting the evening's festivities were two of America's most popular entertainers—Oprah Winfrey and Bill Cosby—a black woman and a black man who had come to honor our history and our victory as represented by the enduring success of *Essence* magazine. Fittingly, *Essence* was the first women's magazine to feature Oprah Winfrey on its cover when her talk show went national in 1986.

Tonight the magazine would be giving out its third annual Essence Awards, a sleek Plexiglas statue in the shape of a pyramid bestowed to seven black women who had made outstanding contributions to their professions or communities. The awards were started in 1987 to further extend the *Essence* brand. They also opened to us the whole new world of corporate sponsorships—another avenue for *Essence* to take in going after advertising.

Corporate sponsorships were not anything new in 1987. Big advertisers like Reebok and Colgate had long sponsored sporting events where their company name might be etched in giant letters at both ends of the football field or flashed on the huge scoreboard overhanging a stadium. It was another way to generate advertising dollars that *Essence* had not yet tapped until a young black woman named Karen Thomas joined the magazine in 1982. Karen came from McGraw-Hill's sales promotion division, and was about to take a job at Time-Life, but changed her mind after a friend suggested she stop by the office to speak with Clarence Smith regarding a sales promotion position open at *Essence*.

"I sat on the edge of my chair listening spellbound as Clarence talked about the black female market," Karen recalls. "He was so passionate, so inspiring, that I knew *Essence* was where I wanted to be." Karen recognized that *Essence* could sell its brand in the sponsorship market by packaging events that advertisers would underwrite, such as an Essence Awards program. That great idea was her brainchild. The first Essence Awards, presented during a dinner program at Los Angeles's Biltmore Hotel in 1987, was sponsored by three advertisers, Coca-Cola, McDonald's, and Procter & Gamble. The event netted $100,000 in profit, and gave the three advertisers public visibility at both the luncheon and in the magazine, which ran a special advertorial that profiled the winners. The sponsorship package included a page of advertising in the advertorial for each of the three sponsor advertisers.

"Sponsorships allowed us to access a pot of money that we hadn't been accessing with print advertising," Karen recalls. Most advertisers have two advertising budgets—one for media advertising and one for sponsoring events. The appeal to advertisers of sponsorships is that they get large public association with the event they are underwriting. The advantage from the magazine's standpoint is that additional revenues can be generated with advertising dollars that are separate from the ones budgeted for print ads.

Sponsorships were enormously successful in extending the *Essence* brand, especially when the Essence Awards went from a dinner event to a televised awards program in 1992, broadcast from the Theater at Madison Square Garden. The Essence name was now seen in living rooms throughout America. The company sold multimedia formats to advertisers, which was a more lucrative proposition that involved several levels of selling. *Essence* might sell a $5 million package to advertisers, for instance, that included print ads in the magazine, television spots on the awards show, and an ad page in the awards program.

Unfortunately, the awards shows never made money, since television production is a phenomenally expensive undertaking. Plus, awards shows of the kind *Essence* did on television had a short shelf life in the 1990s because the nature of such shows changed. Now most awards shows—the Oscars and Emmys, for instance—are supported by either the film or television industries, and have the capability to bring out the A-list celebrities who will draw a viewing audience. *Essence* did not have similar institutional support.

Even so, the fact that a magazine for black women could partner with major television networks to do a nationally televised awards show that ran for five years, first on CBS and then on Fox, spoke to what has always been the singular capacity of African Americans to make a way out of what appears to be no way.

Essence's ability to mount big awards shows staged in glittering venues like Radio City Music Hall and Madison Square Garden was clearly a function of having the cash to celebrate our large milestone anniversaries on a grand scale. Being able to generate additional revenues in the process of doing the shows was the sweetest part of the venture. These splashy, high-profile events enhanced the perception that *Essence* was indeed a major player in the magazine industry. We attracted big names to host our events, gave good after-parties following an event, and had cachet and respect among both our peers in publishing and our people in the black community.

For me, however, the greatest corporate contribution *Essence* made was not in awards shows or splashy parties, but in giving our employees an opportunity to share in the wealth the magazine was generating. In 1991 we replaced the employee stock plan begun in 1973 with an employee stock ownership plan (ESOP) in which the company contributed to the purchase of *Essence* stock for its workers. We started a 401(k) plan in 1993.

I turned to a brother named Ray Gerald to assist me in setting up the ESOP for *Essence*. Ray and I met in the late 1970s when he worked for one of the venture capital firms that were investors in *Essence*. A Harvard MBA graduate, Ray had held jobs in investment banking before starting his own company, and would later do consulting with businesses such as *Essence*. Ray was something of an expert in setting up ESOPs.

ESOP retirement plans are established as trust accounts, and any contribution made by a company into the trust is tax-deductible. This allowed ECI to help fund our employees' retirement and also get a tax break. Because *Essence*'s workforce was primarily black and female, the group least likely to have a financially comfortable retirement, I felt strongly about the company establishing a good retirement program that involved the company making contributions. This was rare in most small companies, to say nothing of a small black one.

If an employee left *Essence* before retirement, she or he was entitled to take the retirement money. There would of course be tax consequences from cashing out early if the money wasn't rolled over into another retirement plan, but that didn't preclude an employee from taking the money when leaving the company. One longtime top editor who moved on to another magazine had more than $100,000 in her ESOP when she left, a combination of the money she invested, as well as the money *Essence* put in.

I also felt strongly about supporting the talents of employees who wanted to launch their own businesses, especially if the business could be of use to *Essence*. When Karen Thomas said she was leaving in 1992 to start her own sales promotion business, we talked about her launching her business *while remaining at Essence.* The deal we struck is that she would have free office space for a year and handle the Essence Awards as a client. A year later, she moved to her own office in Newark, but still kept *Essence* as a client. She then rejoined the company in 1994 for a year to help plan events for *Essence's* twenty-fifth anniversary.

A similar arrangement was made with Terrie Williams, *Essence's* stellar public relations director, when she formed her own firm, the Terrie Williams Agency. She, too, ran her business out of the *Essence* offices for a couple of years. Both Terrie and Karen were valued employees whose desire to run their own businesses I fully understood because I had shared the same dream when I helped start *Essence.* The idea of *in*trepreneurship—allowing an employee to begin a business within the existing business she worked for—was a new corporate idea in the early 1990s that didn't really catch on once the American economy went into a slump. For *Essence,* however, it was one of those novel ideas we took advantage of at the right time for our needs and the needs of the women we supported.

I do believe black businesses have a social responsibility to not only use their cash for good, but to take political positions and leverage concessions if an occasion demands it. Of course, taking hard-line political positions works only when a business can afford to do so. Although it would cost us, *Essence* made a political decision to ban Revlon cosmetics from advertising in the magazine in early 1987, following an insensitive comment by its president, Irving Bottner, in the fall of the year before.

During an interview in the October 13, 1986, issue of *Newsweek* on the subject of competition in the hair-care industry, Bottner said, "In the next couple of years, the black-owned [hair-care] businesses will disappear. They'll all be sold to white companies." This was a particularly galling remark, considering how little attention the general hair-care industry had paid to the black consumer market up to that time. But as black hair-care companies such as Johnson Products, SoftSheen, and Carson Brothers developed a market that constituted a $1 billion industry, white hair-care companies suddenly "discovered" the black hair-care market and jumped on the bandwagon.

With their superior financial resources, it wasn't long before these major hair-care companies were developing their own "black line" of products and beating out the black companies in a competition for the black woman's hair-care dollars. Amazingly, these white companies took the position that they knew more about how to develop products for the special needs of black hair than the black hair-care companies did!

There wasn't anything *Essence* could do about such racist thinking, but we didn't have to tacitly agree with this thinking by running advertising from a company whose president's public remarks suggested a racially smug attitude. In a business story published in the January 23, 1987, issue of the *New York Times*, Clarence and I jointly announced that we would be banning future Revlon ads in the magazine. This was not an easy decision to make—in fact, it took several months—since the move would cost us at least $400,000 in advertising revenue. That was the value of the twenty-one pages Revlon had run in *Essence* the year before, and they planned to increase their advertising budget in the magazine for 1987.

It was not as if we could afford to lose $400,000 in advertising, but neither could we afford to have an advertiser act as if black hair-care companies were expendable. These black companies were our advertisers, too, and like *Essence*, had struggled to get a toehold in American business. As a matter of fact, in the beginning, it was the black hair-care companies that were our advertising salvation. Johnson Products ran thirty pages of advertising during *Essence*'s first year, which amounted to a sizable amount of ad revenue.

Our strong cash position in the eighties became the ace card that *Essence* could play in taking a public and political stand against Revlon. We didn't want to lose $400,000 in ad revenue, but we could absorb the loss if we had to. Bottner apologized for his *Newsweek* comments, and a Revlon company spokesperson said he was "puzzled" by the advertising ban. The magazine didn't have to follow through on the ban after Bottner apologized. *Essence* had made its point: Respect trumps money.

There would be other public positions taken by *Essence* during the coming years, and having the cash resources to put our money where our politics were gave us a winning hand. When *Essence* board members continued to ask, "What are you running here, Ed, a business or a social service organization?" I could honestly answer, "Both, if the business is being run right."

CHAPTER 23

Of Music Festivals and Magazine Fortunes

I was nearly in tears as I stood onstage looking out at the audience in New Orleans's colossal Superdome arena that first Sunday in July 1995. It was the last night of the first Essence Music Festival. There were over 50,000 mostly black women and men from all across America whose presence both humbled and overwhelmed me. "Thank you for being so supportive of what we've been trying to do in publishing *Essence* these last twenty-five years," I said to the crowd. "We don't say that enough—*thank you!* Thank you for spending your hard-earned dollars by coming to New Orleans to be with us this weekend to share a magnificent milestone in *Essence*'s history. Thank you for telling us by being here tonight, 'A job well done.'"

In 1995 *Essence* magazine turned 25. A publication launched in struggle and uncertainty a quarter of a century ago was all grown up, prosperous, and respected. The company was celebrating with a three-day blowout in New Orleans over the Fourth of July weekend.

If I dreamed of a knockout event to mark *Essence*'s twentieth-anniversary year in 1990, I had even grander ambitions for the magazine's twenty-fifth-year celebration. In fact, I started thinking about how to celebrate the twenty-fifth anniversary almost as soon as we had wrapped up the twentieth-anniversary fete with a glittering awards show at Radio City Music Hall. I knew I wanted to celebrate twenty-five years with something even more spectacular. I just didn't know what.

I was having drinks one evening in 1994 with George Wein, producer of the legendary Newport Jazz Festival, and I told him I wanted to celebrate the twenty-fifth milestone of the magazine with something *major*—not just another red-carpet event or splashy after-party.

"Did you ever think of doing a music festival in New Orleans over the Fourth of July weekend?" George asked me. I'd known George for many years. Besides the Newport Jazz Festival, he produced a number of other jazz venues, including the concerts at City College's Lewisohn Stadium, which I used to sneak into as a teenager when my father worked there as a janitor and would unlock the gate to the stadium, letting me slip in before a show started.

A music festival? In New Orleans over the July 4th weekend? No, I told George, I couldn't say that particular idea had ever occurred to me. But I like to think of myself as a big-ideas guy. I thought about George's idea of a three-day music festival in the Big Easy with its rich tradition of jazz, blues, line-stepping bands, and great food. There might be some cultural synergy in pairing the premier magazine for black women with the expertise of a well-known concert producer in doing a different kind of music festival.

I invited George to stop by the office and share his thinking with my top managers—Susan Taylor and Clarence Smith. I also invited Harry Dedyo, my chief financial officer, to the meeting. Harry kept his eye on the cash, and would want to know things like, how much is a music festival going to cost us? What's the profit potential?

George outlined the concept: three nights of concerts in New Orleans's famed Superdome stadium, featuring three or four A-list entertainers each night from all spectrums of black music: R&B, hip-hop, jazz, gospel. Because the Superdome had several smaller, informal theater lounges suitable for more intimate concerts, venues could be staged in these rooms as well. The idea was to produce a festival offering nonstop music for three nights, on both the main stage of the Superdome and in the stadium's smaller lounges—and to get corporate sponsors to foot most of the bill for producing the shows.

Susan and Clarence were initially lukewarm to the proposal. Would three nights of concerts really be enough to bring out a crowd to a hot city in July? What else could we offer that would give added value? I also wanted to move beyond a party for a party's sake in celebrating our twenty-fifth anniversary. *Essence* was known to give great parties, and three nights of concerts did smack of just more partying. I wanted to do more than that to honor the remarkable long-running success of the magazine.

Karen Thomas, the sales promotion manager who had introduced us to the world of corporate sponsorships, helped fine-tune the festival idea. Karen left *Essence* in 1992 to launch her own business, but we hired her back for a year in 1994 to specifically help plan *Essence*'s twenty-fifth-anniversary event. She suggested we think about doing daylong seminars and symposiums on each of the three days of the concerts that would be open and free to the public and held in the city's convention center. Vendor space could also be rented in the huge convention center, which had the capacity to accommodate hundreds of sales booths of every imaginable kind.

Additional revenue would be generated by concert ticket sales. Corporate sponsorships, however, were key to the concert being profitable. Getting big advertisers to sponsor the music festival by underwriting most of the production costs meant more profits to *Essence* and George Wein from the sale of concert tickets and vendor booths. Sponsors, in turn, received huge brand exposure with their corporate logos and products on display at a three-day music festival that had the potential to draw thousands of people to New Orleans over a holiday weekend.

Essence agreed to partner with George Wein's Festival Productions in producing the first Essence Music Festival in 1995. Expenses and profits would be split 50–50. Coca-Cola signed on as the lead corporate sponsor. Anita Baker, Boyz II Men, Luther Vandross, Mary J. Blige, Gladys Knight, and Earth, Wind & Fire, were the lead acts lined up to perform on the Superdome's main stage. Jazz venues in the arena's super lounges ran concurrently with the main stage acts, and featured that first year Thelonious Monk, Jr., Ramsey Lewis, Cassandra Wilson, and Dianne Reeves. Our celebrity hosts over the weekend—Queen Latifah, Sinbad, and the incomparable Bill Cosby—kept the evenings hot and the audience pumped.

The twenty-fifth anniversary of *Essence* was also celebrated in grand fashion with the Eighth Annual Essence Awards program, televised from

Madison Square Garden in the spring of 1995. Oprah Winfrey summed up the celebratory year at the awards program in her reading of an original poem created in special tribute to the magazine's anniversary by writer Khephra Burns, the husband of Susan Taylor. Burns captured the essence of the milestone with these first two lines:

> Girl, look at me! Not even one month old and calling for a revolution. Truth be told, I was a revolution.
> I am 25 now. A woman of my time. A product of my own generation. I know who I am.

As grand as the Essence Awards were, I have to say all of us were completely stunned by the success of the first Essence Music Festival, which became a crown jewel of the company. It drew 145,000 people to New Orleans during the Fourth of July weekend in 1995, and netted $500,000 in profit. The night I stood on stage looking at the 50,000 concertgoers whose presence confirmed the validity of the *Essence* market and the power of the *Essence* message, I knew the music festival was the beginning of something much larger than a one-time twenty-fifth-anniversary celebration. It was the beginning of an annual gathering of black entertainers and thinkers, *Essence* readers and advertisers, that would turn into the company's most profitable and celebrated corporate sponsor event, a distinction it holds to this day.

For nearly twenty years the festival has attracted some of the most popular entertainers in the world, who love doing what has become a major music gig. The Rev. Al Sharpton has attended every Essence Music Festival since the first one as a popular speaker during the symposium sessions. Topics at these free daytime events cover everything from how to improve public schools in the African-American community to financing a business idea or finding a suitable mate. Speakers feature some of the best thinkers and problem solvers in the African-American community, and over the years have included Iyanla Vanzant, Cornel West, Maxine Waters, Steve Harvey, Roland Martin, and Julianne Malveaux.

Over 400,000 people now flock to the city of New Orleans during the Fourth of July weekend, bringing between $175 to $200 million in consumer business to hotels, restaurants, retail stores, transportation services, and the Essence Music Festival itself. It's estimated that about $10 billion in revenue has flowed into the economy of New Orleans since *Essence* held its first festival in 1995. As music festivals go, the *Essence* event ranks among the top ones in the world, and is second only to Mardi Gras when it comes to the number of people who turn out for music festivals in the city of New Orleans specifically.

A second *Essence* festival in New Orleans almost didn't happen, however, because of political events coinciding with the first one in 1995. In the fall of that year, Murphy (Mike) J. Foster was elected governor of Louisiana and announced shortly after taking office that all affirmative action and set-aside programs guaranteeing a certain number of state projects to minority companies would be eliminated. Foster had defeated Cleo Fields, a prominent black Democratic politician, for the governorship of Louisiana in a runoff election. Foster switched his party affiliation from Democrat to Republican that year to better his odds of winning. Besides running on an anti–affirmative action platform, it was disclosed after he came into office that Foster personally paid more than $150,000 for former Ku Klux Klansman David Duke's mailing list of supporters.

The Essence Music Festival had shown in its very first year what it was worth to the economy of New Orleans. The city wouldn't get another cent of our money if the governor didn't back off his anti–affirmative action stance. I had no intention of bringing the festival back to a state run by a governor who was trying to eliminate affirmative action, *and* had ties to an avowed antiblack hate group. The National Urban League was planning to hold its annual convention in New Orleans that summer as well, a week after the Essence Music Festival. I knew I could be more effective in putting pressure on the governor if I got Hugh Price, the Urban League's executive director, to join with me. I gave him a call.

"Hugh, you've probably heard *Essence* is pulling out of New Orleans with our music festival if the governor doesn't give on affirmative action," I said to him. "Why don't you think about holding off on committing to New Orleans for your convention? Let's work together on this. I think we can be a real force here in showing Mike Foster why his affirmative action position is not a good idea."

Word got out to Marc Morial, New Orleans's black mayor, that *Essence* wasn't coming back for a second music festival, and that the National Urban League was also talking about canceling its convention in New

Orleans. This was conveyed to Kathleen Blanco, Louisiana's lieutenant governor, whose office oversaw state tourism. Nobody was saying it, but the idea of both *Essence* and the National Urban League withdrawing their business from the city of New Orleans in the summer of 1996 was unthinkable. Too much money was at stake; too many businesses relied on the black consumer dollar in cities hosting their conventions and other special events. Plus, there would be too much bad press. Bad press for the city of New Orleans, and bad press for the state of Louisiana, run by a governor with racist affiliations. I was ready to use "any means necessary" to deal with this guy. I'd told Hugh we could even threaten to get the Super Bowl to boycott playing in New Orleans if the state had no affirmative action laws.

I soon got a call from Kathleen Blanco, asking if I would come to Baton Rouge to meet with Governor Foster. I did, along with Hugh Price and my partner, Clarence Smith. We were successful in getting Foster to modify his position. I was shocked that he conceded anything at all so quickly.

After meeting with Foster I felt comfortable enough to go ahead with a second festival. But we lost over a million dollars. Because I wasn't sure whether *Essence* would be doing another festival, we had not advertised the event early in the magazine, which meant readers—our festival audience—didn't know until the last minute that there was even going to be a second festival. Advertisers didn't know either, since our sales staff was not out trying to sell corporate sponsorships for an event that might or might not happen. By the time we decided to go ahead with a second festival in New Orleans, it was too late to play effective catch-up. Audience attendance was down that year, as were corporate sponsorships. But the show did go on—and has every year since then to astounding success.

George Wein, however, did not continue his partnership with Essence Communications. My hard-line move in threatening to cancel the second festival if Governor Foster didn't stand down on his affirmative action position made George too uncomfortable. He was a music promoter, he said, not a political activist. Fortunately, *Essence* could afford to be both.

———

Losing a million dollars on the second Essence Music Festival hurt, but it was nowhere close to being fatal. The fact is, by the mid-nineties *Essence* was sitting comfortably on nearly $40 million in cash reserves, an impressive amount for most companies, and absolutely astounding for a small black one like *Essence*. This made us more than flush enough to absorb the financial loss caused by a political victory. We could afford to take a hard-line stand with a state governor, and did so, just as we had with a cosmetics company a few years before.

Whether putting up part of a $25,000 reward for information in the Tawana Brawley case in 1987 in which a 15-year-old black girl in upstate New York accused four white men of raping her, or marching through the streets of New York City for justice as I did following the brutal police killing of Amadou Diallo in the Bronx in 1999, I often made decisions to take political stands in order to make larger political points. Thanks to the superb money management of our CFO Harry Dedyo and my own fiscal prudence as publisher and CEO, *Essence* continued to get bigger and more profitable, giving us greater strength in flexing political and economic muscle.

I always said I wanted *Essence* to be like Time Warner, the publishing empire that had movies, books, and television, as well as magazines in its vast holdings. I saw ECI as a miniconglomerate within the African-American community. But I knew we had to expand our core magazine business into other magazine ventures if we were going to grow the franchise.

That's what drew me to *Income Opportunities*, a nuts-and-bolts business publication that *Essence* acquired in 1992 for between $2 and $3 million. *Income Opportunities* was a small family-owned magazine with a circulation of about 400,000. It appealed to the same small business audience as *Inc.* and *Fast Company* magazines, and also to the nine-to-five paycheck earner who wanted ideas on how to generate additional income.

Income Opportunities seemed like a good fit with the *Essence* magazine model. It provided good service information to a core of loyal readers who were strivers and aspirational, like the Essence Woman. It was subscriber driven, like *Essence,* and profitable. There was also the ego factor: I loved the idea of Essence Communications Inc., a black-owned magazine company, buying a white-owned magazine.

Ego notwithstanding, *Income Opportunities* was not the editorial fit I thought it would be. A basic no-glamour publication printed on newsprint-type paper rather than glossy stock like *Essence,* it had a lowbrow feel at odds with the polished, sophisticated look of the *Essence* brand. Though it made money, it lacked cachet and strong name recognition, two things for which *Essence* was well known. ECI sold *Income Opportunities* after five years.

I would not have even known *Income Opportunities* was for sale were it not for my membership in the Magazine Publishers Association (MPA), the industry's trade organization. Members include the CEOs and publishers of most of the big and small magazine companies—Hearst, Condé Nast, Time Inc., Hachette, Essence Communications Inc. I'd been a member of MPA since 1972. I didn't get much out of the organization in the beginning, but as time went on I began to recognize the value of MPA's programs and networking opportunities.

For my own benefit I started taking courses and going to workshops the MPA offered on advertising, sales, editorial, and circulation. These classes were invaluable to me as a publisher and CEO because I knew it was necessary to have a working knowledge of all areas of the magazine in running *Essence.* MPA membership also gave me access to important contacts, one of whom was the owner of *Income Opportunities,* who told me the magazine was for sale. ECI was not the only suitor interested in buying it, but we won the bid.

I was usually the only black at most MPA gatherings, since there were very few black publishers in the magazine business. And those who were—the big ones being Earl Graves, publisher of *Black Enterprise,* and John Johnson, publisher of *Ebony* and *Jet*—didn't seem comfortable at these all-white sessions. Perhaps this was one reason executive director Donald Kummerfeld reached out to me to join the MPA board of directors in 1988. The magazine industry has never been as racially diverse as it could be, and I think my presence on the board reflected an attempt to correct that.

In 1997 I was elected president of the Magazine Publishers Association, the first and only time in its seventy-five-year history that the MPA has had an African-American president. It was a crowning achievement, to be sure—a testament to the position of respect *Essence* had earned in the magazine industry, and an acknowledgment of my own leadership skills. This was confirmed when I was asked to serve a second term as president of the association in 1998. Until then, MPA presidents were elected to only one-year terms.

Many of my black peers in business say I have been successful because "white people like you." This is always leveled as something of a criticism, as if being comfortable doing business with whites or having whites like and be comfortable doing business with me makes me somehow less legitimate as a black businessman. That's the same reductive thinking that leads misguided black youth to equate doing well in school with "acting white."

Again, I think because my own qualities of quiet strength and steely tenacity tend to be underestimated, it's easier to give credit for my accomplishments to all those white people who reportedly like me. The truth is, no black person can really succeed in America without the support, regard, or alliance of whites along the way. But no whites have ever *controlled* me during the thirty-five years of *Essence*'s independent ownership.

One of the treasured works hanging in the art collection of my New York apartment is the series of twenty-one original paintings done by the African-American master Jacob Lawrence that depict the hanging of John Brown, the fiery white abolitionist for his daring raid on the armory at Harpers Ferry. Brown was considered something of a lunatic. Yet he was willing to pay with his life in the fight to end slavery. Those paintings remind me every day that, crazy or not, whites driven by a sense of decency and fair play have historically been on the side of African-Americans when we needed them to be—whether in business or in war, which at times can seem to be the very same thing. To suggest I would not be the success I am without my affiliations and friendships with whites is to trivialize the complexity of African-American history and human struggle.

———

ECI's next opportunity to expand its magazine brand came from a 27-year-old Hispanic woman with a German name. Christy Haubegger was introduced to me by Stephanie Oliver, the magazine's editor, who was taking her on a tour of the magazine's offices in 1995. They saw me in my office with the door open, as it typically was, and came in. I usually took the time to meet the visitors who came through on informal company tours.

The *Essence* offices were a popular visiting place for everyone from high school students on a class trip to hip-hop celebrities and celebrity wives. Hammer, the hip-hop sensation, stopped by one day with three of his entourage of "boyz" in tow to visit Susan. I heard these young men would courteously stand every time a female staff member came in the office to meet Hammer. Wynton Marsalis showed up another time by himself and wasn't fazed when the executive editor had no idea who he was. I was especially delighted to meet Lonnie Ali, wife of Muhammad Ali, who had stopped by my office when Ali was in town to receive an Essence Award.

On any given day, out-of-town visitors, models, writers, photographers, or entrepreneurs looking for advice on starting their own magazines were likely to be seen passing through the sleek *Essence* offices at 1500 Broadway in the heart of Times Square. Male visitors especially liked looking at all the pretty black women who worked for the magazine. One editor's 7-year-old son told her while he was spending a day with her at the office, "I just love it here!"

Essence had been a particular inspiration for Christy Haubegger, she told me after Stephanie introduced us. Christy was in town to solicit investor interest in her business idea: a magazine for Hispanic women just like the magazine for black women she'd grown up with. "Your last name doesn't suggest you're Hispanic," I told her, impressed with her spunk in turning what should have been a quick meeting into a sales pitch that ended with my asking her to leave her business plan with me.

When she was a year old, Christy Haubegger was adopted by a German family in Houston that had the sensitivity to try to inculcate her with her heritage. She graduated from the University of Texas, then Stanford Law School, and decided to try her hand at publishing. She wanted to create the one magazine she didn't see growing up: a publication featuring women who looked like her. "I didn't know I couldn't do it," Christy would say later in a profile *Texas Monthly* did on her following the launch of *Latina*, the magazine for Hispanic women that Essence Communications financed on the strength of Christy's seventy-five-page business plan.

Christy was pretty much pitching to the converted in selling me on the potential of the Hispanic women's market. I knew how fast the general Hispanic market was growing—and that it was being overlooked by advertisers. I concluded that if I already had a magazine for African-American women with a circulation of more than a million, and if I could develop a magazine for Hispanic women and build its circulation, the two magazines would be virtual powerhouses on Madison Avenue. With *Essence* and *Latina* in its magazine stable, ECI had the potential to reach most of the women in America. Or at least most of America's women of color.

Latina has had slow but steady growth since its launch in 1997. Its circulation is now 500,000. In 2000, 75 percent of the magazine was bought by Molly Ashby, head of Solera Capital, a private equity firm. Solera bought the remaining 25 percent of *Latina* when *Essence* was sold to Time Warner in 2005.

While *Latina* magazine represented the future of a growing demographic, by the end of the 1990s I was interested in securing an owner's position in the hot, new successful publication of the day—*Vibe,* a magazine that was quickly becoming a leader in the exploding hip-hop market. Hip-hop in the nineties was to the Gen-X and -Y generations what R&B and rock and roll had been to the '60s Baby Boom generation. *Essence's* 18-to-34 age group was growing older. A twenty-fifth anniversary for the magazine represented a generation, and the generation that came of age reading *Essence* was aging out. This transition started to occur just as new competitive forces began nipping at the heels of *Essence's* traditional market.

First, after twenty-five years, *Essence* had proved the validity of the black female market, which meant that the pages of many mainstream white women's magazines, especially the fashion and beauty publications, now reflected this reality. Black models were routinely featured in advertising layouts, editorial features, and fashion and beauty spreads in white books. Black celebrities were showing up more frequently on white magazine covers. Oprah Winfrey, with her number one TV talk show, was the perennial favorite in the late 1990s, since her presence on any magazine cover increased newsstand sales that month for the magazine showcasing her.

Barbara Britton, who came from MTV to *Essence* as national sales director in 1988, remembers seeing at least three women's magazines on the newsstands in one month during the early 1990s that featured a black women on the cover. "You had white magazines now going after the young, black female market," she said. "What changed is that the industry recognized the consumption power of the black female regarding beauty products. For most women's magazines, the largest category of advertising comes from the beauty industry."

Secondly, the white women's magazines started to emulate some of the editorial features *Essence* had pioneered under Susan Taylor's leadership: doing special issues on men, featuring plus-sized fashion models, covering international stories, showcasing bold, in-your-face covers. *Essence*'s December 1994 cover was its gutsiest ever, and became the highest newsstand seller in the history of the magazine.

The cover showed a beautiful young woman with a haunting look, staring out at the reader. There was just one cover line, "FACING AIDS," and four stacked accompanying blurbs: "I'm young, I'm educated, I'm drug-free, and I'm dying of AIDS." The woman was Rae Lewis-Thornton, a 32-year-old professional African American who represented the changing face of AIDS in the nineties as black women became the fastest-growing population of people with AIDS.

Diane Weathers, who was *Essence* editor-in-chief from 2000 to 2005, remembers running into *Cosmopolitan* magazine's top editor, Kate White, at a magazine luncheon years after the *Essence* AIDS cover had been published. "That AIDS cover you guys did a few years ago was fabulous," Kate old Diane. "I'd love to be able to do something like that at *Cosmo*, but we'd never be allowed to."

Honey, a magazine geared to black women aged 18 to 34, debuted in 1998, started by two young African-American women, Kierna Mayo and Jocelyn Dingle, who wanted to bring the same unexpected edge to younger black readers that *Essence* was bringing to its demographic. But nine months after debuting, the magazine was sold to Vanguarde Media, a publishing enterprise headed by Keith Clinkscales, a young black publisher who had a couple of other fledgling magazines in his business stable: *Heart & Soul,* the black-oriented health publication started by Rodale in 1994 and sold after two years; and *Savoy,* a general interest magazine self-styled as the "Black *Vanity Fair*." But *Honey* had the potential to be Clinkscales's biggest moneymaker, and represented the most direct challenge to *Essence*'s market.

To be sure, the hip-hop magazines also represented new competition. These publications were young and edgy and appealed to a huge crossover audience of young, black, white, Hispanic, and Asian male and female readers. These readers were the multicultural consumers of bling jewelry and Cristal champagne, Tommy Hilfiger and Timberland, the very luxury goods and youth-oriented fashion advertisers that *Essence* coveted.

I considered *Vibe* to be a hot magazine editorially, and thought the publication with its hip younger audience would be a nice complement to the Essence brand. I had heard through its owner, Bob Miller, who was on the board of MPA with me, that the magazine was going to be up for sale. I told him Essence Communications would definitely be interested in making a bid.

Vibe launched in 1993 as a partnership between Quincy Jones and Time Inc. Three years later the magazine was sold to Bob Miller, who purchased it with a group of private equity investors. Looking to make a quick killing, the group, Miller Publishing, wanted between $200 and $300 million for the magazine in 1999. Maybe we could do a deal in the neighborhood of $75 million, and that was probably a stretch, but $200 to $300 million was out of the question.

I first engaged the services of Goldman Sachs to evaluate *Essence*'s financial strength before we made an official offer to buy *Vibe*. Then we listened to the pitch Bob and his partners gave, providing information on *Vibe*'s advertising sales, circulation, earnings, and future projections.

Editorially, the magazine was first-rate. Respected African-American and Hispanic hip-hop writers such as Greg Tate, Harry Allen, Kevin Powell, Joan Morgan, Jeannine Amber, dream hampton, Michael A. Gonzales, Scott Poulson-Bryant, and Nelson George were regular contributors. *Vibe* would win a National Magazine Award for General Excellence in 2002 under its African-American editor-in-chief, Emil Wilbekin, beating out *The New Yorker* in its circulation category. Emil would later join *Essence* as an editor-at-large. If we could come to a meeting of the minds on price, the magazine looked to be a good investment and nice editorial fit with *Essence* and its new sister, *Latina*.

Then the other shoe dropped. During the annual meeting of MPA in Scottsdale, Arizona, in 1999, Bob Miller came up to me at the opening cocktail reception to say, "Ed, did you know Time Inc. is rebidding on *Vibe*?" Needless to say, I didn't know this, and felt momentarily blindsided. *If Time is rebidding, then we can all step back, because there's no way we can compete with their money and resources,* I thought. Suddenly, I had another thought: *Maybe Time Inc. and* Essence *could work together and buy* Vibe *jointly.*

I ran the idea by Richard Parsons, a friend who was then president of Time Warner, making him one of the highest-ranking blacks in corporate America. He was soon to become *the* highest-ranking black in corporate America when he stepped up to be chairman and CEO of Time Warner. "Dick, am I off the ranch in thinking about the possibility of doing a joint venture with Time Inc. to buy *Vibe?*" I asked him.

"No, you're not off the ranch," Dick told me. "You know Don Logan. Talk to Don and keep me in the loop." Don Logan was the president and CEO of Time Inc. I called him to say I had heard Time was interested in buying *Vibe,* and that *Essence* was too. Perhaps we could do it together.

On the morning of January 10, 2000, we met for breakfast in one of the Time Warner private dining rooms to discuss the matter further. I had asked Rich Wayner, the point person at Goldman Sachs who was evaluating *Essence,* to accompany me. Don asked Michelle Ebanks, a young black woman who was his chief of staff, to also join us.

No sooner had the four of us been seated and were about to place our order than Gerald Levin, chairman and CEO of Time Warner, came up to the table with another man, a much younger guy. "Good morning, Ed," Levin said quickly. "I know why you're here. I just wanted you to meet Steve Case," he said, turning to the man who was with him.

Case needed no introduction. He was the chairman, CEO, and co-founder of AOL, the Internet juggernaut transforming the face of media. "We're about to make a major announcement," Levin added, looking at Case. The two of them then quickly left, heading for another table.

I had no idea Time Warner was about to announce that very day that it was being acquired by AOL in a stunning deal that would leave media pundits speechless. This meant any deal involving the prospect of *Essence* buying *Vibe* in partnership with Time Inc. was off the table, which I didn't know either as I plunged ahead at the breakfast meeting.

"Don, we're here to talk about how we can work together to buy *Vibe*," I said, but couldn't get another word out because Don quickly cut me off.

"Before we do that," he said, "why don't we talk about Time Inc. investing in *Essence*?" I was taken completely by surprise. What was Logan talking about? I was soon left speechless myself as he began to discuss what would become *Essence*'s own stunning deal.

CHAPTER 24

Time on Our Side

No doubt about it, timing is everything, and the timing couldn't have been better the morning Don Logan and I met for breakfast to talk about a possible joint venture between Essence Communications Inc. and Time Inc. It was the first month of the new millennium, January 10, 2000, more than a year and a half before the events of September 11, 2001, would shatter the security of our world as we knew it. A few years afterward there would be the bursting of the dot-com bubble and the convulsing collapse of Bear Stearns and Lehman Brothers, leaving aftershocks of job losses, tanking real estate, teetering banks, a wrecked car industry, and a crashing stock market.

But in that sliver of boom time between the terrorist acts of 9/11 and the Lehman crash of 2008, a little window of opportunity would open just in time for a black-owned women's magazine and the world's largest media company to do a historic deal.

At the time Essence and Time initiated talks about coming together, the American economy was on a bullish upswing, and the fortunes of women's magazines had never seemed better. New titles such as *More*, published by the Meredith Corporation, and *O, The Oprah Magazine*, a Hearst publication, came into the marketplace in 1998 and 2003, respectively. *More* would create a successful new advertising niche for women over 40, while *O* magazine cemented a niche for celebrity brands in women's magazines that had been established by such personalities as Frances Lear, Grace Mirabella, Jane Pratt, Rosie O'Donnell, and Martha Stewart.

The names of all these women, along with Oprah Winfrey's, became the names of *their* magazines, branded in the cachet of their personal celebrity. *Lear's, Mirabella, Jane, Rosie, Martha Stewart Living,* and *O, The Oprah Magazine,* were the titles synonymous with the singular power of a woman's name to label a new category of women's magazines.

Not coincidentally, Time Inc. was the original publisher of *Martha Stewart Living* when it launched in 1990. Acknowledged as the Goliath in the magazine industry, Time Inc., the mighty, cash-generating magazine division of its parent company, Time-Life, had begun something of an expansionist march to acquire and launch new magazines during the 1980s and '90s. In 1980, Time Inc. spun off a little one-page section in *Time* magazine called "People" into a celebrity-driven magazine, also called *People,* that would become a magazine-selling monster. In 1990, the entity Time-Life was dissolved, and Time Inc. merged with Warner Communications to create Time Warner, a sprawling media conglomerate that had 130 titles in its magazine division, making it the largest publisher of magazines in the world.

Among the best known of the magazines were the original "old boys" in what had once been a male boutique of Time Inc. publications: *Time,* the company's namesake newsmagazine and respected elder; *Fortune* and *Money* magazines, and *Sports Illustrated,* which had also started life as a one-pager in *Time* magazine before growing up to become its own publication in 1954. And then there was *People,* the runaway bestseller that accounted for fully *one-half* of the $1.2 *billion* in revenues that the Time Inc. magazine unit was generating by the year 2000.

Time Inc. had picked up a whole magazine operation in the South when it acquired the Birmingham, Alabama–based Southern Progress Corporation (SPC) in 1985. The acquisition cost $498 million, making it the largest amount ever paid for a magazine company at the time, and brought into the Time Warner fold *Southern Living, Cooking Light, Coastal Living, Health,* and *Sunset* magazines, along with a book division.

Don Logan also came with the deal. He had been Southern Progress's executive vice president before becoming its chairman and CEO at the time of the company's sale to Time Inc. Time left its new southern operation intact in Birmingham, and Don would run the division for six years before moving to New York in 1992 to work directly with Time Inc. He was promoted to president and CEO of Time Inc. in 1994. The title of chairman was added to his positions in 1997.

By the year 2000, Time Inc.'s empire extended to not just the American South, but to the United Kingdom as well, with magazines covering everything from celebrities and entertainment to health and fitness, fashion and beauty, golf, money management, hard news, household organizing, and old-house restorations. Under Don Logan's leadership, Time Inc. had eleven straight years of earnings growth. The assault of technology had not yet transformed the world of print media, though ironically the acquisition of Time Warner by AOL, announced the very day of my meeting with Don, would be the seismic act that signaled a transformation was looming.

What the Time Inc. behemoth did not have in its stable of magazine titles in 2000 were any publications geared to the African-American and Hispanic female markets. These markets represented new opportunities for Time Inc., Don was telling me during our breakfast meeting. The black female consumer market in particular had finally been recognized on Madison Avenue as a valuable demographic.

Don cut to the chase: "Ed, you know there are ways Time could be helpful to you, and vice versa," he said. "We have resources, clout in the industry, things that will preserve your business. You can use us. You have access to an arena that Time Inc. doesn't play in, but needs to. Maybe there's an opportunity for us to work together."

It turned out that Don Logan was much more interested in talking about doing a merger deal with *Essence,* not buying *Vibe.* "We took a look at *Vibe,*" he told me when I brought up the idea of ECI and Time Inc. maybe buying the magazine together. "Initially we were interested, but the more we looked, the more we realized it doesn't fit with us that well. We don't know the culture or how to expand on it. Besides, we got out of the music business when we sold Warner Music."

Essence, on the other hand, fit nicely with Time Inc.'s expansion into entertainment and lifestyle magazines. Besides the highly profitable *People* magazine, considered a largely women's publication, there was *Entertainment Weekly,* a guide to popular culture launched in 1990, and *InStyle,* a fashion and beauty magazine started in 1994. *Real Simple,* a women's service magazine on how to do practically everything more creatively and efficiently was published in 2003. Collectively, these female-oriented lifestyle titles became the cash cow of Time Warner's magazine holdings.

Essence was no less a cash cow, sitting with millions in reserves and a virtual monopoly on the African-American female market. The magazine was a proven brand, profitable and popular. This was in no small measure due to the inspiring leadership of Susan Taylor, *Essence*'s charismatic and revered editor-in-chief. A new millennium represented the perfect time to think about mighty Goliath and popular *Essence* perhaps forming a perfect union.

Which made it the worst time for Susan Taylor to say she was ready to leave the magazine.

———

The editor-in-chief position at *Essence* magazine is many things—glamorous and high-paying, respected and coveted, powerful, influential, and certain to confer considerable celebrity on anyone seated in the editor-in-chief's chair. Done long enough and well enough, the job is also certain to lead to exhausting burnout. No other top editor at a women's magazine is expected to be so many things to so many people: a leader and a spokeswoman, a political thinker, as well as a political activist, a race woman, a corporate manager, a creative ideas person, and an enforcer of bottom-line budgets; a "sister" who is down with her readers, and a magazine Houdini who can keep reader circulation perpetually up. Constantly in demand as a speaker or celebrity guest, the *Essence* editor-in-chief's traveling schedule can be grueling and nonstop.

Susan Taylor, like Marcia Gillespie before her, was tired. After nineteen years as *Essence*'s editor-in-chief—ten years more than Marcia had spent in the job—Susan, too, was ready to move on, wanted to pursue other interests. She had written three bestselling books that explored the spiritual themes she had popularized in her "In the Spirit" columns. She was in huge demand as a public speaker, was on everyone's A-list, and had the ear of every A-lister from Oprah Winfrey and Sean "P. Diddy" Combs to Bill Clinton and Nelson Mandela. Most important, she had been crucial to the enormous success of *Essence* magazine during her nearly two-decade run as chief editor. I understood why she was tired. But I wasn't happy that she wanted to leave.

Don Logan and I were in very early talks about a joint venture, and I knew the continued presence of Susan was central to how we sold ourselves to Time. Though Susan was neither the CEO nor a founder of *Essence,* she would often act as if she were both, something I never liked. Nor did I like the fact that many people thought she had started the magazine—and that she owned it. But what became more troubling were her escalating demands for money that seemed to start almost as soon as Don and I started talking about doing a deal. Still, I knew Susan was important to any venture with Time Inc. Consequently, I knew I had to talk her out of leaving.

"You may not want to do that," I said when Susan told me in early 2000 that she wanted to leave the magazine completely. "You may want to continue a relationship of some kind with us. Maybe as a consultant." Just as Marcia had been, Susan was vague about what she intended to do once she gave up the EIC chair. Other than take a much-needed break, which she did do in 2002, with a six-week sabbatical paid for by ECI, it wasn't clear what her next specific move would be.

Susan was quite clear, however, about who she wanted to have succeed her. This was the visionary quality in her that I always liked and respected. Not many top magazine editors think about who will replace them, let alone identify this person at the moment of hiring. Monique Greenwood was the person Susan identified at the moment of hiring as the woman who would one day replace her as editor-in-chief.

Monique started at *Essence* in 1995, at age 36, as the magazine's style director, overseeing the fashion and beauty departments and handling the cover selections and photo shoots. A couple of years later she became lifestyle editor, responsible for the parenting, home décor, travel, and food sections. She would next move up to be the magazine's executive editor before assuming the editor-in-chief title in 2000 when Susan stepped up to become publication director.

It occurred to me that if Susan could move away from the day-to-day running of the magazine—the endless meetings, interruptions, emergencies to deal with—she could have the "think time" she said she so desperately craved, and still be a part of the *Essence* team, especially as the company began talks with Time Inc. Much like the position of editorial director had been when Gordon Parks had that title thirty years before, the position of publication director was created to be something of a "higher authority" in the editorial department.

But unlike Gordon, who was no longer at the office or even working for the magazine during the last year he held the editorial director title, Susan would keep her office, come in on a more flexible work schedule, and focus on ECI's expanding corporate ventures, mainly the music festival and awards program. She would also continue to do her "In the Spirit" column, which had become so popular the advertising sales staff sold ad placements against it. The day-to-day running of the magazine, however, would be assumed by Monique Greenwood, a seasoned editor with the prodigious ability to multitask.

A native of Washington, DC, Monique graduated from Howard University with a degree in communications, and would spend the first fifteen years of her career working for Fairchild Publications in a variety of top editorial positions at the trade press: fashion editor at *Daily News Record,* the men's fashion trade paper; editor of *SportStyle;* and editor-in-chief and associate publisher of *Children's Business,* a publication she helped launch that covered the burgeoning universe of children's fashion, furniture, toys, and licensing. Considered a rising star at Fairchild, at age 31 Monique was named one of the "40 Under Forty" people cited by *Crain's New York Business* as a mover and shaker in the New York City business world.

Monique proved to be a force in her own business world as an entrepreneur running an eighteen-room bed-and-breakfast that she and her husband, Glen Pogue, opened in 1995, just around the time she started to work at *Essence.* The Akwaaba Mansion, as the inn was called (*akwaaba* means "welcome" in Swahili), was an 1863 Federal-style house located in the historic black section of Brooklyn's Bedford-Stuyvesant. The antebellum mansion quickly became a popular place for parties and weekend retreats, as well as traditional bed-and-breakfast lodging.

Susan would say the first time she saw Monique's Akwaaba B&B and toured the artfully decorated mansion that she knew she had found *Essence's* next editor-in-chief. Monique had been asked to host a book party for Susan in the mansion's elegant ballroom, and afterward Monique offered to show Susan the rest of the B&B. "We need you at *Essence,*" Susan said, as she climbed the stairs to the mansion's widow's walk at the end of the tour. "I was flattered," Monique said. "Susan liked that I was marrying contemporary home furnishings with a cultural African flavor in my B&B, which is why she offered me the job of style director at *Essence*."

Monique represented the younger generation of black women who had grown up seeing their mothers' copies of *Essence* on their coffee tables. As a teenager who aspired to be a journalist, she had *Essence* as the model for where a career in the field could take her. "*Essence* was certainly the publication that proclaimed me as beautiful," Monique remembers, "and I probably gave voice that at some point maybe I could be editor-in-chief of the magazine."

Although Monique had been to *Essence* to interview for jobs a couple of times before joining the magazine, ECI could never match the salary she was getting at Fairchild. Susan persuaded her to join the company on the promise that she would quickly move up. "I was used to running a publication at Fairchild," Monique said, "and I didn't make any more money when I came to *Essence*. My name was also lower on the masthead. But *Essence* was a bigger title in terms of audience reach, and I got to write for an audience that meant everything to me. It was an amazing experience to be able to sit around a conference room table and be affirmed as a black woman, knowing that you were working with the brightest, most creative, and most beautiful women in the world."

Yet by 2000, Monique, like Susan, was ready to move on. She had essentially been doing two jobs—helping to run *Essence* as its executive editor, while also running her own bed-and-breakfast operation. Plus, she was planning to open a second bed-and-breakfast, was writing a book, and had a young daughter to raise. Her book was titled *Having What Matters*, and Monique had concluded that what mattered was having family time and the time to pursue her entrepreneurial interests.

After Monique come back from a vacation in early 2000, Susan asked to meet with her. This was right after I had persuaded Susan to take on the newly created position of publication director, a title we both agreed would keep her in a top position, but relieve some of the stress of running the magazine daily. Susan was ready to give her editor-in-chief title to Monique, but Monique, too, like Susan, was thinking of leaving. "I felt in my gut that it was maybe time for me to move on," she recalled, "and I thought I should probably let Susan know that." But that's precisely what

Susan wanted to tell Monique about her own life. "I'm exhausted," Susan said during their meeting. "I can't do this anymore."

"I can't do this anymore either," Monique responded. "I'm ready to move on. I'm about to open another bed-and-breakfast in Cape May, New Jersey."

"Oh, no," Susan said, alarmed. "I want you to replace me. We have this deal with Time going on, and I think I can sell them on you stepping in as editor-in-chief."

Monique admitted she was honored and flattered, and smart enough to recognize that the editor-in-chief position at *Essence*, with its high income and even greater celebrity, would give her B&Bs terrific visibility and a foundation of financial stability. Rather than moving on, she agreed to stay on and move up to the editor-in-chief position.

Succeeding Susan Taylor, however, who had become an icon and even something of an institution during her nearly thirty years in total service at *Essence*, would be a challenge for even the best multitasking editors. Like Gordon Parks and Ruth Ross, the editorial director and editor-in-chief who had gone to the mat before the first issue of *Essence* hit the market thirty years before, there would be an inevitable battle between the new publication director and the new editor-in-chief over who was in charge of running the magazine.

————

"How does it feel to walk in Susan Taylor's shoes?" someone in the audience asked Monique Greenwood during the Q&A session following one of the public speaking appearances she made shortly after her appointment as *Essence*'s editor-in-chief.

"I'm honored to walk in Susan's light, but I wear my own pumps," Monique answered deftly. Indeed, the woman who followed in Susan Taylor's footsteps walked in faith and confidence and a sense of her own personal power. I always trusted the judgment of my senior managers, and I knew that Susan spotted qualities in Monique early on that she felt made her ideal as the heir apparent to the editor-in-chief position.

To begin with, Monique's force of personality was as strong as Susan's. So was her passion, her politics, and her sense of mission. Open and accessible, she had a down-home, nurturing earth mother manner that her staff loved. She was also an unpretentious straight shooter, fully aware of the challenge she had taken on in replacing a legendary editor-in-chief. "How do I create a new face for *Essence* after it has had the same face for nineteen years?" she would ask. "And I'm coming with a new face that I know not everybody is going to be happy to see—light-skinned and full-figured. But I was up for the challenge, and I tried to be sensitive."

The first challenge Monique faced was pressure from our advertising sales department to skew *Essence* younger. Newer magazine upstarts such as *Vibe* and *Honey* were enticing the very market that was eroding at *Essence* as its readers aged out of the prime 18-to-34 age category. The big advertisers in women's magazines come from the beauty industry, and they want the younger market because this is the reader more likely to be experimenting with hair and makeup products, two huge categories of advertising. "The younger girls are the ones going to the clubs on the weekend, trying to look fabulous to get a guy," Monique would tell Susan, who was resistant to making the magazine appeal to a younger demographic. "The young woman constitutes a consuming public; she's in the acquisition phase of her life and represents an ideal market for advertisers."

Internally this presented another challenge to *Essence* because the magazine did not want to lose its older core readers, the readers whom Susan identified with and who were loyal to her. "These were the readers who were trying to figure out how to move into retirement," Monique said, "and the younger readers that our sales team wanted us to go after were trying to figure out how to start their careers after college. How do you speak to both these women? White readers have an endless choice of magazines—*More* if you're over 40, *Seventeen* if you're a young white girl, and tons of magazines in between. *Essence* had to be everything to every black woman, and that was really hard."

Monique found it particularly hard trying to serve two masters: Clarence Smith on the advertising side, who insisted on skewing the magazine younger, and Susan Taylor, who was no longer editor-in-chief, but as publication director felt she had the final say in magazine decisions. Monique chose to follow the directives of Clarence, who was still butting heads with Susan. This would ultimately put Monique in the untenable position of taking on Susan.

I understood the newer black-oriented magazines catering to a younger demographic represented a threat to the *Essence* market, not just in siphoning off our readers, but also our advertising. As Barbara Britton, our national sales director, pointed out, "You had a new, sexy magazine like *Honey* selling a page of advertising for $5,000, as opposed to *Essence*, which sold its page for $30,000. *Honey* didn't have the circulation we did, but it had more of the demographic our advertisers wanted—younger and hipper—so just from a cost-per-page standpoint and the delivery of an audience, it represented a better buy."

Taking her cue from advertising, Monique took the magazine younger and hipper. There was a recurring feature titled "The Date," in which an *Essence* writer was set up to go out with a celebrity, and both the writer and celebrity would then give a she-said/he-said first-person account in the magazine of how the date went. The first date story featured writer Deborah Gregory, author of the popular book series *The Cheetah Girls,* on a date with the irrepressible hip-hop celebrity Fab 5 Freddy, which turned into a hilarious account of bad behavior, mixed signals, and missed communication on the part of Freddy. *Essence* "Contemporary Living" editor Tara Roberts went on a charming date with Heavy D, a rapper who was as gracious and gentlemanly as Freddy had been boorish and insensitive.

Writer Joan Morgan did a story on wearing her hair natural and then putting on a wig to assess what hair means to black women—long versus short, natural versus straight. A fashion page titled "What We're Wearing" was started that showcased how young, fashionably hip women from around the country were dressing. Cover stories on rap divas such as Foxy Brown, Lil' Kim, and Missy Elliott brought the world of rap music to readers who were still largely into Anita Baker, Patti LaBelle, and Mary J. Blige.

The stories were fresh, young, and fun, yet circulation started sliding downward as "request cancels" went up, the surest barometer that a magazine is missing the mark editorially.

"We couldn't make a radical shift without pissing off the older readers," Monique would explain a dozen years later. "They just wanted *their* magazine." So did Susan. Never comfortable with the younger slant the magazine was taking under Monique, the slide in circulation was proof enough to Susan that older was better—at least at *Essence.* "I was hired to lower the age demographic. Everybody knew that had to happen," Monique said, "and I would tell Susan this is what advertising wants, but she was not comfortable with it."

Nor, it turned out, was Susan comfortable with an editor-in-chief who was as strong as she was editorially, yet had her own style of leadership. Susan had always led by consensus. There were mass meetings for everything from reviewing page layouts to coming up with cover lines, and Susan would solicit the input of everyone from senior editors to secretaries. Monique, by contrast, believed that the editor-in-chief is the general giving the marching orders to a staff she entrusts to carry them out. In formulating what direction the magazine should take in the face new challenges from new competitors, Susan wanted to put together a team of editors to figure this out.

"I wasn't comfortable with that," Monique said, "because these editors are the team I have to lead, and they have to believe that I know what the direction should be. I told Susan if you think I don't know, then you and I can work together to figure it out, but I'm not going to be put on the same level with people who report to me also telling me what direction to take. I like group buy-in, but not group direction."

Though I never interfered with Susan and Monique's interactions, I was usually more in Susan's camp just because she had proved over the years to have her finger accurately on the pulse of the *Essence* reader. Plus, the increase in request cancellations on the circulation side indicated that skewing younger may not have been the way for *Essence* to go. On the other hand, Monique had a point when she noted there was never any marketing support for lowering the age demographic of the magazine. "How are we going to let younger women know that *Essence* is no longer their mothers' magazine?" she would ask. "We're not satisfying the older reader and we're not introducing ourselves to the younger reader."

I do believe at the heart of the conflicts between Susan and Monique is what could be called the Michael Jordan syndrome: A star player is not always ready to retire from the game, even when he (or she) says he is. In Susan's case, she moved up to the newly created position of publication director, but was perhaps not really ready to turn over the power of running the magazine and making editorial decisions as editor-in-chief to a successor, even one initially anointed by her.

Nor had the responsibilities of publication director ever been made

clear, a failing on both my part and Susan's. As Monique said of the rock
and the hard place she found herself caught between, "It's never easy to
take on the top job held by someone else when that person is still present.
And if the new job they've been promoted to is undefined, it's easy for
them to slip back into doing the old job. Susan's job was to redefine herself
in her new position, which is never easy, and my job was to be sensitive to
the fact that that's what she needed to do, but at the same time create a
management space for myself." There were not only conflicts of management style, but also issues of respect—or perceptions of the lack thereof.

From the moment Monique announced that she would be walking in
her own shoes as *Essence* editor-in-chief, and not her predecessor's, there
was wary suspicion on the part of Susan, an editor-in-chief whose leadership style had been unassailable for almost twenty years.

In her first editorial column, titled "Within," Monique made it clear
where she expected to take the magazine as the new EIC: "For the last
nineteen years, Susan Taylor has built a skyscraper on a foundation laid by
Marcia Ann Gillespie," she said in the column's opening paragraph. "Now
it's my intent to add a penthouse!" The idea was to say the magazine was
being taken to the next level, though I'm sure it was just as easy for Susan
to think that Monique was also saying she intended to make the magazine
better, which, in truth, any new chief editor is expected to do.

Within a year as EIC, Monique had a showdown with Susan. Monique had returned from a vacation in 2001 and was summoned to Susan's
office to talk yet again about letting the *Essence* editorial team set the new
direction for the magazine. Again, Monique balked at that idea. "I told
Susan we were going to have to lose some old readers to gain new ones—
that we would have to shake off some of the people who wanted the magazine to be like it had been for the past thirty years." Monique also said
she needed to feel empowered to lead the staff, and not be led by the staff.

"Well, maybe this isn't going to work," Susan told Monique, informing
her that she thought her attitude was arrogant.

"Maybe it's *not* going to work," Monique fired back.

"Well, then, I'm going to have to ask for your resignation," Susan said
icily. "You should get your things together and be out in a week."

Monique was stunned. "This is not a good look, Susan," she finally
said. "If you want it to seem like this is an amicable split and we both

agreed to part ways, then I need to finish up the issue we're working on and transition my team."

"No. I just need you to get your things and be out."

Monique called her lawyer.

In an instant, an ongoing disagreement had escalated to the point of no return as two strong-willed black women metaphorically took off their earrings, bared claws, and threw down. The timing couldn't have been worse. Essence and Time Inc. had just entered into a partnership agreement that would give us five years to get to know each other before consummating a final deal. The last thing *Essence* needed was a shakeup at the top of its editorial department.

Time would still be our side as Susan quickly moved to hire *Essence*'s next editor-in-chief. And in time Susan would apologize to Monique for the less than professional way in which she was let go. Yet over time, long after Susan had left the magazine and no longer had a say in the matter, every editor-in-chief who followed her for the next eight years, beginning with Monique Greenwood, would be asked to resign within one to five years. During the thirty-five years of *Essence*'s independent ownership, only two editors-in-chief, Marcia Ann Gillespie and Susan L. Taylor, whose combined leadership totaled twenty-eight years, would prove to have the vision, the commitment, and the stamina to be long-distance runners.

CHAPTER 25

Selling In

I couldn't believe a business publisher like Earl Graves would condone such one-sided, inaccurate reporting in his magazine. Yet there it was, the very opening paragraph of a story appearing in the September 2002 issue of *Black Enterprise,* written by Derek Dingle, the magazine's editor-in-chief, that took this off-the-mark swipe at the agreement made between Essence Communications Inc. and Time Inc. on October 9, 2000: "When Ed Lewis and Clarence Smith cut a deal with AOL Time Warner two years ago, they were offered the promise of fresh capital and new markets for the leading black women's magazine. Little did they know it would mean the split of a 32-year-old business partnership and a fight for the soul of an institution."

It's not as if I wasn't expecting cries of "sellout" when I decided to move ECI forward with a Time Inc. merger. But in 2002, AOL Time Warner had not yet even acquired *Essence.* In fact, when Don Logan and I first sat down to talk, Time Warner was still an independent entity not yet owned by AOL, though that would quickly change.

In 2000 I was still pretty much interested in staying independent. My idea was to buy *Vibe,* not to sell *Essence.* It was Don Logan who broached the idea of Time taking a partnership position in ECI when we continued our talks about working together. He first suggested a 10 percent stake, then 40 percent, and finally offered 50 percent. I said no to that one. "If I'm going to sell you 50 percent of the company, then I may as well sell it all to you," I told him. "And I don't think our [African-American] community is prepared for Time to own 50 percent of Essence."

"Well, Time doesn't do deals in which we don't have at least a 50 percent interest," Don said. I suggested he try to think outside the box. He did. The next time we met he had come up with the proposition that Time Inc. buy a 49 percent stake in Essence; Essence would retain 51 percent, still giving us ownership control, and in the year 2005 we would sit down again to talk about Time taking full ownership of Essence Communications Inc. We would agree in principle to Time buying Essence, but be engaged for five years, getting to know each other to see if we wanted to get married in a merger after that time. Either side could also pull out before consummating a final deal, giving Essence the option to buy back its 49 percent.

Under the terms of engagement an entity called Essence Communications Partners was created that included a twelve-person board consisting of six members from Essence and six from Time. The liaison between the two boards was Michelle Ebanks, the young black woman Don brought with him to our first breakfast meeting. Michelle would be key in shepherding both sides through a tricky deal. The idea that Time was promising Essence "fresh and new markets," as purported in the *Black Enterprise* article, was ludicrous. Essence *had* the fresh and new market Time wanted—the black female consumer.

My real objection to the lead paragraph of that *Black Enterprise* story is that my partner Clarence Smith and I were portrayed as poor dupes who didn't realize that selling the magazine would mean the end of our partnership. My partnership with Clarence totaled thirty years at the time I first sat down with Don Logan to discuss a venture with Time Inc. From the beginning, Clarence opposed the idea of the two companies coming together.

This would mean that as surely as Susan Taylor had to stay to ensure the viability of a joint venture, Clarence Smith would have to go. I knew I couldn't move forward with a Time Inc. deal if Clarence was a part of the negotiation because he had been a recurring problem for quite a few years in both his interactions with Susan Taylor and in his role as president of the company.

For all intents and purposes, Clarence abdicated his position as number one salesman at the magazine when he ceded his title, national sales director, to Barbara Britton a few years after she joined the company in 1988. Barbara was a hard-charging, tough-as-nails manager, yet a superb sales executive whose background in selling ads for both print (she had worked for *Black Enterprise*) and broadcast (she had also worked for MTV) media gave her a strategic advantage in selling corporate sponsors for the Essence Music Festival and the Essence Awards program, as well as selling advertising in the magazine.

While Barbara ably ran the *Essence* sales department, Clarence retained his title of company president and head of the company's entertainment division, which was responsible for the Essence Music Festival and the Essence Awards. But Clarence wanted to move into other high-visibility ventures, some magazine related, some not. He wanted to get into the music business and start a record label. He wanted to buy into other media—television, cable, radio—none of which the company knew anything about. We knew magazines, and that had taken us thirty years to learn. At one point Clarence came to the board with a proposal to do an Internet deal that would have cost us $20 million! I believe that's when the board began having misgivings about his future role at the magazine. I myself had been having misgivings for quite some time.

I was particularly dismayed when Clarence became a licensed boxing promoter in the late 1990s. His son was trying to get a career going as a boxer, and Clarence envisioned himself managing his son's career. As a result, he spent less time at the office and more time going to boxing venues in Atlantic City. My dismay turned to outright disgust in March 1999 when I joined with a group of black businessmen, clergy, and politicians in a march to City Hall to protest the police killing of a young, unarmed African named Amadou Diallo, who had been gunned down just outside his Bronx apartment building. Clarence declined to participate in the march, saying that if he were to be arrested during the protest, he would lose his boxing license, and he didn't want to chance that happening.

Though we would be partners for more than thirty years, Clarence and I couldn't have been more different lifestyle-wise, which is why we rarely socialized outside the office. He was a drinker who on more than one occasion had been accused of sexual harassment by some of the women who worked for Essence. This was a true embarrassment at a company built on affirming black women in the magazine it published. Our legal counsel, Charles (Chuck) Hamilton, would be forced to speak to Clarence a few times regarding his behavior. Chuck was an African-American partner in the law firm of Battle Fowler, which became our general counsel after Suzanne Warshavsky retired in 1994. I went with the firm strictly because of my association with Chuck, having worked with him in the past. I knew I could trust him to delicately handle Clarence. Chuck reminded Clarence that beyond embarrassing, sexual harassment is *illegal*. ECI could be held legally liable.

I've always felt that *Essence* could have continued to benefit from Clarence's enormous talent as a salesman if he had kept his eye on the ball and kept doing what he had a natural gift for doing: selling. But sales was never the profession he wanted to star in. As *Essence* became increasingly popular and profitable, he seemed to desire a role as elder statesman of some sort—as an A-list businessman whose counsel and company were sought in areas outside of sales.

Clarence did become a board member of a few rather prestigious organizations in the health and beauty industry, some of which were key magazine advertisers not known for allowing magazine advertising salespeople into their ranks. For instance, his position as a director on the board of the Cosmetic, Toiletry, and Fragrance Association left other magazine sales directors wondering just how was the president of a black women's magazine allowed such entry. The answer had to do with Clarence's two other assets: street-smart savvy and pure charm.

Clarence and Susan, however, continued to butt heads as he pushed to skew the magazine younger and she pushed to keep the editorial content geared to *Essence*'s core readership, which was growing older. Any stories that hinted at things like menopause, for instance, made Clarence blow his stack. In 1992, when *Essence* assigned former *Washington Post* reporter Jill Nelson to do a Q&A interview with Anita Hill following her testimony during the Senate hearings on the confirmation of Clarence Thomas to the U.S. Supreme Court, Clarence Smith went into a roaring rage. I don't know if Hill's charges of sexual harassment against Thomas hit too close to home for Clarence, or if he just felt the subject was too controversial for the reluctant advertisers he was still pitching to get into the magazine.

Yet during those relaxed, out-of-office moments that occurred when Susan and Clarence had to travel together, going to advertising and health and beauty events that called for the presence of our editor-in-chief and our company president, they would sometimes bond over talking about their children. Susan had a daughter, Shana; Clarence had two sons, Clarence and Craig; and both parents talked about the challenges of trying to raise children as busy, successful executives who were often not home as much as they would have liked.

Most times, however, the two would just individually come to me to complain about the other. Susan, in particular, would routinely come in to my office, saying things like, "Clarence has to go. He's out of control." By 2002, when we were almost at the midpoint in our engagement to Time and it was clear to me that Clarence could not be a part of any final sale "hanging on to the bumper," as Chuck Hamilton put it, Susan and Jim Forsythe, our circulation director, took me to dinner to reiterate once again that Clarence had to go. I agreed. So did the Essence board. But severing the partnership was not going to be easy.

I think Clarence's opposition to an Essence merger with Time had a lot to do with his fear of losing his job at the magazine. He no doubt thought he would die at his desk—that as a magazine founder he had the tenure of a guaranteed position for life. His forays into other business areas were the sort of pursuits he felt he had earned the right to do. After all, he had almost single-handedly sold Madison Avenue on a market that didn't even exist thirty years ago; he made it profitable, envied, and one that was now pursued by advertisers and other media alike.

To a lesser extent Clarence was also a "race man" who didn't want to see a viable black-owned company sell out to whites. In this respect he was like Earl Graves, the proud race man of Barbadian heritage who owned *Black Enterprise* magazine. It was unthinkable to Earl that Essence would even contemplate something as traitorous—or desperate, he thought—as selling its business to a conglomerate like AOL Time Warner. "Why didn't Ed give other black businessmen the opportunity to buy Essence?" he would ask, genuinely perplexed. He thought Essence must be in financial trouble and needed to sell. In Earl's mind, the ownership of Essence Communications Inc. did indeed boil down to what that article in *Black Enterprise* asserted: "a fight for the soul of an institution."

———

I wasn't worried about the "soul" of Essence. I was worried about its staying power. I wanted to ensure the longevity of Essence Communications as an institution serving the needs of black women. *That* would preserve its soul. It was becoming clear to me that independent, one- or two-magazine-titled companies were going to have a harder time surviving in the new millennium. New technologies were transforming how information was delivered. Social media was vying for the attention of mass magazines' traditional reading audience. The Internet was threatening to turn print media on its ear. And there were the ever-escalating production costs that simply made it more expensive for smaller publishing companies to operate.

Fewer small *or* big businesses, for that matter, could afford to ride as Lone Rangers anymore. To make it in the highly competitive, tougher environment in which we independent operators found ourselves, we would have to join a cavalry. Ride together, or die alone. That was the new reality as businesses ranging from bookstores to banking institutions, airlines to accounting firms started to merge, purge, or consolidate at the end of the last century and into the new one.

To ensure the continued existence and growth of Essence it made sense to join with a mighty company that not only desired us, but promised to share with us its considerable resources. "Ed, we're an 800-pound gorilla," Don Logan would say to me, referring to Time's power in the industry. "Use us, and discard what you don't need."

What Time Inc. brought to the table was beyond anything we could ever do alone. Just having Time as a 49 percent partner enabled *Essence* to reduce production costs because we were now part of a consortium that gave us greater efficiency in paper buying, printing, subscription handling, and newsstand placement. As a partner we had the advantage of leverage in dealing with printers and distributors. We suddenly carried partnership *clout*.

Editorially, Time had a better system for color processing, which made our preproduction for processing images much more efficient. Time possessed sophisticated market research resources with opinion-poll capabilities and third-party syndicated research that gave us psychographic information on everything from how many black women buy Toyota Priuses or use Estée Lauder White Linen, to how black women feel about their looks or their relationships with white women at work. Such information was enormously helpful to *Essence* editors in planning and executing feature stories, and to the *Essence* sales staff in selling advertising.

Also, advertising-wise, *Essence* was now positioned as a "buy" with the other women's and lifestyle titles in Time Inc.'s magazine categories. When advertisers made multiple buys in several of Time's women's magazines, for which they got a discount incentive, they recognized it made marketing sense for *Essence* to be one of those buys.

The point person facilitating the "dating" and engagement phase of the Essence partnership with Time Inc. was Michelle Ebanks, the African-American woman Don Logan brought with him to our initial breakfast meeting in 2000. Then 38, Michelle's entire career had been spent on the business side of magazine publishing. Graduating with a degree in finance from the University of Miami in 1984, she took her first job at Knapp Communications in Los Angeles, where she moved up to become director of finance for *Bon Appétit* magazine. When the company was acquired by Condé Nast in 1993, Condé Nast let most of Knapp's business staff go, but kept Michelle, who moved to New York City, where she served as business manager for thirteen Condé Nast magazines.

Both Knapp Communications and Condé Nast are privately held companies, however, and Michelle had developed a growing interest in working for a publicly traded media company, which led her to Time Warner in 1996. She joined Time Inc. as financial director for *Money* magazine. Two years later she was made general manager. When I met Michelle, she was functioning as Don Logan's chief of staff, working on a variety of special projects. "Michelle was basically helping me with all of the businesses [at Time Inc.]," Don said. "She's a pretty smart woman, also very nice, and she represented the African-American talent we were trying to expand on within Time Inc."

Michelle's talent would be indispensable to Essence during our five-year partnership period with Time. She understood editorial and circulation and advertising, and I found her to be quietly fearless as she took the lead in most of the conversations between the two sides, reporting to the boards, negotiating the Time Inc. bureaucracy. "She understands the culture *and* the business," Richard Parsons, former Time Warner CEO and chairman, said of the woman I would make group publisher of *Essence* when she came to work for Essence Communications in 2001. Michelle Ebanks is now president of the company, as well as president of Time Inc.'s *People Español.*

"What you're getting is a first-class manager," Parsons said when Michelle joined us. Parsons, himself a world-class executive, was CEO and chairman of Time Warner at the time of the Essence deal with Time, making him then the highest ranking African American in corporate America. As Chuck Hamilton noted, "There would have been no Essence deal with Time if Dick Parsons didn't want it to happen."

Nor do I think the Essence/Time transaction would have had the synergy it did without a black woman who understood not just the culture of the magazine business but was a part of the African-American female market that *Essence* was serving. "I certainly had a more intimate, direct experience with *Essence*," Michelle said of the strength she brought to the table. "I could say, 'Yes, this speaks to me.' It spoke to a market I knew. I didn't have to go out and read the last twenty-four issues of the magazine to know what *Essence* was about because I was already a reader of the magazine. *Essence* had always resonated in the [African-American] community."

———

Essence signed the deal to sell 49 percent of the company to Time on October 9, 2000. Prior to the closing, there had been months of negotiating as the two sides worked to establish an agreed-upon price for Essence. Because ECI is a privately held company, its value could not be determined by a price set on the publicly traded stock market. Other criteria based on such metrics as cash flow, cash in the bank, current revenues, and projected earnings had to be used to do an independent valuation of the company's worth. This is a complicated, lengthy process involving lawyers, accountants, and investment bankers on both sides; each company's chief financial officers, the boards of the respective companies, and the principals themselves—in this case me on the Essence side of the transaction, and Don Logan on the Time Inc. side.

The sale of just 49 percent of Essence represented a huge payday for the company, and would lead to complicated dealings with my top managers at Essence as issues over money, worth, and value rivaled anything I was dealing with in the negotiations with Time Inc.

The Essence board generously voted to give Clarence and me what was being called a "founders' bonus" following the sale of 49 percent of

the company. Just as the original four partners agreed to share with the company a portion of any corporate opportunity that resulted in monetary profits from our Essence association, the Essence board felt Clarence and I should get a bonus for building Essence into a company that Time Inc. wanted to buy. The amount of the bonus was $1.5 million, to be divided equally between Clarence and myself.

I instinctively knew it would create problems with my other top managers if they were not included in the bonus pool. Clarence and I may have founded the company, but all of my senior managers had certainly contributed to the success Essence had become by 2000. Susan Taylor, editor-in-chief, was the force running a successful engine in editorial; Jim Forsythe, circulation director, kept our newsstand and subscription numbers up; Bill Knight, production manager, kept our costs down, and Harry Dedyo, CFO, kept Essence on fiscal track.

Yet the board initially said no to my request that these managers share in a bonus. Actually, it was just three people on the board who said no. They were part of a board subcommittee I had created to deal specifically with the financial aspects of the Time deal, and they were three of my most trusted advisers and closest personal friends: Camille Cosby, the second largest Essence shareholder after John H. Johnson, and wife of entertainer Bill Cosby; Frank Savage, my buddy of more than forty years, going back to our days in banking; and Bruce Llewellyn, a best friend and father figure who had become a multimillionaire entrepreneur by being a hard and tough negotiator.

I prevailed on the board, however, getting them to agree to give an additional bonus in the amount of $100,000 apiece to the senior management team. It may as well have been $100, because every manager, with the exception of Harry Dedyo, was unhappy with the amount. As a finance guy who had seen companies come and go in his career, Harry, I think, understood the sometimes serendipitous nature of business, and appreciated getting anything at all. He didn't think he had done anything especially remarkable to *deserve* an extra $100,000 in his paycheck.

Susan Taylor, on the other hand, felt $100,000 was far below the value she had brought to the company. I remember John H. Johnson warning me on a couple of occasions about not letting an editor-in-chief accumulate too much power, lest such power go to the editor's head. Indeed, by

2002, when I was negotiating to buy out Clarence Smith, I felt Susan's own demands for money would escalate unreasonably.

On December 21, 2001, a little more than a year after selling our 49 percent to Time, Susan came into my office to say she wanted her salary increased to $300,000, retroactive to January 1, 2001. She wanted another salary increase of $50,000 per year, effective January 1, 2002, and a bonus of $200,000. A year later she asked the company to buy her a three-bedroom apartment in the building she lived in, at an estimated cost of $2 to $3 million. "Hold on," I said, astounded. "You're asking the company to pay for an apartment for you that costs more than the amount of the founders' compensation Clarence and I received?" She didn't answer.

I did talk Essence's financial board members into increasing Susan's salary to $300,000 per year, though it would not be retroactive. She was also awarded stock in 2002 and 2003 worth $1 million for each year. The board was not happy, but it reluctantly agreed to the compensations. "Damn it, Ed!" Bruce Llewellyn thundered. "I told you it wasn't a good idea to give bonuses to your senior staff!"

He was right. Susan still wasn't happy. "It seems like nothing is enough for her," Camille Cosby said. "But we think what we're giving her is enough. So that's it." The board was adamantly opposed to ECI buying an apartment for Susan.

One of my ongoing sore points with Susan was that she refused to share with the company any portion of the speaking fees she made on the lecture circuit or the proceeds she made from her book sales. Both were considerable, and were the direct result of her top position in the franchise *Essence* had created. Because Susan was not an *Essence* founder, however, I couldn't hold her to the same standard of sharing a corporate opportunity as I had the partners. But it always galled me that she wanted ECI to give to her *more* money, while she never wanted to share *any* money.

I know money is the most obvious and agreed-upon symbol of value and worth, and I recognized that Susan's value and worth to *Essence* during her tenure as editor-in-chief were immense. Yet her demands for money felt unseemly for a woman who was well compensated relative to the size of the company she worked for. Yes, celebrity editors like Anna Wintour at *Vogue* and the late Helen Gurley Brown of *Cosmopolitan* magazine, probably make (and made) in the seven figures, but Essence Communications Inc. has never been nor will it ever be Condé Nast or Hearst. Given *Essence*'s size as an independent magazine, Susan and the rest of the senior management staff were paid on par with salaries in the industry.

Once Essence partnered with Time Inc., however, all bets were upped. The perception was that Essence would be making a ton of money on the sale—and everybody involved with Essence at the top levels wanted to get paid a ton of money after the sale. Not surprisingly, Jonathan Blount surfaced immediately after Essence sold its 49 percent on October 9, 2000. Still a shareholder, he knew about the founders' bonus the board subcommittee voted to give Clarence and myself. In a letter he wrote to Susan dated October 13, 2000, he made this telling commentary:

> My Sister Susan . . . The nearly $2 million signing bonus to Ed and Larry [Clarence's nickname] alone appears to be a payoff for the potential sell out. I would be far more comfortable if the signing bonus included a distribution to all top contributing management and certainly, to we founders, Cecil Hollingsworth, Gordon Parks and myself. Certainly, some measure of gratitude and a success fee seems most appropriate to all.

While Jonathan claimed that Essence was "selling out" in its deal with Time, he of course wanted to cash in and get paid from the sale with a "success fee." Never mind that ECI paid him a million dollars ten years before, or that Cecil Hollingsworth and Gordon Parks sold their Essence stock years ago. Even Clarence, never in favor of the sale, wanted to use Time's monetary resources during our partnership phase to fund his many business ideas. He really believed at the end of the five-year period Essence would exercise its option to pull out and buy back its 49 percent ownership. By then, he probably figured he would have spent as much of Time's money as he needed to finance his projects.

As Clarence moved away from the day-to-day running of the sales department and took his eye off the bigger picture, I quietly started buying more Essence stock. This actually began during that stock fight in 1985 when John Johnson tried to take control of the company. Clarence couldn't—or wouldn't—step up to buy more stock himself to help fight off the Johnson takeover attempt. By 2002, I owned more stock than

Clarence did, giving me the control position in our partnership. That was the year I asked him to leave the company.

Firing Clarence after thirty-two years was not an option. He was a founding partner and officer of the company who had spent as many years helping to build Essence as I had. When he was on his game, there was no better player. Although our personal relationship started deteriorating in the 1990s, we still had one of the longest-running partnerships in the history of black business. I couldn't just give him the boot. He would have to be bought out. Respectfully, and for a good price. Susan said she felt he should be happy with $5 million.

It was the full Essence board that finally voted to remove Clarence from the company, though I know Clarence felt I was the one who betrayed him. His decision to side with me during that fateful takeover attempt by Jonathan Blount, Cecil Hollingsworth, and Gordon Parks in 1977 no doubt ate at him twenty-five years later as he was forced to leave Essence. But that decision made twenty-five years before saved us both—and saved our company. Now, for the continued existence of the company, he was the partner who had to go.

After much contentious negotiating, Clarence Smith was bought out for more than $14 million. He wasn't happy either, considering he'd asked for $40 million, and since leaving Essence, we have rarely spoken.

————

"We want to buy out the remaining 51 percent of Essence," Ann Moore said to me over dinner one evening in the spring of 2004. Really? We still had a year to go on our five-year engagement, yet Ann Moore, Time Inc.'s chairman and CEO, was telling me she was now ready to march down the aisle a year ahead of time and take full ownership of Essence.

Ann S. Moore became Time Inc.'s first female CEO when she was appointed to take Don Logan's position after he stepped down in 2002. She had been Don's executive vice president, running the biggest division and the biggest moneymaker in the Time Inc. magazine stable: the lifestyle and women's books.

Starting her Time career at *Sports Illustrated*, Ann took over *People* magazine in 1991, then launched *InStyle* magazine, which became an instant financial success. *Teen People, People Español*, and *Real Simple* magazines soon followed. All were moneymakers under Ann's skilled management, leading Dick Parsons to call her "the launch queen." She had proved that the women's market was where the future and the profits were in magazines. "It was very clear in 1991 that the company needed to diversify, for goodness' sake," Ann said. Selling her on the viability of *Essence* and the African-American female market ten years later was not an issue.

"I loved the idea of making an investment in *Essence*," she said, "because I really believe in diversification. I saw how it made Time Inc. so powerful. We were only making $200 million in profit in the early 1990s, but by the time I became [Time Inc.] chairman and had introduced the women's titles, we were making a *billion* in profit."

Essence, too, continued to be profitable during the five years leading up to the sale of ECI's remaining 51 percent. Following the departure of Monique Greenwood, Susan named Diane Weathers as the next editor-in-chief in 2001. Diane came with perhaps the most all-around solid journalistic credentials of any of the previous EICs: a degree in journalism from Syracuse University, editor and writing positions at *Black Enterprise, Newsweek, Redbook,* and *Consumer Reports*, and a seven-year stint abroad in Rome working for the World Food Programme. She had also done two stints at *Essence*—acting executive editor just before she left for Rome in 1986, and articles editor when she returned.

Susan remained at the top of the masthead, however, and her title publication director was changed to editorial director, making it clear after her tug-of-war clashes with Monique that she had final say in editorial matters. Diane would bring in exceptional freelance writers. So did deputy editor Robin Stone, who brought in Isabel Wilkerson, a Pulitzer Prize–winning reporter for the *New York Times*, whose landmark book, *The Warmth of Other Suns*, was a *New York Times* bestseller and National Book Critics Circle Award winner.

In January 2005 Diane launched an award-winning feature series titled "Take Back the Music," which examined the detrimental effect "gangsta" rap music was having on African-American culture. If the decade of the 1980s was characterized by black men being "bashed" by black women in books and film, the 1990s and early 2000s were marked by misogyny in black music as male rappers talked about all manner of defiling and debasing black women.

Diane's strength as an editor-in-chief is that she saw *Essence* having influence beyond the African-American community. "I wanted it to be a thought leader in all of media," she said of the magazine. "It should generate buzz everywhere." For Diane, being in the position to set the editorial direction for a magazine that had the power, influence, and reach that *Essence* did "was a dream job" come true.

Yet as a manager, Diane could be abrasive and mercurial, known for firing employees on a whim, almost as quickly as she hired them. She groused about how hard the job of editor-in-chief was, and wondered why she could never find any good editors. The tempering influence was always Susan, who not only made Diane hire back perfectly good editors she had fired, but would override some of Diane's other misguided editorial decisions.

For instance, when the magazine was about to publish an already controversial essay by a mother on why she wanted her black son to marry a black girl, Diane wanted to run a companion piece by another mother saying why it was fine for her black *daughter* to marry any man she wanted to—of any race. This kind of double-standard mixed message was not acceptable in *Essence*. Nor was the mixed sensibility of the editor-in-chief pushing the message. In 2005, shortly after Time Inc. acquired the remaining interest in Essence, and Diane had committed a few more editorial and business gaffes, she was asked to resign.

Essence and Time would make an editorial misstep of their own before the final sale. In 2004, the two companies launched *Suede* magazine, a hip and vibrant publication geared to a multicultural audience of women aged 18 to 24. The youth market represented by the rap generation was one that *Essence* still coveted as it looked to reach a younger readership. In this instance, a younger readership of women of color. But *Suede* folded after only four issues, and its failure may have been the result of two mistakes.

First, Time brought in a black Canadian, 40-year-old Suzanne Boyd, to run *Suede*. Suzanne had been the editor-in-chief of *Flair* magazine, the number one fashion magazine in Canada. But Canada is not America, and a black Canadian was not necessarily in tune with the sensibilities—fashion or otherwise—of America's multiethnic market.

Second and perhaps more significantly, our circulation director, Jim

Forsythe, had always argued that the black female market is too small to segment by age increments. "You end up cannibalizing your larger core market," he said. "*Seventeen* magazine can have a million readers because it is segmenting off a much larger population base. But blacks still make up only 13 percent of the total population, and black women are maybe half of that. So when you talk about reaching just the 18-to-24-year-olds in a group that constitutes a little more than 6 percent of the total, you will never get big circulation numbers." The numbers weren't there when other women of color were factored into the equation either.

Suede turned out to be a $2 million mistake, though that didn't stop Time Inc. from wanting to go forward with buying Essence. Then a funny thing happened on way to the final sale. Essence had actually *grown* in value in the five years since 49 percent of the company was sold. That first sale price reflected the value of the company then, or what's known in company valuations as enterprise value. The amount paid in 2000 was 49 percent of the enterprise value, or nearly half of the value. A new valuation of the company would have to be done to set a new enterprise price for purchasing the 51 remaining percent. While other magazines were taking hits during the tougher advertising environment of the early 2000s, *Essence* remained profitable, making the company an even more attractive investment for Time Inc. by 2005.

On October 9, 2000, the day Essence Communications Inc. sold 49 percent of its shares, the company had a value of $143 million. On March 11, 2005, the day Essence sold the remaining 51 percent of its shares, the value had risen to $195 million. This represented a price per share of $410—over *400,000* times the floor value of one cent per share that was set when The Hollingsworth Group issued 180,000 shares of Essence common stock to four partners in 1970. The combined amount of the two sales—49 percent bought in 2000 and 51 percent bought in 2005—came to nearly $270 million, and was the highest price-per-page that Time Inc. had ever paid for a single-title magazine publishing company.

No doubt about it, the Essence Communications Inc. and Time Inc. deal was nothing short of historic.

One of the perceptions people had of me during the time of the sale is that I, too, like the others looking for a big Time Inc. payday, wanted to cash out. I was nearing retirement age, the talk went, and some people believed I had been wowed by the sale of Robert Johnson's Black Entertainment Television to Viacom for a colossal $3 billion in 2000. Selling Essence to Time Inc. would bring me the same kind of instant wealth, the thinking went.

Though certainly not to the tune of $3 billion, the sale of Essence did indeed enrich me, as it did the twenty-six other shareholders who had the business foresight or a sentimental bent to hold on to their shares of Essence stock. John H. Johnson, the largest of the shareholders, cashed in for $38 million. The smallest of the shareholders, Jonathan Blount, with 500 shares, walked away with $205,000. And the rest—the twenty-five of us between the biggest and the smallest payout, most of whom were black women—did very well, indeed.

Dozens of other employees and investors had sold their shares of Essence stock over the years for a variety of personal and monetary reasons. But money was not the sole motivating factor driving my decision to sell Essence. Selling *in* was clearly the surest way to ensure the longevity of a business I had spent more than half my life helping to build.

The bigger story here is that *Essence* magazine has not only been a source of inspiration and affirmation to black women for two generations, but has empowered black women and men everywhere, beginning with those who worked for the magazine. Many of them have taken the skills they acquired at *Essence* to new ventures and new possibilities. Many cut their teeth as writers and editors, graphic designers, photographers, account executives, public relations and finance professionals, models and stylists at Essence Communications Inc. and have illustrious careers to show for it. Many will retire with comfortable benefits because of stock plans and 401(k) programs Essence put in place more than forty years ago to ensure "golden years" for its predominantly black female employees.

And twenty-seven Essence employees, board members, or investors achieved wealth or great financial reward when Essence was sold to the biggest media company in the world after thirty-five years as an independent black-owned business. No other black-owned business has ever created such opportunity for those in its workforce to share in company profits of this magnitude.

I have always said that the larger goal of any black-owned business should be to not just do good business and make money, but to do good work with the money it makes and be of service to the larger black community. I believe Essence has done this. Starting as a magazine "For Today's Black Woman" four decades ago, *Essence* is still standing, now as a powerhouse within a powerhouse, poised to affirm and celebrate a third generation of African-American women. The magazine continues to prove that these women matter—in the American marketplace and on the scene of American culture.

Afterword

When Time Warner announced in early 2013 that it was selling its magazine division, the news stunned the media world the way the announcement of AOL acquiring Time Warner had jolted everyone at the start of the new millennium. It wasn't that long ago that Time Warner's magazines had been its mighty profit center. Yet by 2013, as the onslaught of technology continued to decimate huge sectors of the print industry, city newspapers in particular, the very future of print media was being called into question. The favored jewels in the Time Warner crown were now the cable divisions—HBO, Time Warner Cable, and CNN—as print lost luster, and perhaps its reason for being.

But isn't that what they said about radio after television came on the scene? The fact is, radio is still here, playing strong, its future secured. And Time Inc.'s magazines continue to carry clout and make money. While recent profits may not be as great as they were in the heady days of the 1980s and '90s, Time Inc.'s most popular and successful publications are still making around 10 percent on the bottom line. It's not the 40 percent they were used to making, but a 10 percent return is hardly shabby.

By the end of 2013, Time Warner's plans to sell Time Inc. had fallen through, and the magazine division was spun off into a separate corporate entity that would have to rise or fall on its own merits and capacity to be relevant. The bigger question regarding the future of print media is how successful will it be in keeping an audience of readers and advertisers who are constantly being seduced by new media. I know as a former magazine publisher that if you create an editorial environment that your readers want to come back to, advertisers will want to be in that environment as well, regardless of other competing media. A large part of *Essence*'s editorial success has been in having strong and charismatic editors-in-chief who *lead* a community of women, in addition to editing for an audience of readers.

A *community* of readers is perhaps the best way to describe the *Essence* audience. This is an audience rooted in the specifics of race and gender. Being a woman matters. Being an African-American woman matters. And being part of an African-American community matters. I think this accounts in no small measure for the enormous success of the Essence Music Festival, still the biggest corporate sponsor event in the Time Inc. franchise.

The festival was originally conceived by jazz promoter George Wein and myself as a three-day "Party with a Purpose" special twenty-fifth-anniversary event for *Essence* magazine. But over the last twenty years it has grown into a national black gathering that celebrates African-American culture through its music, arts and crafts, writing, and intellectual thinking. Last year's festival drew 543,000 African Americans who spent a whopping $231.6 million in a single weekend. It was a remarkable display of a magazine's power to galvanize a community of readers.

I have always been very clear that I sold *Essence* to Time Warner with the expectation that the magazine would continue to exercise its power to galvanize black women—to inform, affirm, and empower them. There have surely been internal challenges since the sale. One acting editor-in-chief and three editors-in-chief have run the magazine in the eight years following its acquisition by Time Inc.: Angela Burt-Murray (2005–2010); Sheryl Hilliard Tucker, acting editor-in-chief and a former executive editor at Time Inc. (2010–2011); Constance C. R. White (2011–2013), and Vanessa K. Bush (2013–present). Four editors-in-chief in fewer than ten years has arguably resulted in a sometimes less than steady leadership.

But the *Essence* reader remains ever faithful. Circulation has consistently stayed at just over a million since 2005, the year the magazine was sold. Total readership, which includes "pass-along" readers who pick up the magazine in places like beauty parlors and nail salons, is close to 8 million. The principal players on the *Essence* team have moved on, however, something change inevitably brings.

Clarence Smith, who left the company in 2002, went on to launch a record label and start a travel business. Both Susan Taylor and I left Essence Communications Inc. in 2008 after fulfilling our three-year contracts with Time Warner following the sale.

Susan, who received a Henry Johnson Fisher Lifetime Achievement Award in 1998 from the Magazine Publishers of America, and was inducted into the American Society of Magazine Editors' Hall of Fame in 2002, left the magazine business entirely to launch National Mentoring Cares, an organization that places mentors for at-risk black youth with mentoring organizations.

I became a senior advisor to Solera Capital, a private equity firm that owns *Latina* magazine, the second magazine Essence Communications Inc. launched for women of color. I am also chairman of Latina Media Ventures, the holding company for *Latina*. I am the only *Essence* principal still standing in the industry I joined nearly fifty years ago when I helped start a magazine for black women with three other black men.

In 2002 I, like Susan, received the Henry Johnson Fisher Lifetime Achievement Award given by the Magazine Publishers of America. In 2009 Time Inc. honored me with its Henry Luce Award, given annually to a Time executive who is considered outstanding. In April 2014 I was inducted into the sixty-fifth Annual Advertising Hall of Fame, administered by the American Advertising Federation.

Though I am no longer involved in the magazine business on a day-to-day basis, I continue to live by many of the rules I learned running a business for nearly forty years, beginning with the four points of personal advice dispensed by my mother, Jewell Spencer Lewis Clarke. They are as follows:

1. Be a proud black man.
2. Take care of your family.
3. Get a good education.
4. Always try to do the right thing.

Here are a few business rules that are also useful, whether owning and managing a business or simply managing your own work life:

• ***Share power.*** Real power is always shared. The *Essence* partnership worked in the beginning because the four of us partners recognized and respected the individual strengths of the others and were comfortable sharing and drawing on those strengths.

- *Listen, don't just hear.* It is not that difficult to hear what someone is saying. The greater challenge is *listening* to what's being said—understanding the point of view or the thinking that went into a decision-making process.

- *Know the difference between being silent and being clueless.* As someone who has always been described as quiet, I can tell you it's not because I have nothing to say. Silence allows me to focus on the speaker and on what's being said, to listen and to carefully process so when I do open my mouth, I am making informed commentary. Additionally, there is much to be learned in moments of silence about yourself and others.

- *Trust your managers.* If you hired them, allow them to manage and not try to second guess or micromanage them. Their style may not be your style and you may not even agree with their management tactics, but if they are successful at what they do, leave them alone.

- *Listen to your gut.* Instinct is real. Trust it. It is difficult to define, but through experience I have come to recognize, respect, and value this "inner voice."

- *Cash rules.* Whether it's personal savings or corporate cash reserves, money in the bank represents leverage, power, and options. The key to *Essence*'s financial success after its initial rocky start was keeping debt down and cash reserves up.

- *Surround yourself with smart people.* They not only make you look good, but are most likely to be open to new concepts, to think outside the box.

- *Always look like you're the boss.* My mother liked to dress well because she instinctively understood that how you present yourself says everything about how you see yourself in the world. A good presentation says "I am in control and in charge."

• *Do the right thing and be a good man.* As a businessman, I've always strived to run a venture that does good work in the community as well as does good business on the bottom line. But my mother also instilled in me the importance of doing the right thing by being a good man—a man of integrity, honor, discipline, and responsibility. "Sonny, no matter what you do," she would tell me, "whether you travel the world or get to be a man who has influence, always remember to do the right thing. That's what really matters."

• *"Don't let me stay at the party too long."* That's a quote from Johnny Carson, who recognized the danger of hanging around anything too long, be it a talk show you host or a magazine you own. Knowing when to change up is crucial. As my buddy Frank Savage likes to say, "If you don't change, you die." I sold *Essence* because I wanted the magazine to live—to be in business long after the original founders had moved on. That is how businesses become institutions.

• *Never ever underestimate your opponent.* He or she could very well turn out to be the last one standing.

Index

S

Safeway, 176

Samuels, Annette, 122–23, 132–34, 135

Sant-Angelo, Giorgio, 215

Sapphire, 22–26, 27, 38, 161

Satterwhite, Sandra, 129–30, 152–53

Savage, Frank, xiv, 16, 184, 207, 282, 295

Scott Paper Company, 148–49, 150–51

segregation, xi-xii, 64

Sepia, 217

September 11 attacks, 261

7-Eleven, 176

Seventeen, 269, 288

Shange, Ntozake, 203, 215

Sharpton, Rev. Al, 249

Shaw, Bernard, 235

Shaw, Linda, 232, 233, 235, 237

Shay, Michele, 205–7
  as actress-model, 206, 207, 225
  marriage to author, 206–7, 225, 237
  miscarriage of, 226, 229
  separation and divorce, 229, 235
  and therapy, 225–26, 228–29

Shearson, Hammill and Company, 29–30
  business advice from, 5–6, 10–11
  and *Essence* startup, 6, 19, 29, 30, 31,
    35, 38, 98, 99
  and First Harlem Securities, 7
  merger of, 30

Sheperd, Kathy, 213

Shriver, Sargent, 84

silence, 294

Simmons, Martin, 204

Simon, Neil, 57

Simone, Nina, 101

Sinbad, 248

Skeeter, Sharyn, 123, 153

Smart-Grosvenor, Vertamae, 215

smart people around you, 294

Smith, Clarence, 207
  and advertising, 103–6, 112, 119, 127,
    160, 165, 168, 178, 216, 226–27,
    229, 245, 269
  after the sale, 292
  and Blount, 127, 136, 139, 141

and boxing promotion, 276
buyout of, 283, 285
and control, 140, 181
and the Essence Woman, 103–4, 127
and financing, 36–37
founders' bonus to, 281–82
and Gillespie, 123, 161
income of, 32
and music festival, 247, 251
and partnership, 18, 19, 118–19,
  140–42, 143, 155, 171, 183, 275–78,
  283, 285
as president, 148, 275
and Ross, 113
and sales, 13–14, 17–18, 103, 119, 122,
  148–49, 168, 211, 241, 275, 277
and Scott Paper, 148–49, 150–51
and stock fight, 181, 182–84
and Taylor, 197, 226–27, 275, 277–78
and Time deal, 278, 283, 284–85

Smith, Cydya, 23

Smith, Elaine, 25, 40

Smith, Phil, 40–41, 93, 113–14

Smith, Tommie, 8–9

Smith, Willi, 195

Smothers, Kirk, 87, 89

SoftSheen, 244

Solera Capital, 256, 293

Soul Train, 170

South Africa, political coverage of, 221

Southern Christian Leadership
  Conference, 163

Southern Living, 262

Southern Progress Corporation (SPC), 262

Spencer, Charles, 50

Spencer, Mary, 50

Spencer, Tracy, 15, 51, 55, 56

Spielberg, Steven, 203

Spillers, Hortense, 189

Sports Illustrated, 262

Stans, Maurice, 10

Stein, Bob, 27

Steinberg, Phil, 60, 61

Stephens, George "Kingfish," 24

Sterling/McFadden, 217

Stewart, Martha, 261–62

DISCARD